Buy Black

BUY BLACK

How Black Women Transformed US Pop Culture

ARIA S. HALLIDAY

UNIVERSITY OF
ILLINOIS PRESS
Urbana, Chicago, and Springfield

© 2022 by the Board of Trustees
of the University of Illinois
All rights reserved
Manufactured in the United States of America
1 2 3 4 5 C P 5 4 3 2 1
∞ This book is printed on acid-free paper.

Library of Congress Cataloging-in-Publication Data

Names: Halliday, Aria S., 1990– author.
Title: Buy Black: how Black women transformed US pop
    culture / Aria S. Halliday.
Description: Urbana: University of Illinois Press,
    [2022] | Series: Feminist media studies | Includes
    bibliographical references and index.
Identifiers: LCCN 2021046453 (print) | LCCN 2021046454
    (ebook) | ISBN 9780252044274 (hardback) | ISBN
    9780252086359 (paperback) | ISBN 9780252053269
    (ebook)
Subjects: LCSH: Consumer behavior—United States. |
    African American women in popular culture. | African
    American consumers. | African American women—
    Social conditions. | Group identity—United States.
Classification: LCC HC110.C6 B89 2022 (print) | LCC
    HC110.C6 (ebook) | DDC 658.8/3430973—dc23

LC record available at https://lccn.loc.gov/2021046453
LC ebook record available at https://lccn.loc.gov/2021046454

Contents

List of Figures

Acknowledgments

It is difficult to include all of the food, people, places, prayers, songs, and conversations over the past decade that helped create this book, but I will definitely try. To Rayvon Fouche for keeping me focused when I wanted to burn it all down, for being supportive in more ways than I thought I needed, and for always asking the questions nobody wanted to answer; I am abundantly grateful for your mentorship and friendship, Ray. Thank you Marlo David, for always asking about and supporting my life beyond academia; you've taught me so much about life purpose, vision, and graceful balance. To Shannon McMullen and Cheryl Cooky: thank you for supporting an "ambitious" dissertation project. To Ms. Juanita Crider, Mr. Bill Caise, and the rest of the Purdue Black Cultural Center family: you all kept me grounded when I felt lost in a sea of whiteness; thank you for embracing me and always encouraging me to bring all my talents to bear. To the cutest family that kept my love for sweets and great debates intact in Indiana: thank you Stephen and Melissa Horrocks. All of my love to my Delta Sigma Theta Sorority, Inc., sorors, especially Nadia Brown, for mentorship, insomnia talks, and sisterhood; and Veronica Rahim, for friendship chicken and so much more.

At the University of New Hampshire and in the New Hampshire community, thank you to: (the late) Burt Feintuck, Katie Umans and the UNH Center for the Humanities, Michele Dillon, Brett Gibson, and Reginald Wilburn for support and resources; Siobhan Senier, Avary Thorne, and all of my Women's

Studies students, especially Peri Sanechiaro. Many thanks to Nora Draper for so many chats about book development and for reading chapters, Elyse Hambacher, Kabria Baumgartner, Chanda Prescod-Weinstein (and, Michael Burnham), Jade Caines Lee, and Kristen Butterfield for all our lunches and dinners; Dennis Britton, Chryl Laird, Tamsin Whitehead, and Tonya Evans (WE MADE IT SIS!) for community. Loretta Brady, thank you for freedom seders, pandemic flour delivery, and joy.

At the University of Kentucky, I am abundantly grateful for communities that embraced me and reminded me how important this work is with enthusiasm and genuine interest despite Zoom fatigue and a global pandemic that made personal interactions rare. Special thanks to DaMaris Hill, Melynda Price, Anastasia Curwood, Regina Hamilton, Elizabeth Williams, Srimati Basu, Jackie Murray, Nikki Brown, Nazera Wright, Frances Henderson, Blanche Bong Cook, Mel Stein, Ellen Riggle, and Michelle del Toro (you are the best!). I am appreciative of the UK–AAAS Summer Writing Group for helping me stay focused on many Fridays when I would rather have been in bed. Cheers to brunch buddies, Jazmine "JWells" Wells and Lauren Whitehurst; I can't wait to celebrate this accomplishment with y'all and an absurd number of drinks—WE GOT PHDs AND $HIT!

For the Barbie chapter, specifically, many thanks to the Strong National Museum of Play staff, especially Michelle Parnett (curator), Tara Winner-Swete (cataloger), and Beth Lathrop (director of libraries) who made sure I had everything I needed during my February 2016 and June 2019 Strong Research Fellowship visits. The Strong's financial support for research on Black dolls and Black girl play illustrates how important this work is and that there are institutions that are interested in and encourage it. Thank you to the Children's Museum of Indianapolis staff for their assistance during my visit in 2015 and for followup emails and images, specifically Jennifer Noffze (collections manager) and Andrea Hughes (lead curator); Lori J. Durante, founder of the Museum of Lifestyle and Fashion History in Delray, Florida; Darlene Powell Garlington, PhD, consultant for the Shani doll collection; Stacey McBride-Irby, creator of So In Style dolls, for our great conversations and all your lovely ideas; Stephen Sumner, creator of the Nicki Minaj charity doll and designer for So In Style dolls, for your brilliance and creativity; Dr. Ann duCille, author of *Skin Trade*, for your encouragement, interest, and suggestions; Elizabeth Chin, author of *Purchasing Power*; Yla Eason, creator of Olmec Toys; Tuesday, Lynne, and Doris Connor, seamstresses for Shindana Toy Company; Robin Bernstein, author of *Racial Innocence*; Vinay Harpalani, for guidance on *Brown v. Board of Education* research; Debbie Garrett, Black doll historian and enthusiast; and Lagueria

Davis, Black Barbie documentary filmmaker. Special thanks also to readers and editors of the journals *Departures in Critical Qualitative Research* (University of California Press) and *Girlhood Studies* (Berghahn Books)—especially Tori Cann—for helping me develop and for publishing sections of what is now chapter 4.

Many thanks to Jasmine Cobb, Marlon Bailey, Therí Pickens, the Duke Summer Institute on Tenure and Professional Advancement program, and my Duke SITPA cohort, especially Randi Gill-Sadler and J. T. Roane. Thank you Ashley Payne, co-conspirator and protector of my time. Thank you, Ritu Mukherjee and the Woodrow Wilson (now Institute for Citizens and Scholars) Career Enhancement Fellowship for Junior Faculty 2020–2021, my mentor Riché Richardson, and my fellows' cohort for your support in finishing this book. Our writing group, spearheaded by Kwami Coleman and Amaka Okechukwu, really made the difference in the last few months of this project; thank you Ester Trujillo, Maria Firmino-Castillo, Elva Orozco Mendoza, Renee Hudson, Crystal Donkor, Nicole Burrows, Kwami, and Amaka for allowing me to be in community with you—what a privilege it has been. Thank you to attendees of the Race and Identity Matters Symposium (at University of Connecticut in February 2020) and the Black New England conference in 2017 and 2019 for allowing me to talk through various aspects of this project and for your generative feedback.

I am also grateful for sister scholar-mentors like Ruth Nicole Brown, Kyra Gaunt, Keisha Blain, Ebony Elizabeth Thomas, Kinitra Brooks, and Mireille Miller-Young. Thank you, Rebecca Wanzo, editor/reader/encourager at every stage; and Dawn Durante, editor extraordinaire for seeing the promise in this project from our first conversation in 2015. Thank you Kristen Elias Rowley, at The Ohio State University Press, who let me talk about this project and cheetah-print shoes endlessly, with appreciation and interest. Ashleigh Greene Wade, you already know what it is!

Thank you doesn't even seem like enough for you, Candice Robinson, Heather Moore Roberson, and Tina Beyene, for the best kind of friendship a Black woman in academia could imagine and Rev. Dr. Twana Harris for prayers and songs of healing. Thank you, Dr. Sheree Rainbow, for your visionary genius that created SisterFriends, and my phenomenal therapist, Porsche Lockett. Thank you to my Upsilon Mu sisters, who have supported me even when they didn't know what I was doing, and to Rachel Means for your beautiful artwork and understanding my vision. To all my Davidson homies, especially Aaron Goodson and Rayna McKenzie, and my Institute for the Recruitment of Teachers (IRT) fam that have been there for everything, you already know.

To my family and cheerleaders: Mommy aka Beverley Francis-Gibson, Vernon Gibson, Djarta "Dja" Halliday (for talking me through this one as well as all the other books I have yet to write), and Gabrielle "Gabby" Halliday. To my honey, Delta, and the Thach/Yeap family, thank you for keeping me fed and centered. To Granny and all who came before in the US/British Virgin Islands and beyond: for your dedication to education, for your love of Black culture and Black women, for your grandiose stories and space-filling laughter, for curry chicken and johnnycake that did more than feed the stomach, and for life lessons that will never fail me, thank you. I love you. I miss you dearly.

Buy Black

Introduction

The Making of Black Womanhood

I am what many journalists these days disparagingly call a Millennial.[1] Naturally, this label heightens the labels already associated with me as a Black woman. A Millennial Black woman: I am supposedly assertive and entitled, sexually liberated (or promiscuous depending who you ask) and therefore unwilling to marry or have kids when socially appropriate, outspoken and unwilling to use phrases like "racially charged" to describe racist incidences.[2] My shopping and eating habits have destroyed capitalist industries like dairy farms, buffet restaurants, and department stores, while growing others like poke bowl restaurants, brunch with avocado toast, and outsourcing rides/meals/dates to people who create algorithms from my choices.[3] I am highly educated and expect quick responses to issues or injustices, and will easily leave a job that does not promote me within a year so I can travel whenever I want instead of buying a house.[4]

Born between 1980 and 1994, we are the generation of consumers that have changed marketing, production, and social media use. We are the children of late Baby Boomers and early GenXers who taught us that if we worked hard enough, everything would be available to us. We came of age in what some consider the golden age of hip-hop, girl power, and multiculturalism, in which tokenism in television shows, films, and consumer products made us feel hopeful about shifts in representation and access to wealth for which GenXers and Baby Boomers protested. We partied to the Spice Girls and Missy Elliott and sought out visual media that looked like the world we lived in. These shifts in consumer products and visual media, however, were not separate from the growth in multicultural marketing during the Civil Rights Movement and the Black Power era. The celebration of difference and the acceptance of women in the workforce through their educational aspirations throughout the United States pushed corporations to produce consumer products for our changing society. The largest corporations worked to create products for us, marketing products directly to children in service of the development of lifetime consumer attitudes and habits. Particularly, Mattel and Disney became conglomerates that narrativized ideas about love, happiness, legacy, and difference that was the background to Millennial childhoods; the full-blown power of princess culture—the consumptive world of becoming the Disney princess of your choice through owning every film, outfit, houseware, soundtrack, adapted television show, or game featuring her—took hold in the late 1990s.[5] Popular television shows on Nickelodeon, ABC Family, and the Disney Channel as well as animated and live-action films by Disney, Pixar, and DreamWorks worked to create the reality that Sarah Banet-Weiser, Susan Douglas, and others call popular (or post)feminism.[6]

As a young Black girl in the 1990s, I remember playing with my sisters, traveling to various cultural events, and participating in summer camps. I was not a child who was interested in Barbie dolls (except one baby doll I had named Maria for whom my grandmother made a cloth diaper with the US Virgin Islands flag) or princess culture. I remember wanting to spend as much time as possible with my older sister, five years my senior, who was always thinking of things to do. We were constantly riding bikes around our large yard, playing imaginative games in the wooded area behind our house, or making pillow forts and sliding down the stairs in sleeping bags. As she recalls, "we were living life," meaning that we spent less time concerned with stereotypically girly things even as we wore and owned all the trappings of early 1990s girlhood including bows, barrettes, itchy taffeta dresses, and lace-trimmed socks. My mother was determined to expose us to the world around us and therefore made sure we were involved in as many dance, piano, and cultural foundation classes that the Durham, North Carolina, Arts Council or Edison Johnson Center offered. When I turned seven, Mommy enrolled me in a summer/afterschool program called "Sisterfriends."

A group geared toward Black girls ages six to sixteen in the Durham community, Sisterfriends introduced us to service-learning, self-esteem building, African and African American history, domestic skills (i.e., cleaning, cooking, baking, setting a table), physical activities (i.e., African dance and drumming, step, swimming, basketball, volleyball), and event planning (i.e., girls planned the year-end event including all performances and agendas). Founded by a

Black woman (a former corporate financial analyst turned charm school and model consultant), Sheree Rainbow, Sisterfriends started as an afterschool program to help Black girls in the community learn about Black history and culture; as the program grew into Saturday and summer meetings, Sister Rainbow was able to enlist local Black women college students to volunteer. I remember meeting some of my closest friends those summers, calling all girls and adult women "sister" and learning steps proclaiming the legacy of African queens like Nzingha and Nefertari. We learned how to play chess and checkers and ask hard questions about the community we lived in while visiting various places in town and across the South. Sisterfriends was transformative for me and planted the seed for my Black feminist consciousness.[7]

Perhaps this program, and the various other activities my mother forced my sisters and me to attend, shielded me from the rise of Barbie and princess culture that occurred in the late 1990s. Also, having a mother who made sure that we knew we were beautiful Black girls and our voices mattered just as much as anyone else's I believe helped guide me through the formative years when, scholars have argued, white girls fall prey to society's constructions of heteronormative femininity and the primacy of white womanhood within the Barbie/princess cultural landscape.[8]

While I, like many other girls, questioned the desirability of my body, my hair, my voice, and my skin and complexion as they developed, I recognize now how important a group like Sisterfriends was to a healthy self-esteem. In addition I loved the many shows and movies that centered the experiences of girls and women of color. As scholars like Ruth Nicole Brown, Bettina Love, Venus Evans-Winters, and Elaine Richardson discussed in the late 2000s, I recognize how these formidable experiences in youth shape much of the self-concept that Black women have in adulthood.[9] Forces like the media (especially Black Entertainment Television and Music Television—BET and MTV), popular television shows and films such as *Moesha*, *Clueless*, and *Boy Meets World*, and boyband and teen heartthrob music taught Black girls who and how they should be. With the exception of shows and films tailored to Black youth in particular—which Patricia Hill Collins points out proliferated because "African American youth are not marginalized but rather remain essential to new consumer markets, both as suppliers of commodities that are bought and sold, and as reliable consumer markets"[10]—Black girls were few and far between, although generally outspoken, well-dressed, and desired by at least one boy (usually the buffoon of the group).

While many shows and films were crafted with Black girls as accessories to the main narrative, *Buy Black: How Black Women Transformed US Pop Culture* examines how Black women in representational industries, like toys, films, and music, actively worked to craft a position for Black girls at the forefront. My book is about Black girl playthings, but not necessarily about Black girls' experiences with those playthings. Others, such as Kyra Gaunt, Bettina Love, Treva Lindsey, and Ashleigh Greene Wade, have considered how Black girls respond to and create alongside representations and material products of Black girlhood that exist in popular culture.[11] I center this text on the ways that Black women as creative intellectuals, or what I call cultural producers, envision the necessary tools of Black girl development. These women actively shaped whiteness and the white gaze in a Black woman's image and therefore manifested their own ideas about blackness within popular culture. Accordingly, I investigate: what becomes of Barbie if and when Black women actively devise her as Black Barbie? What ensues in a Cinderella story if and when Black women engineer the narrative and the image of the princess? What emanates from and also holds back Black women in the rap industry as they attune their personas to the lack of representation in the industry, and their fans who may not mirror their own identities? What becomes of the products Black women create when they are no longer the main consumers of those products? I explore, according to Black women, which dolls, which princess stories, which rags-to-riches narratives, which characteristics represent the repertoire of Black girlhood. Although the narratives of self-making and responses to whiteness I include throughout are global in some ways, this project is based squarely in the imagined space of "America" and the cultural attitudes, discourses, and concepts that produced a Black American sensibility. These chapters explore Black representation and consumerism to better understand how Black women have made themselves visible in the present, while also imagining a future and reimagining a past through objects, images, sounds, and lessons necessary for Black girls to become who Black women cultural producers believe they should be.

Buy Black considers the material, visual, and digital archive of Black girlhood that Black women in the twentieth and twenty-first centuries created in response to discourses on feminism, respectability, and blackness. These new narratives took place in the popular sphere to reflect on and shape Black girlhood. While I am not writing about Black girls' reception of these consumer products as Elizabeth Chin and Erica Rand have, Black consumptive practices work in tandem with the Black women cultural producers' creative processes.[12] All of the creators I interviewed—from the founder of my beloved group Sisterfriends, Sheree Rainbow, to Black women who worked for two of the most important fantasy-making companies, Mattel and Disney—noted that the lack of options as consumers led them to create so-called authentically Black products for their children and themselves. Yla Eason, founder and creator of the late 1980s company Olmec Toys (credited with the term "ethnically correct" and the first Black action figure, Sun-Man), noted that her desire to create action figures and dolls was based in a lack of consumer product options for her then three-year-old son and other mothers like her who complained about options for their children; Eason's son's statement, "I could never be He-Man because I'm not white," during a family trip, put Eason in a frenzy about the child's self-concept and ability to imagine a future for himself without limitation.[13] Although *Buy Black* does not focus on Black boys and their reception of the products devised by Black women cultural producers, the need to address a lack of representation and how it in turn limits Black children's self-concept and imagination frame the motivation for every creator within these pages.

Black women have been concerned with creating different narratives of who they are (or who they wish to be) through their influence on popular visual and material culture for some time. The rise of multicultural marketing in the 1960s—a response to the growing financial capabilities of Black people in the United States and the inclusion of more Black people in the sale of products, goods, and services after the end of state-sanctioned discrimination—defined a new opportunity for Black women to capitalize on narratives that they could create to change public attitudes about blackness, womanhood, and sexuality. Black women's role in creating and changing public opinion through capitalist multiculturalism is the center of this text. In the creative process, though, Black women built material objects and commodified themselves; these objects, in many instances, represented and stood in for actual Black women in spaces in which they were ridiculed or disallowed access. Racial play—via dolls, princess narratives, and the appropriation of Black women's bodies online—became the ways that Black women could move their beliefs about themselves, womanhood, femininity, and blackness into the hands and minds of Black children (and many others). The objects they created were not merely for themselves and the Black girls and women they imagined as the ideal consumers; there were always others who were intentional about purchasing products that reflected Black cultural attitudes and experiences—a precursor to the social media ad campaigns we see today that encourage all consumers to support Black businesses or "buy Black."

Authenticity in Representation

The politics of respectability for Black women, particularly in the ideological field of representation, has been about bestowing dignity and respect upon Black girls and women.[14] Historically and presently, Black women's stake in the ideological work of respectability is about making space for themselves in a world where they do not see themselves or their experiences reflected. As visual and material "embodied discourse," the images I engage in *Buy Black* uncover how and why some Black women cultural producers are arbiters of authenticity masked as respectability despite the diversity in their creations.[15] From 1960 to 2015, the push for dolls, princess narratives, and celebrity Black women that are supposed to accurately represent and depict everyday Black girls and women falls in line with the intellectual work on stages and in images Black women created of themselves and each other at the turn of the twentieth century. The seeming obsession with creating authentic representation for Black people, representation that reflects and supports a holistic vision of blackness worthy of dignity and respect from white people and the government, is rooted in the stronghold of white supremacy via stereotypes, or what Melissa Harris-Perry calls the "crooked room," that constrain the everyday and popular culture experiences of Black people.[16] Authenticity in the form of representation favors certain phenotypes, idioms, and aesthetics to perform blackness or some close proximity to blackness; a "real" Black woman, for example, always looks, says, feels, and acts in certain ways. While we know Black women who can be many different things, a material or visual representation of those things has historically and presently had to behave and look a certain way.

As a result, products are sold to women and marketed to children in the form of selling so-called authentic representation and meeting the desire of Black people generally—and Black women in particular—to have examples of themselves in popular culture. The Black women creators, designers, artists, and producers in this book articulate the yearning for Black representation in popular culture and they see their alignment with corporations like Disney and Mattel as a means to representation. For Black girls, these cultural producers say, corporate alliances allow for greater access and representation—the development of products in which Black girls can see themselves and imagine possibilities beyond their current experiences or those of their families. Companies like Disney and Mattel, too, find these imaginative possibilities compelling for different reasons (mainly generating income and access to new consumer populations), yet use the rhetoric of authenticity and representation derivative of multiculturalism discourse to further expand potential consumers from the cradle to the grave. As I show in later chapters, Black women championed the corporate rhetoric of inclusion via multiculturalism in the 1990s and diversity in the 2000s because it allowed for more of us to spread authentic (read: respectable) images of Black female identities.

Saidiya Hartman notes that "the decades between 1890 and 1935 were decisive in determining the course of black futures" so here I take up the futures created from the makings of Black respectability politics in the post-Reconstruction period to consider how the success of *Brown v. Board of Education* shifted the discourse of rights and liberties to those of multiculturalism, diversity, and representation.[17] Black self-making (and the history of it) is part of the American Dream and the concept that the whole system is built upon ideas; in particular Black women—like Pauli Murray who was involved in crafting Thurgood Marshall's rhetorical *Brown v. Board of Education of Topeka* defense strategy that illustrated separate was not equal—have been instrumental in intellectual discourses of self-made Black people. Outside of the legal sphere, the role of whiteness and white supremacy in the lives of Black people has resulted in the use of the image economy or the use of representation as currency to make themselves known outside of the white gaze. Black Power evolving into Black/multicultural identity has pushed use of images to make ideas of blackness and beauty, power, prestige, exclusivity, and talent knowable through sight. Early twentieth-century Black intellectuals celebrated New Negro womanhood, the mid- to late twentieth century coaxed discussions of Black is beautiful, and now twenty-first-century ideas have turned to explore the diversity in blackness.[18] While all of these discourses are distinct in the particular intellectuals and concerns present in each respective moment, these ideas hinge on two major aspects of Black identity: representation and authenticity. From the use of daguerreotypes, magazines, and portraits to minstrel shows, television, and hip-hop culture, much of the intraracial intellectual debates about how Black people are represented have taken up the accuracy (or lack thereof) of Black characters that mimicked the lived experiences of Black people as well as how many or the diversity of Black characters that are available in any given moment in the service of uplifting the race.[19] Since before the end of enslavement, Black people in the United States have been concerned with how to be themselves, and the tension between how to represent themselves for each other and for white audiences. As *Brown v. Board*'s legal decision illustrates, the apex of these discussions refer to the concern for children and what harm is done to children's self-concept based on these images. Therefore, the discussion of Black girl play items exposes the foundation of how adults and children manifest ideas about authenticity and representation in blackness. I wonder as Ann duCille did in the early 1990s, why does a doll need to be authentically Black?[20] Why does a princess narrative need to be authentically Black? Why does it need to mirror us to help us imagine a future beyond our present circumstances?

The Political Life of Black Dolls

While Mamie and Kenneth Clark manufactured the most famous studies related to dolls and Black children in the 1940s, Black dolls had been of particular importance to the project of Black racial politics since enslavement.

Sabrina Lynette Thomas maps the timeline of mass-produced Black dolls by Black doll companies as well as Black intellectuals' investment in Black dolls for racial uplift. The Rev. Dr. Richard Henry Boyd's National Negro Doll Company, formed in 1904, was the first Black doll company and began importing dolls from Germany in October 1907.[21] R. H. Boyd and his son, Henry Allen Boyd or H. A., worked to bolster the sale of Negro dolls through Boyd's other ventures like the *Nashville Globe* newspaper and National Baptist Publishing Board (which worked closely with the National Baptist Convention). As a formerly enslaved man, R. H. Boyd saw all of his ventures—including One-Cent Savings Bank—as working toward independence and racial uplift, a feat that would stave off Jim Crow discrimination. In a December 18, 1908, front-page editorial in the *Nashville Globe*, R. H. Boyd responds to an editorial by Dan W. Baird (an older white man and editor of the *Southern Lumberman*, a trade journal) in the white newspaper *Nashville Banner*, which highlighted how Black dolls currently on the market were not fit for "a gorilla, a chimpanzee, or even a baboon."[22] Although he had not talked to Boyd or anyone involved at the National Negro Doll Company, Baird argued that "respectable Negro mothers" would not buy Boyd's dolls despite a resolution of support for the manufacturing of Negro dolls by the "Colored National Baptist Association."[23] Because the dolls allowed the child to "understand fully the conditions he will encounter on account of his race and color," however, Boyd argued that racial development stemmed from Black mothers to Black children, connecting the consumption of Black dolls with the overall parenting project of children's "positive" identity development.[24]

Despite success in reaching Black consumers, the Boyd entrepreneurs continued to challenge white disparagement of Black dolls (and perhaps Black reluctance to buy them) through advertising in the *Globe* (see figure 0.1). In a November 1, 1912, advertisement, H. A. Boyd is quoted saying that "when you see a Negro doll in the arms of a Negro girl, then you know that the child is being taught a lesson in race pride and race development which will not result in race suicide."[25] His statement acknowledges two major concerns of Black folk at the turn of the century and still today: (1) the need for children's understanding and acceptance of their racial history and culture, and (2) the threat of Black children disowning their complexion, history, or culture as a result of white supremacy. Ultimately, the National Negro Doll Company solidified in a material product the angst that Black intellectuals like E. Franklin Frazier, Anna Julia Cooper, Booker T. Washington, and others made clear on lecture stages and in pamphlets. Beyond assimilation and racial violence, Black middle- and working-class people across the United States were concerned with the ways that Black children would inherit racial struggles and advance the race. Laila Haidarali explains that Black people in the early and mid-twentieth century worked hard to cultivate beauty as racial pride so that in addition to illustrating "social mobility through . . . respectable waged labor" and "personal happiness" through sexual appeal to others, they cultivated beauty as "an ultimate challenge to white cultural beliefs in the physical inferiority of African American people."[26] This cultivation was made possible through consumer products like dolls, where the stakes of racial pride were not only imparted to

FIGURE 0.1. National Negro Doll Company ad, *Nashville Globe*, November 22, 1912, Holiday Edition, part three, page 21, image 21. Source: Courtesy of the Tennessee State Library & Archives.

children as an ideological means of racial progress, but also instilled in them an understanding of which complexions, hair styles, and bodies were held in high esteem.

Evelyn (Victoria) Berry and Victoria Ross established the first Black woman–owned doll company, Berry and Ross Doll Manufacturing, in Harlem in the early 1910s. Marcus Garvey later bought the company in 1922 and it became the UNIA Doll Factory.[27] While similar in mission and scope as the NNDC, the UNIA Doll Factory contended that the "mulatto" dolls that NNDC manufactured were not representative of the race and did not bolster racial pride, especially for darker-complexioned people. If, as Boyd argued, objects like toys taught children higher intellectual development, Garvey and the UNIA Doll Factory were disturbed by the lack of intellectual development for dark-skinned children since NNDC only sold light-complexioned dolls.[28] For UNIA, darker dolls promoted acceptance of "African roots as elements of children's race pride" whereas "the fair complexion of the NNDC's dolls implied an acceptance of miscegenation as a pathway to race progress."[29] The dolls' complexions alone were imbued with social and political importance for children's development as racialized citizens, as Black people in the United States.

One of the most resonant examples of doll complexions as political warfare in the project of racial uplift in the Civil Rights Era is the development of Sara Lee dolls. The brainchild of Sara Lee Creech, Sara Lee (sometimes Saralee) dolls were produced by the Ideal Toy Company in 1951 as the first, according to Zora Neale Hurston, "anthropologically correct" Black dolls.[30] Developed from over one thousand pictures of Black children (mirroring Boyd's claims about how his dolls were developed some thirty years earlier), Sara Lee dolls represented a major shift in toy production based in white stereotypes and attitudes of Black people. As a white woman, Sara Lee Creech was able to get support for her dolls from Eleanor Roosevelt, Zora Neale Hurston, Ralph Bunche, Lester Granger, Walter F. White, and several historically Black college and university presidents from Atlanta University (Dr. Rufus Clement), Howard University (Mordecai Johnson), Morehouse College (Dr. Benjamin Mays), Morris Brown College (Bishop Richard R. Wright Jr.), and Bethune-Cookman College (Mary McCloud Bethune) through an active campaign to create "the Ultimate Negro Doll."[31] Roosevelt hosted a reception for these Black scholars and intellectuals to determine the complexion that the Sara Lee dolls should have to be the most marketable to Black people; the jury decided on a soft brown complexioned doll, markedly different than the "high brown" dolls of the NNDC and "dusky" dolls of the UNIA Doll Factory as well as the Patti-Jo (sometimes Patty-Jo) and Amosandra dolls sold in the 1950s by white-owned doll companies. Despite the political endorsement Sara Lee dolls received from prominent Black and white leaders at their inception, they were produced for only two years. Ideal Toy Company was much less invested in manufacturing racial reconciliation, as was rhetorically symbolized by the doll. The same fate befell the Patti-Jo dolls created by famed cartoon designer Jackie Ormes, based on her critical cartoon character. Patti-Jo was manufactured by the Terri Lee Doll Company in 1948 with much less fanfare and was better received on an international scale as representative of Black people and racial harmony in the United States.

All of the Black dolls created in the 1950s, from Sara Lee to Patti-Jo and Amosandra, were all saturated with notability across the color line. These dolls, like those from the early twentieth century from the NNDC and the UNIA, marked the ways that Black people became invested in material products of play to instill racial pride. Additionally, the shift in the manufacturing and aesthetic of Black dolls over time—from Dinah and Topsy servant dolls made of cloth during enslavement until the turn of the nineteenth century to "anthropologically correct" Black baby dolls that highlighted a variety of political and social issues around race and beauty—illustrated a growing Black middle class that could afford, and in turn demand, dolls that reflected their social, political, and economic concerns.[32] The idea that Negro children required "Negro dolls" for positive racialization abounded and also merged intellectual conversations about assimilation and miscegenation into consumerist ideals.[33] Alongside other massive (and controversial) cultural events that featured Black people in the United States—such as television shows like *Amos 'n' Andy*, Jackie Robinson playing for the Dodgers in 1947, and the murder of Black people and destruction of Black businesses all across the nation throughout the first half of the twentieth century—Black people used dolls to engage ideas of uplift on multiple fronts.

As duCille notes, racial uplift was a foundational part of the "African American Dream" in the 1950s and 1960s; remarking on her parents' adherence to respectability politics albeit without religiosity and elitism, duCille argues "racial uplift was nothing other than a black version of the desire—the determination—most parents hold for their offspring to do better than they. In this case, doing better wasn't simply for the sake of the individual or the family, but rather, for the race."[34] DuCille's construction of racial uplift as the expansion of parental desire for offspring to do better is a symptom of enslavement and politics of representation created about Black people. The servants, buffoons, and monsters that represented Black identity in popular culture of the 1950s and 1960s created sociopsychological minefields that Black people worked constantly to deride in their daily presentation and attitudes. Like their enslaved and free forebearers before them who worked to stylize themselves as "not a slave," Black people in the mid-twentieth century toiled every day to represent themselves in stark contrast to Black (and blackface) characters on television. The struggle over which representation of blackness was more "accurate," indeed most "authentic," took hold specifically alongside the long Civil Rights Movement and then exploded within the convergence of various political attitudes of the Black Power and Black Arts Movements. The whole twentieth century was marked by the ideological amalgamation of authentic blackness, product production and consumption, and political alignment with racial uplift and progress.

Black Popular Imagination and Corporate Alignment

Exploring the racial aspects of consumption in the early twentieth century, Erin Chapman contends that "African Americans' new conspicuousness made race popularly relevant on a national scale. While the burgeoning entertainment industries were quick to capitalize on this new consumer group and source of entertainment commodities, African Americans themselves utilized new technologies such as film and publishing to articulate evolving expressions of racial identity and advancement politics."[35] Stepping into the role of consumer, producer, and consumable object in new ways, New Negroes hastened to shift their representation on their own terms. Factions of Black people worked to align their representation with their uplift politics—complexly situated in middle-class politics through "high brown" beauty aesthetics and middle-class leisure activities or those of the "folk" who populated juke joints, blues clubs, and other so-called licentious activities. This tension shaped the political discourses encircling Black people at the turn of the century as well as the social spaces "respectable" people *should* occupy. From the racial uplift ideologies of Nannie Helen Burroughs to Zora Neale Hurston's celebration of folk culture, the first half of the twentieth century aligned consumption, leisure, sexual behaviors and politics, and modernity in ways that opened up as well as curtailed self-determined expression.[36]

The wake of *Brown v. Board of Education* and the marginal desegregation of public places like department stores, buses, pools, and schools created some opportunities for Black people to expand their reach in the realm of representation they worked to efface in daily interactions. Building on the representational work that intellectuals, artists, and working folk advanced during the New Negro period, the Civil Rights Movement generation used the arts as well as corporate interests in Black consumer markets to drive greater integration despite white (and Black) concerns of "race mixing" in a changing world.[37]

During the long Civil Rights Movement, the concern for racial mixing proliferated as Black consumption gained momentum at the nexus between consumer,
producer, and consumable object. Traci Parker illustrates how American citizenship, especially for Black people who were subject to Jim Crow treatment at every
location of leisure, was contingent upon one's access to consumption as a form of
democracy; she argues that public leisure environments like department stores
"enthroned consumption as the route to democracy and citizenship and invited
everyone—regardless of race, gender, age, class, and country of origin—to enter,
browse, and purchase often superfluous material goods."[38] As is true today, the
ability to buy consumer goods illustrated one's own class (and race) status and
therefore fed mass social change. Alongside *Brown v. Board of Education* and in
the aftermath of the Great Depression, which stymied many Black businesses,
Black consumers and producers worked to take advantage of war surplus as well
as the general desire of many companies to make money. In this way, the 1950s
through the 1980s saw the inclusion of many "firsts" for Black people in corporate
environments, especially in popular culture. Some of the most remarkable shifts
in representation occurred through television and the marketing of consumer
culture as the interest convergence between Black people's own demonstrations
against racist treatment as consumers and corporate environments that saw an
increased number of Black people as employees and marketplace competitors.
There were those, Black women especially, who used beauty culture as a means
to create independence for themselves and other people they employed; others still turned to white-collar work—in corporations that were increasingly
marketing to Black populations—to position themselves as equal partners in
the American consumption project of the twentieth century.[39]

The remaining chapters of this book consider the ways that Black women, in
particular, worked within corporate environments to navigate their own ideas
of Black racial politics through embodiment. Considering the advancement
of Black dolls at Mattel, Black princesses at Disney, and Black women in rap
stardom on the global stage, my argument lies at the tensions I have explored
in this chapter. I provide contemporary evidence for Erin Chapman's argument
about Black people in the 1920s: "liberation via the marketplace was ultimately
ephemeral. And yet the satisfactions of participating in it remained real."[40] While
the venue for discussions of racial uplift and Black consumerism has changed
somewhat (such as social media, more than churches or public lectures), I
explore how Black women as consumers, producers, and consumable objects
propelled discussions of Black consumer practices, Black beauty, and identity
development for children in the United States from the 1970s to the Obama era.
My hope in contextualizing the role that some American Black women play in
the global project of Black consumption is to think with and against the terms

of Black uplift in the late twentieth century, forcing us all to consider what happens after Black people get their idiomatic slice of the corporate pie.

Structure of the Book

Chapter 1, "Theorizing Black Women's Cultural Influence through Consumption," examines the tensions between Black women cultural producers as repositories of Black symbolic power and Black women consumers who are intentionally hailed by their products. Black women within the corporate environment of making imagination—specifically within Disney, Mattel, and on social media—create a means by which Black women are known; as cultural producers, they create objects that then stand in for Black women's bodies. I coin "embodied objectification" to describe the process through which Black women cultural producers infuse products for mass consumption with their experiences, aesthetics, and intraracial politics while specifically seeking Black girls and women as their target consumers. This understanding of Black women's self-objectification must be foundational to how we theorize the relationship between producer and consumer, race and the mass market, and Black women's and girls' consumption of mass-produced products. Centering Black women's consumption in the haircare industry—specifically with two major formerly Black-owned hair companies, Carol's Daughter and SheaMoisture—I illustrate how Black women cultural producers bridge ideologically-based relationships with consumers based on their embodied objectification. This ideological relationship is developed and at times severed between Black producers and consumers through identification, signifying, and reification in capitalist markets.

Using interviews and archival research from the Strong National Museum of Play and Indianapolis Children's Museum as well as interviews with Black women designers who were employed by Mattel, I recover Black women's role in the creation of Black Barbie dolls from 1980 to 2015 in chapter 2, "From Riots to Style: The History of Black Barbie." I argue that while testing their project to commodify blackness in their relationship with Watts-based and Black-owned Shindana Toy Company (1968–1978), Mattel's foray into multicultural markets was fortified by Black women employees—Kitty Black Perkins, Deborah Mitchell, and Darlene Powell-Hopson—who imbued each doll with the embodied knowledges they have as Black women. An example of the theory of embodied objectification and the tension between Black women's vision of creation for Black girls and white corporate interests, Black women cultural producers' experiences illustrate how Mattel's rise to and maintenance of doll industry fame occurred through Black women's harnessing of Black symbolic power for corporate gain. Through these women's influence, Mattel became the arbiter of material multiculturalism, creating consumer markets based in the phenotypic stereotypes and the aesthetic creativity of different groups. Their decisions to claim beauty and femininity, alongside disco or urban fashion, cultural vernacular, and afro-styled hair, shifted the cultural imagination of Black womanhood to include America's most beloved doll, Barbie.

Chapter 3, "From Bootstraps to Glass Slippers: Black Women's Uplift in Disney's Princess Canon," turns to Disney's competing investment in multicultural marketing through the narrative of Cinderella as a Black woman. Outlining a discursive convergence of ideas of Black citizenship through uplift and the American Dream, I examine how Black women cultural producers created, funded, and characterized popular princess films featuring Black women through their own embodied objectification. Alongside the rise of "multiculturalism" as a commodification of blackness and the harnessing of Black symbolic power to sell Black culture back to Black people, I argue that Black women cultural producers used Disney's *Cinderella* (1997) and *The Princess and the Frog* (2009) to shape the imaginative space available for Black girls within popular princess narratives as well as the ideological relationships that Black women and girls have to them as Black women cultural producers. Birthed from narratives of racial uplift and self-sufficiency through consumer citizenship promulgated in the twentieth century, these films illustrate how Black women have been integral in creating stories that present Black women as hyperindustrious, further perpetuating lessons that Black girls and women learn in US popular culture across generations. *Cinderella* and *The Princess and the Frog* present possibilities for Black women and girls to see themselves outside of the norm of Hollywood representation while also capitulating to narratives that bind our blackness and desirability to our labor and attractiveness to men.

In chapter 4, "A Black Barbie's Moment: Nicki Minaj and the Struggle for Cultural Dominance," I analyze how the construction of Black Barbie and Cinderella frame the rise of Black woman rapper Nicki Minaj. The only mainstream Black woman in hip-hop from 2009 to 2018, Nicki Minaj substantially dictates an opening of representations of Black women that privileges sexual freedom and social dominance through self-determination and empowerment for Black women and girls, while also illustrating the symbolic value of white iconography through the playful use of Barbie, Cinderella, and the white gaze. I contextualize her performances, albums, and lyrics within narratives of Black authenticity, uplift, and beauty via Barbie and Cinderella that Black women producers, designers, and consumers curated within the mass consumer market from the 1970s to the early 2000s. I argue that other cultural producers and consumers appropriate the symbolic value of Minaj's images on social media—based in her embodied objectification and the ideological bridge she builds to Black women and girl consumers—therefore, reifying Black women's experiences and bodies to facilitate their own cultural relevance and popular culture success. Nicki Minaj, as a Black woman–produced cultural product, helps us visualize the ways Black symbolic power established through embodied objectification is harnessed for other means, including sociopolitical posturing in twenty-first-century US popular culture.

In the final chapter, "The Stakes of Twenty-first-Century Black Creativity," I consider how Black women cultural producers face new challenges in the promulgation of Black women's stories. Mired by twenty-first-century Black Twitter commentary prior to any release dates, Black women cultural producers not only have to consider the ways their ideas and images may be used by non-Black consumers, but also how the desires of Black women consumers have changed. Revisiting major social media controversies that affected the reception of Kasi Lemmons's *Harriet* (2019), I argue that Black women cultural producers must shift their ideological relationship to their consumers. In the aftermath of the 1990s and 2000s multicultural push and the rise of Black women's role in social media discourse (as well as mass incarceration and Black women's political exigencies), the stakes of Black women's creativity are even higher than generations past because Black girl and women consumers want more.

Buy Black as a cultural text brings together Black history, literature, visual culture, and digital discourses to consider the national (and global) impact of Black women's labor within entertainment-based consumer markets. Focused on creating for the Black women and girls with whom they find community, Black women cultural producers teach all of us the parameters of Black symbolic power by harnessing intraracial ideals of blackness, womanhood, beauty, imaginative play, and sexuality through Black women's eyes. While they compete in the consumer market for the attention and loyalty of Black consumer dollars, their capitulation to white corporate interests and audiences requires propagating historical tensions in discourses of Black consumer citizenship and multicultural inclusion. Negotiating the line between "sell out" and "for us, by us," Black women cultural producers further Black women's historical position as the moral compass and arbiter of Black racial progress in the United States. Beyond the ability to identify and play with conceptions of blackness through their products, Black women cultural producers will need to go further than conventional representation and "Black is beautiful" rhetoric to secure financial gain and maintain Black women's consumer loyalties.

CHAPTER 1

Theorizing Black Women's Cultural Influence through Consumption

Black women's role in creating and promoting representations of Black women all too often continue centuries'-old racist and intraracial imaginative possibilities about who Black women are and can be. These imaginative possibilities are built within the ideological apparatus of the United States and therefore promulgate its politics in everything that is imaged and everything that is not. In a capitalist society, Louis Althusser argues, "all ideology hails or interpellates concrete individuals as concrete subjects" and therefore individuals and subjects are co-constitutive through interpellation.[1] A Black woman is made a subject of white supremacy even as she is an independent and free-acting individual—her individuality and subjection are in concert with one another. I, for example, was constituted within this system at birth and also work to make the system real in my daily actions, or what Althusser calls practice, and become a "Subject" once "hailed." My hailing makes me visible to the structures of domination that deliberately work to incorporate me into its system. Therefore, as a spectator, the process of seeing yourself represented causes you to become part of the "visible," since you are hailed by the images. I am hailed into supporting and regurgitating white supremacy through practice, particularly through daily interactions with language and images.[2]

The argument that marginalized people make for greater inclusion as a response to historical erasure is usually made at the level of visibility, partially because finally seeing ourselves communicates some level of inclusion in the mainstream.[3] We recognize the process of interpellation that happens through language and images daily and, therefore, argue that seeing ourselves is important to societal acceptance. We find pleasure in language that replicates our communication styles and images that show us, even as tokens. This recognition allows us to perform differing levels of what José Esteban Muñoz calls disidentification (recognizing the ways we do not identify with the image), even while celebrating the singular opportunity to see ourselves.[4] For example, Katherine Sender shows the development of niche marketing for the LGBTQ community on the national level made some feel that "we are everywhere," representing greater visibility and awareness of gay lifestyles; yet the consummate murder of Black trans women illustrates that greater visibility and acceptance for some does not translate to all.[5] The interpretive connection between visibility in marketing and real-life acceptance then contextualizes the importance of niche marketing as a marker of inclusion within American citizenship for marginalized people. For many, the incorporation of one's community or likeness into the US market system means that they have been accepted into US citizenship. Consumerism and the ability to buy products that you can identify with, in some ways, communicates social acceptance.

In the project for the social acceptance of Black people, Black women are producers and repositories of Black symbolic power. Black symbolic power means the images, sounds, aesthetics (as well as the dis/identifications) that resonate with and permeate throughout Black communities as well as the ideologies that undergird the images, sounds, and aesthetics we hold dear. We can understand the work that Black women cultural producers do within culture as creators of wealth through Black symbolic power—cultural capital that gets converted into economic capital for white corporations. This wealth, however, commodifies the embodied discourses of Black femininity and reproduces them for a public, and many times unknowing audience of spectators. Even for those who reject the logics of empowerment via visibility or visibility within the consumer market as a marker of acceptance, the neoliberal ideologies built within the system mandate their participation (hails them through language and images). As oppositional spectators in a system that Sarah Banet-Weiser calls the visual economy, marginalized people must utilize similar logics of visibility to make their plight known. Because popular culture maintains itself via this attachment to capitalism, empty signifiers—such as the one token marginalized person in a television show or film like Storm (played by Halle Berry) in *X-Men* (2000) and Susie Carmichael and her family in the Nickelodeon show *Rugrats*—promote representation as a stand-in for political struggle. Visibility becomes an end in itself, or as Banet-Weiser argues, "economies of visibility do not describe a political process, but rather assume that visibility itself has been absorbed into the economy; indeed, that absorption *is* the political."[6] Therefore the push for multicultural representation, particularly in corporate entertainment environments like Mattel, Disney, and the music industry, rests on the desire to create potential capitalist subjects from "emerging" markets.

For corporate executives, the only reason to promote a multicultural cast, create a token character in a mostly white show, or promote older racialized caricatures is the possibility of consumers buying with their dollars or viewing hours (and, with increasing regularity, their data) the representation with which they identify. The push for inclusion is the push to connect to emerging markets, because if people feel represented, meaning they are visibly marked in the products that companies use to try to signal to them, they are more likely to participate in an economy that reduces their political struggle to mere visibility. The use of rainbows, or curly haired ambiguously brown children, or even the voices of assimilated popular Black celebrities like Morgan Freeman, Dennis Haysbert, or Samuel L. Jackson, purposefully inject a consumer product with the cache of marginalized people. The goal for consumer industries, then, of getting people from the fringes to the center is less about greater representation and more about getting them to spend more and more money, increasing the company's overall market share of consumer dollars.

This chapter reveals the tensions between Black women as producers and a racial marketplace where commodifiable blackness is a product to be bought, sold, and exchanged. Black women's role in what has become the visual economy is at the center of this book, as are the questions I seek to answer about the popularity of certain images, bodies, and femininities over others, especially as they are authored by Black women. As creators, producers, actors, and designers, what images and narratives are Black women invested in reproducing and why? What factors constrict the decisions that Black women cultural producers make as they pertain to learning about Black womanhood, femininity, and race through consumer products? I consider the politics of visuality for Black women—as both consumers and producers—and the ways that Black women working within corporate environments narrate the imaginative possibilities for Black (and other) children through play.

Black women cultural producers do not solely create for the benefit of Black girls, Black women, or Black people writ large, but rather actively struggle with and against popular constructions of Black femininity which cavort with white supremacist images. Black women seemingly create and harness Black symbolic power for consumer products for two goals and with two audiences in mind: one is to generate a sense of pleasure through visibility for Black people while the other is to shift ideas and assumptions about Black femininity for non-Black audiences and buyers. This tension sometimes spawns conflicting messages about blackness, womanhood, beauty, and other topics that exist and proliferate simultaneously.

Therefore, I am attentive to this creation process and tension by constructing a Black feminist theory of consumption that better reads and interprets Black women as both cultural producers and consumers as well as identifies the ways that they use identification, reification, and branding to further their own aims within the construction of Black consumer products for mass consumption. Their use of identification, reification, and branding, I argue, is contingent upon their own ideals of blackness; I expand on the play of Black symbolic power within Black women's cultural production to understand how Black women infuse their own ideals of what constitutes blackness within their creation and marketing of products for Black people as well as what happens when those brands become mainstream, and the ways they reify and reinforce stereotypes of Black people.

Consumption as Ideological Renegotiation

Consumption is typically considered from two perspectives in academic scholarship: from corporate institutions that are creating products, marketing, and narratives to lure consumer dollars, and from consumers who consider how and why they use their dollars in particular ways. Many scholars of consumption foreground the theoretical constructions of consumption on identification. Louis Althusser, Stuart Hall, Grant McCracken, Jagdish Sheth, Bruce Newman, and Barbara Gross, and other scholars conceptualize representation and consumption through the ways that people are able to align themselves with consumer products and in turn how consumer products—as physical manifestations of a society's cultural ideologies—hail and make use of people as subjects.[7] Industry executives are interested in the idea of difference and representation only as it becomes sellable, and therefore consumable, to a mainstream, popular audience; Leonard Steinhorn and Barbara Diggs-Brown explain that "putting black executives in high-profile but not very significant positions serves a number of corporate needs," mainly "for public consumption to portray a corporate image of diversity and tolerance, very important in a society that wants to see itself as integrated" as well as to "help the company compete for business, particularly when affirmative action laws or other diversity imperatives apply."[8] However, with the turn to more so-called niche marketing after the Civil Rights Movement, the possibilities for what and whom are consumable have changed drastically. McCracken, for example, argues that "hippies, punks, and gays" constructed the lower-class perspective that the fashion industry appropriated to create "edgier" clothing for the mass market.[9] Sarah Banet-Weiser considers the ways that the ideology of branding—a marketing tool that started as simple differentiation in a crowded market and became a structure that makes certain ideologies, expressions, or tastes synonymous with a particular consumer product—has changed how certain aspects of culture (politics, religion, feminism) are understood by consumers; for example, "natural haircare" has become synonymous with Black women and representations of Black women. Brenda Wynn Greer establishes the ways that Black men, specifically John J. Johnson (founder of *Ebony* and *Jet* magazines) and Gordon Parks (famed photographer), convinced marketing executives at companies like Coca-Cola to invest in marketing to Black consumers as Black people and as premier citizens of the American polity.[10]

Let us take as a case study the production of black hair as a signifier for authentic, or at times, respectable blackness (or a combination of the two). Studied for the ways that Black women find meaning, articulate political beliefs and ideals, and connect with each other through styling practices in person and digitally, hair has served as a marker of beauty, socioeconomic status, and commitment to Black communities' struggle for acceptance. Ingrid Banks, Ayana Byrd and Lori Tharps, Maxine Leeds Craig, Noliwe Rooks, Tanisha Ford, and others have written about Black women's hair and the ways it has been used for political and social means.[11] Judged for their proximity to the ever elusive ideal of "good hair," Black women whether wearing their hair natural or straightened have worked to exude kempt and coiffed beauty with their hair. Ford argues that Black people's styling practices, which extended beyond the sartorial to all aspects of presentation, worked to "[re-aestheticize] blackness, which created new value and political power for the black body."[12] Hair took on new political meaning during the mid-twentieth century as Black women positioned themselves as worthy of respect in the public sphere. These coiffed looks located Black women at either side of a divided intraracial sartorial politics, communicating allegiance as well as sedition.

Extending age-old arguments about Black women as representatives of the race, the 1960s and 1970s marked a politically volatile moment for Black women's hair. Black women navigated, and are still navigating, their beliefs in uplifting the race, their own beauty rituals and individualized aesthetic desires, and Black men's desire.[13] Leeds Craig shows how Black women's hair choices positioned them as either beautiful or "invisible" because of their adherence to Black intraracial hair politics; unlike Black men who moved from conks to

Afros as a marker of (masculinized) racial pride, Black women "who chose to express proud black identity by wearing a natural felt that they diminished their identity as women by doing so."[14] Black women's hair, historically and contemporarily, has been articulated as their "crown" and therefore the marker of their beauty, desirability, perceived worthiness of respect, and affinity for Black culture. With a short cut or without any hair, Black women are constantly questioned about their preference for heterosexual relationships and chastised by men and women alike for not performing their so-called feminine duties of attractiveness. While this idea goes beyond hair to other aspects of the sartorial, Black women's hair has always retained its importance in the making or breaking of their individual and collective beauty.[15]

Black girls' hair and hair play has been equally endowed with symbolic importance. From Black girls wearing braids being suspended from school for not adhering to the dress code to the popularity of Willow Smith's 2010 song "Whip My Hair" and its *Sesame Street* counterpart, Black girls are invested in the political and socioeconomic attitudes toward Black hair, and how they construct themselves alongside Black women as "consumer citizens."[16] With Ann duCille who argues that hair play with straight-haired Barbies creates the desire for straight hair, Elizabeth Chin contends that Black girls braiding their white Barbie's straight and blonde hair is a radical political project that brings "blonde-haired and blue-eyed dolls into their own worlds."[17] Because Black girls understand the ways that straight hair is associated with whiteness and how that association further shifts perception of their other phenotypes, they learn to recognize and emulate white beauty standards even while venerating the braids, twists, and styles that they see celebrated in their communities.[18] Both in the ways they wear their hair and the ways their hair is perceived in social and educational settings, Black girls, like Black women, are constantly embroiled in the political and socioeconomic symbolic power of hair.

Beyond the political and interpersonal aspects of hair, Black women are historically known for their mass consumption of hair products. A running joke about this aspect of Black women's consumption is to guess how many barely used products are under their sinks, casualties of the buy-and-try method typical of Black haircare. Beautifying, as Kathy Peiss calls the process of making oneself up for the day, has always been a particularly important aspect of Black women's bodily presentation. The growth of mass-produced products easily accessed at mainstream stores has shifted Black women's relationship to the beauty industry and their hair ever since Madame C. J. Walker and Annie Turnbo Malone started selling hair products and face creams in the 1920s and 1930s.[19] Even as Black women navigated the difficult relationship to their own hair, to other Black women's judgment, and to beauty shop politics, they were also faced with the difficulty of finding products that suited their hair. The smorgasbord of hair products under a Black woman's sink has only grown alongside the access to more hair products.

The growth of Black entrepreneurship, advancements in mass production (including small-batch production), and changes in Black hair product consumption have made billions of dollars from Black women's search for haircare products that will keep their hair moist and manageable. Brands like Carol's Daughter, SheaMoisture, and others have risen to financial heights unachieved by Black beauty brands previously and shifted many other brands' targeting of Black women consumers. The naming and aesthetics of Black beauty brands arguably illustrate each brand's ideal consumer. The hair texture, skin complexion, product label, product description, and price point communicate the brands' intentional hailing of certain Black women consumers. Phrases like nappy, kinky, coily, and textured in the names or descriptions of brands or their products, for example, differentiate for whose hair it would be best suited. Likewise, the company owners' style, hair, complexion, and overall sartorial practice harnesses Black symbolic power for sales. Carol's Daughter and SheaMoisture are the most recent examples of these processes and ideological underpinnings. Despite both Carol's Daughter and SheaMoisture being acquired by large white corporations—L'Oréal in 2014 and Unilever in 2017 respectively—their owners argue their continued commitment to Black women consumers through new partnerships with Black women celebrities, new product lines that specifically name and describe textured hair, and the types of ingredients used in each product. However, the acquisition of these brands by large white corporations has unearthed historical tensions between Black consumers, Black producers, and white-owned corporations over representation and marketing. I present Carol's Daughter and SheaMoisture, specifically, as contemporary evidence of the ways Black women (and sometimes men) producers attempt to create a relationship with Black women consumer-spectators based on ideological beliefs about blackness, hair, beauty, and complexion. These ideologically bridged relationships not only structure the development of products, but also the growth of the companies through a fragile and tenuous commitment to the same political and socioeconomic concerns that are foundational to Black women's lived experiences and representational politics. In their attempt to grow and entice consumers beyond the Black diaspora, Carol's Daughter and SheaMoisture learn how and why the haircare industry exemplifies the ideological renegotiation inherent in Black women's consumptive practices.

Encouraged by her mother Carol and the success of products within her family, Lisa Price expanded her haircare products beyond her Brooklyn kitchen and began selling them at local markets and regional festivals in 1993.[20] Her success led her to opening boutiques where women could come in and test products, get advice, and see the results of products on shop workers and the founder herself. Testing products and seeing results immediately were an important part of Price's business success because consumers had the ability to perceive the applicability of products on Price's hair as well as the hair of her sales associates, eliminating the buy-and-try method; consumers believed they could not only emulate the styles, but also the textures of hair they saw. Price was able to utilize the growth of internet sales, faster shipping options, and Black haircare blogs to begin selling her products online, which resulted in launching into a larger market beyond New York. After being highlighted on Oprah Winfrey's show in 2002, selling products on the Home Shopping Network in 2008 (including an exclusive fragrance bearing singer Mary J. Blige's face and name in 2011), and reaching mass-market production with Target and the financial help of Pegasus Advisors Group, Lisa Price filed for Chapter 11 bankruptcy in 2014, then sold Carol's Daughter to personal care conglomerate L'Oréal.[21]

As one of the first major companies to launch natural haircare products after the rise of Black women's "natural hair movement," Carol's Daughter represented a substantial opportunity since the 1970s for Black women to buy products that would help them as they transitioned from relaxers to more regularly wearing afros, twists, and braided styles. Price, as a Black woman cultural producer, was in step with a global movement in which some Black women were not only shifting their hair routines, but also creating counterpublic spaces—principally online—to learn about their hair and trade best practices. Carol's Daughter, subsequently, cultivated a substantive following among Black women. With the name "Carol's Daughter," the haircare line not only represented Price's personal relationship with her mother, but more importantly provided a tangible and accessible Black woman with whom to associate the company. As representative and a material manifestation of Lisa Price, the haircare line itself was the daughter of a Black woman—the object that was cared for, prayed over, and made real through many years of cultivation and care. Price's decision to name her product line after herself essentially, while also constantly hailing her mother and her relationship to her mother within the product's name, aligns with many Black women's narratives of their hair. Recalling their memories of being young Black girls taught to sit patiently between the legs of their mothers who combed, braided, straightened, or relaxed their hair, Black women could connect epistemologically with Price's narrative of starting the company as well as her products as they stood in for her own embodiment. Said differently, Black women consumers were ostensibly becoming Carol's daughter, becoming Lisa Price, through their purchase of her products.

Like many Black haircare producers, Price's body—her hair specifically— exemplified the power of her products. From her appearances at markets and festivals to her debut on the Oprah show and interviews with *Essence* magazine, Lisa Price became synonymous with her products. Particularly in the visual economy of the late twentieth and early twenty-first centuries, the Carol's Daughter brand was reified by Price's own hair; Black women consumers saw and identified with Price as a Black woman who discussed her own struggles with her hair and finding the right products to manage it. Black women consumers also identified with other celebrities who had invested or publicly supported Price's products, including Jada Pinkett and Will Smith, Mary J. Blige, and Gabrielle Union. In every single interview, Price's hair is out and visibly

FIGURE 1.1. (L-to-R) Investor Steven Stoute, artist Mary J. Blige, and Carol's Daughter founder Lisa Price. Source: Courtesy of AP Images.

curly. Unlike Black women beauty culturalists of the early twentieth century (or even the well-known slicked back, long ponytail of Mary J. Blige), Price's hair was not pulled back or slicked down in a way that historically would be ideologically mapped onto ideas of professionalism or respectability. Instead, in a visual economy of Black women's hair where the condition, texture, and luminosity of the founder's hair becomes representative of what could happen with their products, Lisa Price is never seen without her hair (and hair texture) in a noticeably curly afro in an interview or at a public event.[22]

Price's hair and body exemplified to Black women consumers the aesthetic that Black women celebrities and everyday people hoped to style for themselves—confident, business-minded, modern, and aesthetically Black. Her hair emphasized and affirmed the move that many Black women were making to use natural products and to "go natural" or transition their hair from a chemically relaxed state; in many ways, Carol's Daughter came into prominence because of the shifts culturally occurring for Black women. Black women, since 2010 especially, have shifted toward using natural products for their natural hair and have founded "more than 133 million 'natural hair blogs,'" in addition to products, conferences, and workshops.[23] Carol's Daughter, buttressed by celebrity investors and the "Oprah Effect," was able to capitalize on the niche market of Black women's haircare, and, through embodied objectification, reification, and branding, became the number-one haircare line for Black women, based on units sold.[24]

Despite the success story of Price and her brand, the L'Oréal USA acquisition made many Black women turn away from Carol's Daughter and make their own products or use other upcoming brands.[25] While Price celebrated this achievement and marked it as the fulfillment of her entrepreneurial dreams, many Black women consumers were dismayed. Some noted and confirmed that the products changed with the acquisition, resulting in watered-down products that no longer worked the way they had for years, a typical complaint of natural products when large corporations find cheaper ingredients to replace more expensive ones (for example, vegetable glycerin in place of shea butter).[26] Others disagreed with Price's choice to "sell out"—a Black euphemism for becoming a token of diversity in a white company or for literally selling one's product to white people and letting their companies produce the same product. An extension of arguments about cultural appropriation or Black-owned and -operated brands that sell to white companies, "selling out" is one of the most denigrating comments to be slung at any Black entrepreneur or performer.[27] Still others disliked the idea of buying hair products from white companies, on the ideological principle that to "go natural" should also be linked to supporting

Black-owned (especially woman-owned) businesses; this is another aspect of Black women's haircare that aligns with politically expedient beliefs, albeit still built within capitalist paradigms. Overall, Carol's Daughter suffered some loss of its popularity among Black women consumers, but supposedly gained white consumers with L'Oréal's shift toward more broad-based advertising strategies for the line. This too turned away Black consumers who felt "their" products were now being steered toward others in place of them, recapitulating other ways that white people are always positioned as the principal marketing audience and the ideal consumers.[28]

Much like Carol's Daughter, its competitor SheaMoisture has led an even more aggressive campaign to create opportunities for Black women consumers in the haircare industry to buy their products at every consumer goods store. Founded by Richelieu Dennis, his mother Mary Dennis, and a friend Nyema Tubman in 1991 (approximately the same time Lisa Price founded Carol's Daughter), SheaMoisture and its parent company Sundial Brands promoted shampoos, lotions, and soaps on Harlem's streets.[29] Gleaned from Dennis's grandmother's recipes for women in her community in Liberia, SheaMoisture's brand has specifically targeted Black women with the aim of shifting the global market for skin and haircare products. Major retailers like Macy's and Target started selling SheaMoisture in 2007, a major undertaking that like Carol's Daughter aligned with the change in Black women consumers' attitudes about their hair and haircare products, but also forced retailers to sell their products beyond the "ethnic hair" aisle. After investment from Bain Capital in 2015, SheaMoisture began to shift its marketing to increase its consumer base; marketing campaigns like "Break the Walls" and "What's Normal" targeted the segmentation of the haircare aisles and the ways that "normal hair" was almost always synonymous with straight, long, and kinkless hair. SheaMoisture retailers now include pharmacy chains like CVS and Walgreens, big-box stores like Costco, and consumer goods retailers like Target and Walmart. It is almost impossible to go to a consumer goods store and not be confronted by at least one line of SheaMoisture's products. However, this broad-based success and marketing has turned away Black women consumers for several reasons: the desire to support Black women's entrepreneurship, changes in SheaMoisture's products and marketing, and Unilever's acquisition of the brand.

Unlike Carol's Daughter, which was Black woman-owned and -operated, SheaMoisture and its parent company Sundial Brands are run by Black men. While Richelieu Dennis argues that Black women occupy over 70 percent of SheaMoisture's employee base, Black men hold the top leadership positions in the organization. Some Black women consumers have turned specifically to Black women-owned brands; this attitude within Black women consumer markets to support Black women entrepreneurs in particular, perhaps shows a growing number of Black women who want to support their friends, sorority sisters, and mentors in more financial ways, investing in those brands and products that directly speak to their sartorial concerns and representational politics.[30] Exemplified by SheaMoisture's faltering social standing in 2017, when Black women consumers feel neglected by a brand, they will seek alternatives.

SheaMoisture's marketing expansion to target women in both the "regular" and "ethnic" beauty aisles made their loyal consumer base of Black women feel snubbed. A commercial "Hair Hate," part of SheaMoisture's new #EverybodyGetsLove campaign, released in April 2017, featured five women, none of whom were dark-skinned or had hair considered typical of Black women. Without a model that represented kinky textures in the commercial, Black women consumers argued that SheaMoisture had wholly left them out of the "everybody" the company wished to target with the campaign. Deeply angered and confused, Black women responded on social media.[31] Some argued that in its attempt to appeal to white audiences, SheaMoisture had completely disregarded its base and left Black women where all other brands had, making white women their ideal consumer. Others called for boycotts of the brand to signal their displeasure and Black women's buying power. Still others simply asked for the names of other companies to support as a way of separating themselves from a brand that no longer catered to them and their hair. While Dennis and

FIGURE 1.2. SheaMoisture #HairHate ad still.
Source: Courtesy of SheaMoisture/Twitter User @girlswithtoys.

his team apologized for the ad and assured Black women consumers of their commitment, the damage to their reputation was resounding.[32]

A few months later in late November 2017, Unilever announced it had acquired Sundial brands and would be appointing Esi Eggleston Bracey to assist Richelieu Dennis in growing SheaMoisture's production and distribution to sell in markets in Africa and South America.[33] Dennis and Eggleston Bracey were hyperaware of the visual branding needed to convince Black women consumers of Unilever and SheaMoisture's commitment to them; unlike Carol's Daughter, without a Black woman's body to physically mark the ways that Black women were central to the mission and vision of SheaMoisture after the acquisition, and especially after a marketing campaign that wholly excluded darker-complexioned Black women, the social media commentary was less than celebratory. Met with criticism akin to that of Carol's Daughter of selling out to white companies in hopes of white consumer dollars, Eggleston Bracey (a Black woman now the executive vice president and chief operating officer of Unilever's North American market) and Dennis aggressively interviewed with major Black magazines and news outlets like *Essence*, *The Root*, and *MadameNoire* to clarify the vision and mission of Unilever's acquisition. However, making a Black woman stand in for the global British-Dutch company after the "Hair Hate" commercial faux pas was not enough for some Black women consumers. On counterpublic spaces, especially on digital blog platforms like CurlyNikki .com, Nappturality.com, and Blackgirlwithlonghair.com, Black women argued that the commercial communicated a dismissal of the very communities that made the company $700 million as well as the communities they used in Liberia to source the ingredients. SheaMoisture instituted listening sessions to smooth over concerns about product changes and brand loyalties, trying ultimately to reconnect the fragile relationship based on ideological beliefs about blackness, beauty, and citizenship that had bridged Dennis and Black women consumers from the beginning.

Over the course of six months, I collated responses to SheaMoisture's #HairHate commercial on the aforementioned blogs and Facebook and Twitter posts. In reviewing over 50,000 uses of the hashtag across all the sites, I found that some Black women consumers continued to buy products from Carol's Daughter or SheaMoisture after news of their acquisitions spread. While they expressed concern over the acquisitions of the companies by larger white-owned corporations and new marketing campaigns that focused on non-Black consumers, they remained loyal to the products (rather than the brands) that kept their hair and skin happy and healthy. Others, however, turned to smaller, Black woman–owned brands like Aunt Jackie's, CurlMix, Mielle Organics, and

Tailored Beauty. These brands and others have capitalized on the models Carol's Daughter and SheaMoisture have used in highlighting Black (woman) ownership, harnessing the visual economy of Black women social media influencers, models, and celebrities in their marketing campaigns, and focusing on the concerns of Black women as their ideal consumers. Black women consumers in turn continue to search for Black women cultural producers who maintain their ideological relationship as Black women as well as craft products that keep their hair in a healthy state. Through the production of new haircare products, Black women cultural producers and consumers struggle to find the right mixture of premium-quality products, mid-range price point, and company political ideologies that keep their hair, bodies, and political affinities aligned.

The case studies of Carol's Daughter and SheaMoisture illuminate how two aspects of twentieth- and twenty-first-century mass culture—the appropriation of oppositional cultural markers for consumption and the process of branding through marketing to Black consumers in particular—further shift what Stuart Hall calls identification.[34] Identification or the process through which consumers can project themselves into the marketing of a product relies on fantasy and play; the relationship between consumers and the consumer product is materialized through the identification of consumers with the images surrounding the product and the ability to imagine themselves as the consumer to whom a product is marketed—the subject who is intended to be hailed. As Adrienne Shaw shows, there are multiple and complex ways in which consumers identify with a consumer product in the media; the larger construction of both whom consumers and corporate institutions are as well as to whom and for what purpose consumer products are made needs to be further theorized to illustrate the ways Black women and girls navigate the consumer landscape.[35]

For Black cultural producers like owners of Carol's Daughter and Shea-Moisture to break into a saturated market, they must encourage consumers to renegotiate their relationship to consumer goods (as well as the cultural ideologies that underlie them) through repetitive cognitive connections (linguistic and visual practice). Grant McCracken explains that cultural producers are responsible for connecting a consumer good with already occurring cultural ideologies to create consumer buy-in. A cognitive connection between a consumer good and a particular company is created through the regular exposure of a consumer to the marketing of a good.[36] Following Stuart Hall, I concur that meaning is contextual and understood in different ways in differently distinct moments. For example, through extensive marketing (and in these days, social media retweets or what McCracken calls "ritual"), consumers renegotiated their identification between haircare products made for them and SheaMoisture with the release of the "Break the Walls" and "What's Normal" campaigns.[37] For some time, haircare generally and the haircare aisle in particular has been ideologically underpinned by the idea that Black hair and haircare were not "normal" or Black people were not the targeted consumers of products. Companies like Unilever (which owns Dove and TRESemmé) and L'Oréal (which owns L'Oréal Paris, Garnier, and Redken) have worked to create a fixed meaning (Stuart Hall's "stereotypes") of what constitutes quality haircare; so much so, that companies like Carol's Daughter and others that focus on women of color as their main consumer base have not worked as hard to unfix those meanings. SheaMoisture, contrastingly, released its #EverybodyGetsLove marketing campaign and encouraged consumers via social media to embrace a narrative that shifted the cultural meaning of so-called normal hair. While the older connection was not necessarily removed, the new connection broadens the consumer imagination about which products signify a particular experience. New connections, which I also understand as new ideological pathways or meaning creations, are made through the appropriation or imitation of a preexisting consumer product. Particularly in a world that is saturated with cultural meaning and markers, marketing and brands must recontextualize preexisting meaning to shift consumer reception to their products. How, though, do cultural meaning and markers attached to preexisting meanings of blackness, femininity, and beauty get negotiated over time? How, particularly when Black women are the cultural producers, are new ideological pathways created within the cultural landscape in which the "metalanguage of race" encapsulates all cultural production?[38] If, as Evelyn Brooks Higginbotham notes, "we think we know [the soul of blackness], when we see it because of its beat, its feeling, its movement," then how do material and visual presentations of blackness retain the soul of their producers?[39] Does the recontextualization of blackness dismember the soul?

While this book cannot address all cultural productions created by and produced for Black people by Black women, I render visible Black women cultural producers' use of universal representations of femininity and beauty. Through the appropriation of the symbolic power of these so-called universal images and the suturing of Black symbolic power to them, Black women cultural producers have worked to disaggregate the fixed meaning of representations, the stereotypes that put on pedestals thin, white, blonde, able-bodied, busty, and tall heterosexual women that dominate popular television shows, films, and music. By using the images that many US institutions hold dear, Black women shift the process of identification and reification through the manipulation of symbolic power, moving Black women and the ideas they have of themselves to the center of US imaginative consciousness. Said differently, Black women cultural producers renegotiate stereotypical ideas of femininity to include themselves, in turn shifting national (and at times global) representations of Black people, especially women.

Black Bodies in the Fight for Symbolic Power

Nicholas Mirzoeff explains white heteropatriarchal oppressors constructed visuality to function in three main ways: it "classifies [people] by naming, categorizing, and defining," it "separates the groups so [that they are] classified as a means of social organization," and it "makes this separated classification seem right and hence aesthetic."[40] Furthering Pierre Bourdieu's explanation of "symbolic power," Mirzoeff contends that the power of visuality is the power to produce identities, include or reject those who do not fit, and position them as inherent or already determined. In a Baudrillardian sense, visual culture makes the ideological work of images common sense and therefore difficult to decipher the original referent in any context. In a system of symbolic power in which so-called commonsense explanations justify representation, subtextual information can be demonized, constructed as individual interpretation rather than a larger pattern of symbolic dehumanization and erasure. However, the ideological work of visuality, the symbolic power of images that construct and constrict Black women, is exactly the level at which change is shaped.[41] Black women cultural producers use symbolic power, particularly at the level of children's play, to challenge the overdetermined ways that Black women's bodies are grouped, defined, and positioned as monstrous, sexually deviant, and abnormal in US popular culture. Like Lisa Price's persistent positioning of herself and her hair at marketing events, in addition to creating sponsorships with prominent Black women celebrities such as Solange Knowles, Cassie, Mary J. Blige, and Gabrielle Union as well as Carol's Daughter's 2009 release of Disney's *The Princess and the Frog* shampoo, conditioner, and bath set (intended for Black girls viewing the film), the shift of representation for Black women and girls challenges erasure and dehumanization at the symbolic level.[42]

Symbolic power is the harnessing of the power of images to represent people, places, and ideas. Underlying every representation are the attitudes and beliefs of the imagemakers and the institutions that are invested in selling certain images. Through the use of images, historically, people have had the ability to create or disband groups of affiliation by constituting beliefs about in-group and out-group membership. The work of images, especially over time, by powerful groups is to justify their power and to conscript others in maintaining their power. In the United States, the ideological power of images has been used by colonial settlers turned enslavers turned US politicians and businessmen to construct Black people as continually outside the American politic as well as unworthy of the rights, liberties, and cultural representation secured for others in closer proximity to whiteness or wealth. These images, however, do not have power in their own right; instead, symbolic power is wielded through the interpretation of images as well as the regular shifting of signifiers (and their meaning) to communicate the same information—the making and unmaking of normal hair and haircare, for instance. These symbolic systems are constituted and made real through their sociohistorical contexts and by who is interpreting them. The struggle among meanings, importance, and interpretation creates the visual landscape in which Black women cultural producers establish their own products as well as communicate the ways that Black women are interpreted and therefore constituted.

Society provides the means to both create and maintain knowledge about people generally and each of us specifically. In this way, popular culture provides one arena in which we receive confirmation or disconfirmation of the identities we are developing. Despite the diversity of people in the United States and around the globe, stereotypical and simple characterizations constitute many of the representations of nonwhite people in popular culture. The images used to represent different people throughout the history of images—such as minstrel shows—formed a global narrative of interpretation about who Black people were, in contrast to white people and the ideas, behaviors, attitudes, lifestyles, and desires that they had. These images and the ideological work within them have constructed the overall livelihoods of many white people across the globe—enfolding many other people and places in projects of settler colonial ideologies as arbiters of white supremacy—but also the ways Black people within cultural products and in their lived experiences understood themselves and the world around them. The power to dominate the creation and circulation of images therefore undergirds the ideological dominance necessary to squelch rebellion and civil discontent. A major site of contestation, then, images and their meaning are foundational to shifting cultural attitudes, especially over time. The ability and right to see yourself reflected as you imagine yourself is the struggle between visuality and countervisuality within the realm of cultural production.

Carla Peterson contends in the foreword to *Recovering the Black Female Body* that the Black female body was considered both masculine and feminine because of its multiple sites of labor (i.e., reproductive, domestic, physical); the Black female body, she says, has been "immutably fixed" as "grotesque."[43] Rooted in the fact that "the black female body served as one of the prime technologies of reproduction and commodification," Black women's own ideological work about their bodies highlights other aspects of their identities, in which their consumer products become the material and discursive strategies they use to fashion themselves against and within the gaze of others.[44] Whereas Stuart Hall concludes that "there is no escape from the politics of representation," uncovering the ways that popular images create, distort, and proliferate images of Black women and girls illuminate how these images shape our understandings of what is popular—and therefore inherent and abnormal—about Black femininity and sexuality.[45]

In the realm of the visual, Black cultural producers labor to rework the stereotypes that populate all images of Black people in popular culture. In many cases, these popular stereotypes of Black people replace the lived experiences and embodied knowledges of actual Black people; therefore, Black cultural producers' ability to harness the power of symbolic blackness equates to the reshaping of stereotypes that override any lived experiences of Black people. Historically, Black men and women, however, differed in the ways they approached the development of Black consumer marketing and products. Since the early 1900s, Black men media entrepreneurs like Anthony Overton and John H. Johnson became wealthy, formidable producers through their use of Black women's ingenuity as editors and writers as well as the main images in magazines' pages; in the 2000s, Black entertainment businessmen like Tyler Perry and Russell Simmons constructed empires by impersonating and attacking Black women. I have argued elsewhere that Black women like Katherine Williams Irvin and Olive C. Diggs constructed New Negro womanhood, the positioning of Black women as modern, beautiful, and respectable, through editorials and images in the Black press owned by Anthony Overton prior to the Great Depression.[46] Brenda Wynn Greer furthers this conceptualization of Black men cultural producers who created ideals of blackness and womanhood for their financial benefit.[47] While Black men cultural producers during the postwar period worked to create corporations like the Johnson Publishing Company (parent company of *Ebony* and *Jet* magazines), shifting the corporate interests of Coca-Cola to illustrate Black people as ideal consumer citizens, and harnessing the steady increase of Black buying power, Black women were only active as models of the sexiness and beauty of Black people, especially in *Jet's* "Beauty of the Week" spreads.

Mirroring the strategies of the visual used in white magazines and marketing, Johnson in particular framed Black families and individuals as similar to white counterparts in other magazines; Greer argues "his tactics reveal that the representation and marketing strategies of the most powerful black media- and image-making institution of the postwar United States did not emerge purely out of black culture or a set of black sensibilities or politics, or even from methods and models defining black publishing or the black press at the time."[48] Black men like Johnson juxtaposed popular representations of Black women as ugly or hypersexual against both celebrity and everyday Black women as sexy-yet-wholesome pinups and cover girls within his magazines. Black men imagemakers crafted their own ideal of beauty for Black women, alongside and in contrast to white women, using these images; desire for both men and women was crafted through the creation of beauty hierarchies, realized by the women who made the cover or other pictorials and those who never did.

Conversely, due to their lack of capital or social autonomy, Black women found limited possibilities within these environments to enact their ideals of Black womanhood; beyond the choice to be a model for a publication, writing letters in support or protest of images, and starting or ending subscriptions, Black women had seemingly little positionality within marketing industries due to misogyny and lack of opportunity. Therefore, the imagemakers prior to the 1970s were principally Black men whose own ideas of Black womanhood, suggestively hinting at sexuality yet bound by homemaking roles and traditional beauty standards, constructed and constricted the avenues through which Black women could shift popular understandings of who they were.

Within the corporate image-making environments of the mid-twentieth century, Black women were represented "in excess of idealized white femininity," which was foundational for the ways womanhood, femininity, and sexuality were understood.[49] Through the images crafted of Black women's bodies, all men, women, and gender-nonconforming individuals have been socialized to understand their body's proximity to "excess" and "ideal." Black women as consumers and as cultural producers made note of the symbolic power of these images and responded through the creation of their own images. Janell Hobson argues that Black women cultural producers resist the racist iconography of Black women's bodies through a process called "un-mirroring," in which they reinterpret the ways their bodies have historically been represented.[50] To "un-mirror" or change what one sees, even when the image itself is in excess of the so-called proper representations of femininity, is a highly volatile practice that complexly adds to the struggle over which images are more accurately representative of Black women in the cultural sphere. Black women's ability to shift their representation in the cultural sphere has been both contentious and greatly successful, especially on the big screen; Hattie McDaniel's Oscar-winning performance of Mammy in *Gone with the Wind* in 1939 is a vastly different representation of Black women than Regina King's Oscar-winning performance of a determined mother in *If Beale Street Could Talk* in 2018. The possibilities for children to see Black women are much vaster, in this contemporary era, and yet Black women's creation and use of material and visual products to perform this representational work is still necessary to understand.

In the next section, I further my explanation of Black women's role within the visual economy as *self-objectification* to better grapple with the ways Black dolls, princesses, and popular personas put Black women on display to harness the power of the symbolic. While dolls and princesses are not sexual per se, their presence as womanlike objects created specifically for girls maps a critical cognitive continuity between girl and woman that fetishizes the possibilities of teaching girls how to be women, including stepping into their role as caregivers and objects of desire. The desire—of people across racial lines—to communicate girls' so-called proper position in life through imaginative play with symbolic images proves to be the impetus for many Black women's involvement in corporate multiculturalism; Black women worked within corporate entertainment environments to increase images of people of color, thereby broadening the consumer base (and consumer revenue from niche markets) of corporations. This desire too coincides with the sharp uptick of corporate interests in Black consumer markets since World War II. Therefore, I construct the theoretical terrain in which Black women wade into crafting "authentic" representation through self-objectification for corporate interests and Black consumer dollars.

Black Women's Self-Objectification

As embodied objects, Black women create space for the selves we cannot be as well as the selves we wish we could be. Black women, as cultural producers, make abstractions of their lives and thereby map the aesthetic terrain of their productions with their experiences. The process of self-abstraction or turning one's life into an object extracts critical information from lived experiences and memories for the purpose of creating a product. The information that underlies a product, then, is built on and with the ideological perspectives of the subject—the Black woman who makes a Black womanlike object uses her own ideas about what makes someone Black, as well as a woman, beautiful, and worthy of having an affinity to, as the basis for her creation. The work to infuse oneself into a product becomes an uncanny representation—one that mirrors but is not like the original. Uri McMillan argues that Black women performance artists "reimagine black objecthood as a way toward agency rather than its antithesis, as a strategy rather than simply a primal site of injury."[51]

Through strategic performances of self-objectification, as avatars, Black women reconstitute the spaces Black female bodies are allowed to occupy while also complicating the ways they have historically and contemporarily been gazed upon. These avatars "act as extensions of our agency, while also revealing a persistent slippage between real and virtual worlds . . . avatars, in short, act as mediums" because they dislocate subjecthood to allow for other possibilities of existence.[52] This conception of self-objectification is one aspect of the ways I understand Black women's role in image-making industries within which the struggle to create so-called authentic representations typically encourages Black women to infuse their representations with the very details of their lives, experiences, and aesthetics.

For many of these Black women cultural producers, their motivations were to create for themselves: the girls they were who did not have things that looked like them to play with or their children who struggled with their own subjection to white supremacist notions of hegemonic beauty and importance. Like the Black entrepreneurs of early periods, the haunt of racial uplift (or working for the race) stood over the world that they wanted to create as well as the imaginative space within which they worked to create. Therefore, Black women used their own struggles with racial identity, with hair, with complexion, with "Black cool" to craft consumer products that spoke to the experiences of other Black women, to the children they were raising, and also to the greater white majority who ultimately bought and popularized their products more than Black consumers did.[53] Their self-objectification served to build multiple consumer bases for their corporations, while also shaping the popular attitudes and beliefs about objects like dolls, princesses, and mainstream pop stars that had only been white, in color and culture, in the US cultural imagination and consumer sphere.

There must be a distinction made, however, between the objectification of oneself in a performance and the objectification of oneself to create a mass-produced material product. Whereas McMillan's avatars are crafting "geographic representation of a person—a human-like figure, usually—controlled by a person via a computer" or "of a spiritual reincarnation and an alternate self," the cultural producers in the pages that follow create humanlike figures in the form of dolls, animated princesses, and gifs or memes that they no longer control after production is complete.[54] These objects, personified by the lives of their Black women creators, then become more Frankenstein's monster than avatar. They are neither the abstraction of Black women nor the representation of their memories or lives; instead, they are a mass-produced amalgam of Black women's ideas about themselves, the marketing agendas and financial interests of the corporate industries that fund their creation, and the symbolic power that undergirds how consumers read, interpret, and affirm or reject their physical manifestation.

Their objecthood becomes the basis for dis/identification for Black children, Black mothers, and others interested in holding Black womanhood to their skin or watching a Black woman become a princess. The objects' objectification of Black womanhood forms the proximity for pleasure based in the consumption of Black female narratives, bodies, and histories. These products enliven a desire to eat the Other as well as the pleasure of Black women producers to be made real, or to make the unknowable (of blackness, womanhood, beauty, etc.) known through the real or imaginative performance of play; the products provide the pleasure of play and imagination through which the "specialness" of blackness and Black womanhood feels knowable and therefore replaces conversations or interactions with Black women in the everyday.[55] Black women producers, in some ways, form an autoerotic pleasure from producing consumptive objects that are like them. Their creations, like those of any other creator especially in children's entertainment industries, bear the creative mark of their producers as well as the ideological scaffolding that makes the products sellable. The consumption of objects that form physical, visual, and representational proximities to Black women—objects that look like, feel like, sound like, or act like Black women—particularly in a cultural space that had only previously marked Black womanhood in very particular ways (i.e., Mammy, Sapphire, Jezebel, Welfare Queen, etc.) not only teaches others what approximates Black womanhood, based in the imaginations of some Black women, but also narrates how others should act in response to Black women.[56] For example, dolls that instruct a particular type of hair play (using a pick versus a comb or brush) communicate ideas about Black women's hair and the ability to use "normal" styling tools in it, but more importantly, it imparts what Black women believe to be true about our hair and provides instructional information on how to play with our hair. These ideas and instructions make not only our ideas (and more importantly, ideals) apparent, but also provides the premise for future interactions with Black women and their hair. Therefore, Black women's cultural production in which the creators use their lives, experiences, and aesthetics as the foundation of consumer products produce, too, an ontological mapping of Black womanhood that is distinct from the self-objectification of performers or artists.

This distinction in self-objectification, between producers of cultural products and performers, however, extends the work of Black women in the public sphere in the nineteenth and twentieth centuries. Exemplified in "embodied

discourse," Black women intellectuals made their bodies into "racial spectacle" and "drew on common assumptions about who they must be and refig-
ured those assumptions in ways that allowed their message to be heard more
effectively."[57] Black women intellectuals' ability to navigate, use, and then shift
national and international discourses about their intellectual abilities, their bodies, and their aesthetics provide fertile ground to better contextualize the use
of self-objectification for the creation of consumer products. Much like Black
women before them, contemporary Black women cultural producers are well
versed in the ways the world constructs stereotypes of them, especially against
white women and Black men, and how those constructs scaffold a "crooked
room."[58] Knowing the warped space of cultural production and representation
affords Black women cultural producers the ingredients required to fashion
representations for themselves, from themselves. Like Anna Julia Cooper and
Mary Church Terrell, Black women cultural producers in the late twentieth and
early twenty-first centuries worked to make their lives visible by utilizing the
stereotypes and assumptions already present in the US (and global) imagination. Black women producers making a spectacle of the racialized body for the
purposes of consumer products perform a similar function as Black women
intellectuals inserting their bodies into their speeches; in what Brittney Cooper calls "negression," or "an embrace of transgression as a legitimate strategy
for making clear one's politics and a simultaneous refusal of regression," Black
women subjectify their objecthood to challenge and reshape the bounds of
representation.[59] Said differently, Black women enmesh their subjective experiences within cultural products in a strategy to refute racist representations
that mark them as ugly, manly, or an unsellable product.

This subjectified objecthood, or what I call "embodied objectification,"
recasts the terms of Black women's involvement in their own objectification
for consumer cultural production within a larger historical genealogy of Black
women's embodied discourse. By embodied objectification, I mean that Black
women cultural producers infuse their products with their names, their experiences, and aesthetics in ways that create Black womanhood within the bounds
of polyvinyl chloride (the plastic used to create doll bodies and hair), animation,
and memes. Black women's self-objectification for consumption requires a distancing of the self and the creation of materials with the intentional purposing
of self.

In many ways, Marxist scholars of capitalism (and the present articulation
of capitalism via neoliberalism) argue that we all become mere pawns of the
system, so-called cogs in the wheel of production, so that any products that
are made by us are owned solely by the company; we, as workers, become

estranged from the things we make and our humanity in the process.[60] However, considering Black women's embodied self-objectification as the aesthetic object of consumer products means also considering a different relationship to consumption and consumer products that goes beyond Karl Marx, Max Weber, or Emile Durkheim. It means considering how those whose subjugation and dehumanization created the system of capitalism from which many contemporary companies, universities, and individuals benefit make sense and use of this history in the creation of consumer products.[61] As those who were formerly not allowed to articulate personhood or love, aesthetic preference or family, Black women creating of themselves for mass consumption should be understood differently in critical interpretations of capitalism. Those who were once made and used as capital deciding to create of themselves is a consideration that navigates the human and nonhuman, the animate made into the inanimate. The ability to think and create is the essence of humanity, and therefore became activities in which Black women were particularly invested.

Black women cultural producers made objects like themselves in the hopes that mimesis—the process by which art imitates life—works in two ways. Black women, with the purpose of changing the public perception of Black women at the intersections of blackness, beauty, and womanhood, make themselves into objects and therefore animate objects. The relationship between cultural producer and product translates the process by which producers envision how children will interact with their product; imbued with cultural information and idioms, Black cultural products made in the image of their creators can whet the appetite for a desire to further identify with or use the Other. Particularly in the case of children, whose exposure to Black women writ large could be limited to only their mothers and aunts or Black women celebrities on television shows and films, Black cultural products shape the present and future ways that children form opinions about and proximities to blackness, womanhood, and beauty. Understanding the relationship between creating for Black children while also adhering to both white and Black standards of beauty for representation are central in the next section.

Consumption for Black Girls: Objecthood, Desire, and Play

The way Black women cultural producers themselves as well as their products—any products that physically represent a Black woman's body—must embody the contradiction of beauty has particular significance to any Black feminist conceptualization of consumption. The dolls, princesses, and public personas that are created from their embodied objectification for the purpose of children's play align various ideals of beauty within one product and must speak to the visual economy of desire. Black women's embodied objectification situated within the system of "Big Beauty—the structure of who can be beautiful, the stories we tell about beauty, the value we assign beauty, the power given to those with beauty, the disciplining effect of the fear of losing beauty you might possess," illustrates the conflicting gazes that Black women's cultural products have been made to address.[62] Exemplified by the products and images created and promoted by John H. Johnson and other Black men from the postwar period to the Black Power/Black Arts Movements, Black beauty ideals aligned Black women's allegiance to Black cultural politics through their ascription to and distancing from particular beauty rituals, as evidenced by the hair industry example I provided earlier. The structures of desire, for Black women as consumers and producers, have always been filtered through multiple lenses of interpretation—the dominant cultural attitudes of beauty, intraracial counterparadox of beauty, and Black women's own ideas of how and why they should ascribe to either level of beauty or some conflicting merging of both. Black women have had to navigate the white world of beauty for mass consumption as well as the Black world of beauty that Black men author.

Theories of Black women's pleasure and fantasy buttress Black women's embodied objectification for Black children's consumption.[63] Children's consumption of Black women's self-objectification is regulated within contemporary and historical ideas about Black women's bodies—I mean here that the ways children perceive and understand Black womanlike objects are situated within how and why Black women have been presented conflictingly in hypersexual or asexual ways. A child's personal proximity to blackness and womanhood occurs through the lens of desire cultivated through play. That relationship, however, is also affected by what embodied aesthetic performances Black women creators use for their products.

By investigating the ways that Black women experience pleasure in "embodied racialization," Jennifer Nash locates Black female pleasures in the same space where racial logics constrain how their bodies are looked at.[64] Mireille Miller-Young theorizes the "black feminist pornographic gaze" as a method for reading Black women's agency within the complicated and, many times, racial-sexual mythologies that construct their performances on the pornographic scene. Her method acknowledges the ways in which Black women inherit the racial, sexual, and political logics of slavery, especially as performers.[65] This means that Black women always have agency and create agentive situations, even as they are subject to the racialized logics of desire and pornography. The possibilities for

Black women to experience pleasure, then, can exist within self-objectification. As actors in what I have called embodied objectification, Black women cultural producers actively imbue their products with their aesthetics as well as their pleasure. Therefore, the pleasure they derive in the creation process—the excitement of seeing one's sketches or ideas became plastic or animated as well as the pleasure in making a creation like you—is then translated to the pleasure that accompanies play in children's consumption, especially when Black girls are the consumers.

As Aisha Durham points out, "from hand-clapping games, cheers, to double [d]utch, girls' play has always involved vulgarity."[66] While I argue in "Envisioning Black Girl Futures" that the relationship between Black women performers like Nicki Minaj and Black girls, particularly around the performance of vulgarity, could be considered the "pinkprint" to pleasure for Black girls, here I would like to think more concretely about the definitions of vulgarity and pleasure for Black women and girls and the ways that consumption allows a blurring of those ideas.[67] How and why is vulgarity activated in girls' play? And, what exactly is considered vulgar about hand-clapping games like Miss Mary Mack for example?

According to Kyra Gaunt, the cheers, dances, and hand-clapping games of Black girls illustrate a connection between body and sound—what she calls kinetic orality—gestures and music that inform dances, songs, and music videos in hip-hop. Gaunt makes a profound connection between the lived experiences and imaginative play of Black girls with those of Black women when she argues that Black women in hip-hop and women who enjoy the music/culture "are actually attracted to their own sphere of musical practice subverted within hip-hop practice" because they are ultimately "dancing to their own beats."[68] Derived from Black girls' games, hip-hop culture and the ways that gender is performed within the culture illustrate a similar connection to Black girl pleasure and vulgarity that I argue is present within Black women's cultural productions writ large. Often Black women, specifically, draw on and extrapolate from their experiences within girlhood, as girls, to sustain the embodied objectification they use to create products for mass consumption. In this way, on a continuum of Black girlhood becoming, Black women create for the Black girls they were, the women they are, and the Black girls who are yet to be born.[69] This multigenerational, epistemological engagement of production forges a formidable psychic relationship between Black women and Black girls as both producers and consumers. In the ethos of Toni Morrison, many Black women cultural producers create the object that they desperately wished they had or that they acknowledge is missing from the lives of the children they know.[70] Whether or not reflective of what current children wish to play with, Black women cultural producers' embodied objectification has diversified the world of imagination through their use of their own experiences and the knowledge they have of those who wish to play with objects and in fantasy worlds that match their social conditions.

If Black women, and by extension Black girls, craft products based on their epistemological knowledge of play, then the objects of play become representative of where Black women find pleasure by seeing, hearing, and feeling themselves in the objects. The aesthetics of Black womanhood, such as hair, bodies, and idioms that could be rendered in Black girl play and imagination are brought to bear when Black women create. While I do not mean that objects can stand in for the lived experiences of people (i.e., playing with a Black doll does not tell you what a Black woman is like or how she feels), these objects of Black women's creation convey information about how and why at least some Black women think and articulate themselves and the objects of their representation in particular ways. Relatedly, the choices that Black women make in how they create certain products, and every aesthetic choice built into that product, results from both individual and collective Black women's epistemology as well as the psychic work of the memory of Black girlhoods and the heightened awareness of the future of play for Black girls. Like Lisa Price's aesthetic design and personal personification of Carol's Daughter as the daughter of her mother, Carol, and the imagined girls/women who would become "daughters" through the use of Carol's haircare recipes, Black women cultural producers generally harness the symbolic power of Black girlhood (as a collective experience) as well as their individual lived experiences to create for present and future generations.

In this way, the market for Black girl consumption is constituted, at least partially, by Black women and what they believe Black girls want. As Catherine Driscoll notes, "consumption articulates identities and communities" yet "marketing strategy works by trying to manipulate conformity," meaning that Black women as cultural producers partially construct the consumptive market for Black girls by the aesthetic choices they make for products and by making assumptions about the desires of Black girl consumers.[71] Black girls, in this sense, do not exist within marketing schema outside of what others create as markers of girlhood, unless they are the cultural producers themselves. Therefore, Black women cultural producers, as well as focus groups with Black mothers and Black girls, create the assemblage of Black girl consumption and the products ultimately available for Black girl play. Constituted by Black women and the idea of girls as always becoming, Black girl play objects are more about the Black women that create and consume them than the Black girls for whom they are intended. Black women cultural producers enmesh their ideas of womanhood, girlhood, and the imagined space between those configurations in the products they create. Like the early doll creators I mention in this book's introduction, Black women cultural producers imbue products with the ideals they wish to impart to Black girls, establishing what aesthetics are representative of Black girlhood and the ideas that they hope Black girls will embrace through play.

The psychic relationship between Black women cultural producers and Black girl/women consumers, then, is substantively ideological, made real through the creative processes of embodied objectification; Black women and Black girls often play together, experiencing a cross-generational reciprocal relationship of sharing, but also learning, which is then sometimes translated into the producer/consumer relationship. More precisely, though, the producer/consumer relationship is more so between Black women—some of them being the creators in concert with focus groups and celebrity Black women and others as the consumers whose responses in writing (and on social media) and dollars frame the reception of consumer products. Herein lies an important aspect of the false dichotomies created between creators/producers and consumers/spectators. The relationship between Black women as producers and consumers for Black female consumption centers the ideal consumers as Black women—not as "welfare queens" or what Elizabeth Chin calls "combat consumers" (the popularly constructed "brand-crazed" crack dealers or users).[72] Black women wrestling over the aesthetic construction and symbolic meaning of Black womanhood via the boundaries of Black girl play within the public sphere ultimately position the Black woman's gaze—as well as her desires, energies, and pleasures—at the center of production and spectatorship. Positioned differently than Black men cultural producers of the early and mid-twentieth century, Black women creators have worked to unveil Black female spectatorship as a means to Black creativity and self-knowledge. As the conduit for what Stuart Hall calls a "second-order mirror held up to reflect what already exists, [as well as] constitute us as new kinds of subjects and thereby enable us to discover who we are," the products of Black women's creative labor produces self-knowledge and an oppositional gaze that is made available to others through the consumer market.[73] Black women as consumer-spectators and creators, then, act "as critical spectators, [participating] in a broad range of looking relations, contest, resist, revision, interrogate, and invent on multiple levels."[74]

Signifying to each other through the use of particular aesthetics and idioms coded as Black and woman, Black women cultural producers and consumers' ideological relationship forms a complex web of meaning. In some ways, this web of meaning is a conceptual proliferation of infrapolitics—the resistance of marginalized groups disguised within the stereotypes of the dominant.[75] Because nearly 75 percent of Black women use at least one social networking site, Black women's infrapolitics occur face-to-face and on digital platforms as a counterpublic; the so-called echo chamber of social media presents a multinational, multiethnic, and multigenerational coalition of Black women discussing the products, spaces, and producers who are made for us and by us as well as the ones that portray Black women poorly or displace them as their directed audience in hopes of currying favor with white (mostly women) consumers.[76] Black women's ability to engage one another in digital spaces frames and reframes our multifaceted sociopolitical existence and our relationship to consumer products.

Conclusion

From Angela Davis's halo afro to Willow Smith's "Whip My Hair," Black women's consumptive choices around hair have presented the most controversial political statements. Constrained by beliefs about Black women's desirability and racial uplift politics (embodied in the mid-twentieth century by large afros), Black women utilized intraracial hair ideologies in ways that exemplify an ideological relationship between producers and consumers, embodied objectification and consumption. I used the examples of two major Black-owned beauty companies, Carol's Daughter and SheaMoisture, to illustrate embodied objectification as well as the ideological relationship that is developed and at times severed between Black producers and consumers through identification, signifying, and reification. I also highlighted the ways that contemporary shifts in Black cultural attitudes weigh heavily in how producers and consumers navigate the visual economy.

Drawing from performance studies and cultural studies as well as theories of consumption and pleasure, I presented embodied objectification to describe the process of Black women infusing objects for mass consumption with their experiences while specifically seeking Black girls and women as their target consumers. This understanding of Black women's self-objectification must be foundational to how we theorize the relationship between producer and consumer, race and the mass market, and Black women and girls' consumption of mass-produced products. Throughout this chapter, I have outlined the ways that Black women as cultural producers have reshaped the contours of self-objectification for Black women and for public consumption. These ideas become the basis for the rest of *Buy Black* and the case studies of embodied objectification that follow.

The next chapter on blackness within Mattel's Barbie history considers the ways that Black women cultural producers have envisioned a Black girl future based on the 1950s icon of white American wholesomeness. It considers questions such as: how have Black Barbie dolls created and maintained blackness as a material aesthetic? And, in what ways do Black women and girls curate and cultivate these images? These questions help frame how Black women as cultural producers utilize and reshape the symbolic power of Mattel's most iconic doll using their own experiences to instruct Black girls and the world at large on beauty, femininity, and blackness.

CHAPTER 2

From Riots to Style

The History of Black Barbie

The history of Black Barbie is the history of Black women cultural producers' embodied objectification for the purpose of selling dolls. By embodied objectification I mean that Black women cultural producers go through the process of harnessing their own experiences of blackness, womanhood, and beauty, within the US—collecting and then parsing out the intraracial idioms, aesthetics, symbols, and cultural knowledge of Black diasporic cultures that they cherish—to create consumer products that narrate an identity of blackness that major markets can easily identify and consume. They proliferate the symbols of Black identity within Black cultures and within the larger consumer marketplace—what I call the process of aestheticizing blackness—to in turn make products that hail Black consumers, especially Black women and girls, through the use of ideologies, aesthetics, and idioms with which they already identify. Black Barbies, then, are the manifestation of Black women cultural producers' ideologically based bridges to Black women consumers, a bridge assembled by their embodied objectification and consumers' practices of identification, within a white capitalist market and under the auspices of a white cultural icon, Barbie. However, this process predates Barbie's emergence in 1959; as I illustrate throughout this chapter, Barbie's antecedents in Black communities in the United States primed consumers, corporate markets, and retailers for the emergence of Black products in children's toy aisles.

As I argue in the introduction of this book, the call for baby dolls made in the image of Black children was grounded in the idea of "racial play"—the

opportunity for kids of a specific race to play with and see dolls, action figures, and material reflections of themselves because it would benefit their self-
concept—a concept directly linked to Jim Crow segregationist rhetoric.[1] For
Black children, especially, this encouraged the push for playthings that not only
mirrored their skin tones, but replicated their facial structures, as well as hair
and body measurements. Within thirty years of the *Brown v. Board of Education of Topeka* decision—the landmark 1954 Supreme Court case that ended
legalized racial segregation in public schools, shredding the earlier 1896 case
Plessy v. Ferguson that legally upheld racially separate public facilities if they were
equal—this call was embraced at one of the fastest growing doll companies in
the world: Mattel. Black women were an integral part of that shift because of
the ways they utilized embodied objectification—the process of imbuing Black
cultural idioms, artifacts, and ideas into products for mass consumption—to
shape Mattel's relationship to Black consumers. This chapter, then, examines the
history of Black people generally, and Black women specifically in the production and marketing of Mattel's "ethnic" dolls since they were first painted brown
in 1967. I explain not only the aesthetic choices that Black women designers
like Kitty Black Perkins and Stacey McBride-Irby made to mark dolls as "Black"
or "African American," but also the ways that Mattel worked to build relationships with Black companies, organizations, and celebrities, and learn cultural
practices to further ingratiate Black consumers to their products. Specifically,
I provide background on Mattel's inspiration for its first Black dolls through
the corporation's relationship with Watts-born Shindana Toy Company and
the hire of their first Black designer, Kitty Black Perkins, in the late 1970s. I
reveal the historical tension between Black women cultural producers' vision
for products tailored to Black audiences and the commodification of difference
occurring in the mass production of consumer products at one of the largest
companies dedicated to making children into consumers.

Olmec Toy Company founder Yla Eason prides herself on developing the
first "ethnically correct" action figures and dolls from 1985 to 1995.[2] Eason's niche
market had already been created and catered to for over eighty years when she
decided to make action figures motivated by her son's inability to see himself
as a hero within the imaginative world he created with his playthings. Even if
unbeknownst to her, Eason's Olmec Toy Company was rooted in a history of
Black dolls created by Black men and women for the building of confidence
and self-concept for Black children as well as a market that has been fruitful
for Black-owned companies as well as white ones. The rhetoric of "ethnically
correct" dolls in the 1980s mirrored that of Sara Lee dolls developed in the early
1950s, which were advertised as the "ultimate Negro Doll for Negro Children."

Although developed by a white woman with the ear of historically Black college and university leaders, Zora Neale Hurston, and Eleanor Roosevelt, Sara Lee dolls were not new in their desire to create a plaything for Black children that looked like them, either. Sara Lee dolls reinvented rhetoric that already existed about doll products made for Black consumers; their advertising merely replicated the 1904 slogan of R. H. Boyd's National Negro Doll Company: "Negro Dolls for Negro Children."[3]

I contend that Mattel's foray into the production of Black dolls in 1967—built on the ideological relationships Black women have to each other as producers and consumers—not only illustrated a major shift in employment opportunities for Black women in corporate environments (from cover girls and models to designers and production managers) but also the confluence of niche marketing and twentieth-century Black uplift ideologies. Despite the oppositional, and perhaps revolutionary, form that Black material culture has taken over the past half-century in response to white production and curation of caricatures of Black people, Black women cultural producers (and by extension Black cultural producers generally) maintain many of the hegemonic aesthetics of white products because of the ways industry has stereotyped and then commodified blackness. As employees of institutions like Mattel that control the production and distribution of their visions, Black women designers' dolls illustrate how white aesthetics still control forms of consumption in the twenty-first century. These products force us to consider how these representations can both affirm the self-concept and racial pride of Black girls while also affirming white hegemonic norms of beauty and femininity. In this chapter, I examine how blackness became commercialized from the waning of the Civil Rights Movement into the new millennium because of Black women's own relationship to consumption and desires for representation in a capitalist society. This visual mapping of Black aesthetics beckons larger questions about the choices that Black cultural producers, as well as Black consumers, in the United States make to craft a material world that validates and celebrates their racial background and cultural experiences while also attempting to make decisions that are profitable.

Barbie and Other Material Girls:
Mattel's Early Black Dolls

Ruth Handler created the first fashion doll named Barbie in 1959. Her motivation for the doll's creation was based in her own issues surrounding gender identity, concern for passing along the process of becoming a woman to her daughter Barbara, and a lack of representation of these ideas in the baby doll and paper doll markets.[4] Handler's motivation created a different institution—a doll—to symbolically impact values through girls' leisure activities with a material object; Handler wanted to assuage anxiety over becoming a woman for girls, while also creating a doll that girls could imbue with their own ideas of themselves in the future. Unlike other dolls on the market, Barbie was not a doll that needed a mother or to be taken care of in the way that taught girls how to change diapers, clean up baby spittle, and nurse a baby with a bottle. Barbie was created as a womanlike figure with breasts, many accessories, and eventually professions that would provide ample opportunities for girls to imagine themselves as adults, using Barbie play as the imaginative launching pad to their adult personalities, behaviors, and consumer habits. Barbie play taught girls about the glamourous life of (white) womanhood, through the ever-growing attachment to fashion and other consumer products. In this way, girlhood and the development into womanhood became intrinsically tied to consumerism. A proper woman, like Handler from whom the doll's fashion was initially inspired, had many outfits and accessories, and outings to attend to showcase them.

Because Barbie play was built on Handler's ideological standards and personal anxieties about how to be "female," Barbie's symbolic purpose was to teach US-based gender ideologies to anyone who played with the doll and even those who never did. Barbie's early popularity in the toy market affected many childhoods because of the ways that girlhood is constructed in relationship to people and things, but also the ways that mothers hoped to socialize their daughters. Kristina Gottschall and her coauthors explain that girlhood is an assemblage of relationality wherein images, bodies, and subjectivities collaboratively craft personhood for girls.[5] Girls, therefore, shape and are shaped by the material conditions and visual representations with which they interact. Each Barbie, then, imparts ideas about societal values, which in turn shape girls' affective relationships to their bodies, each other, and material culture writ large; as a key part of girl culture, whether one has a doll or not, Mattel developed Barbie as a womanlike plaything that is supposed to stand in for a girl's imaginative projection of herself into the future. Even more so than dolls made before her that stood in for human playmates or human babies, Barbie dolls represent a girl's future adult self. Particularly for girls of the early Barbie years, ideas about who and what constituted a fashion model were communicated in the commercials, catalogs, and packaging; as many feminists have argued, the aesthetic choices used to promote Barbie also promoted body issues stemming from her thin, petite, and busty shape.[6] Mattel, also, made sure to show girls how to play Barbie through some of the first commercials in toy marketing history targeted directly to children.

The first Barbie commercial in 1959 showcases ten different Barbie dolls and a spinning wheel of accessories. Even though the image is in black and white, it is obvious that all of the dolls are white. They are represented in the traditionally feminine ways of the 1950s—poodle skirts, furs, and gowns. At the end of the sixty-second commercial, an offscreen male announcer notes her price of "only $3" (almost $27 in 2019) and her accessories are between $1 and $5. It closes with a woman's voiceover singing, "Someday, like you, I'm gonna be, until then I know just what I'll do—Barbie, beautiful Barbie—I'll make believe I'm you," as the camera zooms in on a dark-haired Barbie in a wedding gown with a bouquet.[7] The sing-song style of the jingle and the lyrics communicate Mattel's aim in forging identification with and personification of Barbie. "Someday" as the song goes, the girl playing will be Barbie, but until then, she will use Barbie to create an imaginative landscape for herself. It must be reiterated, however, that the imaginative landscape where a girl becomes Barbie and Barbie is a girl is one that only people who look like Barbie can occupy; the girl and Barbie become synonymous, although not the same. Commercials like these and the ideologies that undergird them frame what Ebony Elizabeth Thomas calls the "imagination gap," in which white people are the only subjects or objects of fantastical worlds; even when the girl being represented is nonwhite, the imaginative space she is required to occupy makes white girls and boys the heroes.[8] This ideological connection between material object and girlhood, between make-believe and future embodiment, inform the ways that girls of color and their white girl counterparts understood in the late twentieth century—and still understand contemporarily—themselves, each other, and the futures they will inhabit.

On a global scale, "playing Barbie" has become a process of socialization, of habitus formation, that continues to shape the ways that girls (and other children) understand themselves individually and in relation to their ability to acquire and use material objects like Barbie dolls. Furthermore, if Barbie was created to communicate womanhood to girls in the process of becoming, then the first brown-painted Barbie in 1967 not only taught these principles but also communicated ideas about race and ethnic difference to these same girls. Because there had been no doll that wasn't white in the first eight years of Barbie's existence, the addition of dolls with different colors (and eventually hair) constituted both who and what Barbie was and who these new additions are in relationship to her. In many ways, Mattel's "ethnic" dolls from 1967 to the late 2000s communicated to girls of color and white girls that there was no aesthetic difference between the consumption of white and brown dolls; these dolls shared the same clothes and hairstyles, had the same bodily proportions, and had the same desires (shopping, being the romantic companion of boys, and having fun at the beach); the dolls, and perhaps also the girls, were the same in aesthetic presentation. However, the first brown doll created by Mattel was not African American in the sense that she was not an American at all. "Colored Francie" was included as a doll in the Barbie family under a different name and through cultural differentiation.

Francie Fairchild—Barbie's "MODern" British (white) cousin—was modeled after British rock and pop artists who had risen in popularity in the United States in the 1960s. Mattel hoped to re-create that cultural hysteria over "the British invasion" in the doll business, while also increasing their hold in the capitalist market. "Colored Francie," the brown version of Barbie's cousin Francie, was released in the fall of 1967 in the United Kingdom.[9] Her "mod" fashion, hair, and face shape replicated other European and American Barbie styles.

FIGURE 2.1. Mattel's 1967 Colored Francie. Source: Courtesy of the Indianapolis Children's Museum, Indianapolis, IN.

Mattel articulated the British cultural difference through choices in clothing, hair, and a Black version of Barbie's cousin, while maintaining the ability to transfer aesthetics from the British doll to the American one by making it easy to swap clothes between the dolls; Colored Francie was released in the US in early 1968, but her lack of sales made Mattel discontinue her production.[10]

Unlike Colored Francie, who is not considered the first "Black" doll for many US doll collectors because of her British roots, Mattel's first brown-painted doll released in the United States was based on Diahann Carroll's character in the critically acclaimed television show *Julia*, which premiered in September 1968 and ran for three years.[11] The show featured a widowed Black woman, Julia Baker, raising a son alone. Julia's husband, a pilot, was killed in Vietnam, which made Julia the first representation of a Black single mother and professional. Julia worked as a nurse for a doctor at an aerospace company and raised her son in a predominately white middle-class neighborhood. Diahann Carroll became the first African American actress nominated for an Emmy for her role on the show.

For Black audiences, the *Julia* show illustrated a shift in representation in Hollywood, particularly in the ways it displayed Black people outside of stereotypical roles. Unlike popular comedy shows like *Beulah* and *Amos 'n' Andy*, or fantastical action roles like Bill Cosby in *I Spy*, Greg Morris in *Mission: Impossible*, and Nichelle Nichols in the original *Star Trek*, *Julia* presented Black people—specifically a single Black woman and her son—beyond the popular conceptions spurred by Daniel Patrick Moynihan's 1955 report on the Black family or boycotts around the United States. And yet, the show and Diahann Carroll were met with criticism for its lack of connection to real life for Black people and the effects of racism.[12] For some, it sanitized the regular hostility and discrimination that Black people faced as well as the feelings of contempt and hopelessness that took hold in Black America especially after the murder of Dr. Martin Luther King Jr. in April 1968. Carroll, however, worked within and beyond the show to illustrate her commitments to Black people. Therefore, Mattel's sponsorship of the show and, later, the release of the doll positioned the company as a potential site for Black consumers to see themselves represented in its products. Mattel attempted to capitalize on the show's popularity—taking advantage of consumers' desires to commodify their respect for Diahann Carroll and love for her character.

Like Carroll's character, the Julia doll came dressed as a nurse with a stethoscope and a white uniform that could be swapped with other dolls. She, too, had real eyelashes like other dolls of the period, but her hair and eye color differentiated her from other Mattel dolls on the market; she had short reddish hair and hazel eyes, replicating the *Julia* character. The doll was considered a

(a)   (b)

FIGURE 2.2a and 2.2b. Mattel's 1968 Talking Julia doll and
1968 Talking Christie doll. Source: Courtesy of the Indianapolis
Children's Museum, Indianapolis, IN.

facsimile of Diahann Carroll in the role of Julia, and therefore marked Mattel's
embrace of Black popular culture to help sell dolls. A photo of Diahann Carroll
was prominently displayed on every Julia doll box, which like Colored Francie's
box was blue and green. The prominence of Diahann Carroll's picture and the
blue-green box colors distinguished this doll from the typical Barbie doll.

Mattel differentiated both Colored Francie and Julia from other dolls, especially because their names were never Barbie and they existed outside of the
commercials, products, and worlds made real through Barbie play. While the
clothes could be swapped between dolls—making Barbie a nurse and Julia a
fashion model, for example—the different boxes, hair, and motivations for
each doll's creation position them differently in Mattel's doll pantheon. Mattel's decision to produce this doll solely illustrates their recognition of Black
popular icons' ability to sell products as well as the possibilities for marketing

dolls to Black consumers, the broad development of a niche doll market; with the release of Colored Francie and Julia, Mattel began to articulate blackness as a viable commodity through their products and sponsorship of television shows like *Julia*. Similar to companies like Coca-Cola that used Black people in commercials to appeal to Black people's desire for so-called positive representation, Mattel embraced new marketing schemas by underwriting a television show featuring a Black actress and releasing a doll in her likeness.[13] Mattel helped pioneer the marketing associations between television shows, products, and celebrities that we see prominently in the twenty-first century.

Shortly after its release of the Julia doll, Mattel also released a brown version of their Malibu beach-themed Barbie, Malibu Christie. The "doll with the suntan look" was aesthetically similar to the mod-fashioned British doll, Francie, and the well-received Julia doll; she had short black hair and was marketed as a bendable doll with hand-sewn eyelashes. Like the Julia doll, Christie was released in "talking" and "kissing" versions popular at the time. Marketed as Barbie's friend, Christie came in a bright pink box, signaling a visual connection between the brown-painted dolls Mattel had tested previously with the original Barbie dolls. Doll collectors credit Carol Spencer, a white woman designer who was employed by Mattel for over thirty years to design Barbie, as the clothes and props designer of the brown Malibu Christie as well as Colored Francie's designer. Spencer represents a possible early design connection between Colored Francie and the brown Malibu Christie in Mattel's history.

Christie's design, release, and popularity are particularly important because they dovetailed with Mattel's relationship with a Black-owned toy company, Shindana, which intentionally created Black dolls with Black consumers in mind. While it is unlikely that Colored Francie's designs were influenced by the Mattel-Shindana relationship, Mattel's subsequent Black dolls—including Julia, Malibu Christie, Black Barbie, and Shani—were directly impacted by Shindana's designs, marketing schemes, and failures. The success of Mattel's foray into multicultural Barbies came as a direct result of its sponsorship of and working relationship with the Shindana Toy Company (sometimes called Shindana Toy Factory).

Learning Black Self-Determination: The Rise and Fall of Shindana Toy Company

In October of 1968, the Shindana Toy Company emerged as a subsidiary of a Black-owned corporation, Operation Bootstrap. Operation Bootstrap— inspired by Booker T. Washington's "Atlanta Compromise" speech and contemporary Black Power discourse espousing self-reliance and racial uplift ideologies—focused on providing jobs for Black people in and around Watts after the uprising in 1965.[14] With the confusion and anger that stemmed from the murder of Malcolm X in February and ongoing tension with the local police, the rebellion that occurred in Watts April 11 through April 16, 1965, centered on an incident of police violence against an unarmed Black man, Marquette Frye, and his mother. Black citizens in Watts protested unjust policing, housing discrimination, poverty, and deteriorating schools. The uprising also prompted the establishment of new Black organizations like Bootstrap to address community problems.

Lou Smith, a Philadelphia activist who had moved to Oakland as regional director of the civil rights organization Congress of Racial Equality (CORE), led the effort within Operation Bootstrap to develop toys that were "Brother and Sister dolls made by brothers and sisters."[15] Like many African Americans in the mid-1960s, Smith looked to Black cooperative economics and Afrocentric aesthetics to promote Black identity development.[16] Following Maulana Karenga in the belief that pan-Africanist ideals like the learning of African languages would unite African Americans, Smith and Bootstrap members called their toy company Shindana, a Swahili word for "competitor."[17] Reframing the Watts rebellion chant "burn, baby, burn" to "learn, baby, learn," Smith saw toys as an opportunity for children to learn and appreciate their cultural heritage by studying history from a Black perspective.[18] Smith's decision to develop toy manufacturing reflected a larger discussion in Black communities about representation in popular culture as well as Black self-determination through entrepreneurship and cultural knowledge; because of the ways that stereotypical beliefs about blackness were communicated to children prior to and alongside the *Brown v. Board* (1954) ruling, Black cultural producers like Smith found it of great importance to show that Black people could compete in the same capitalist market with white-owned businesses as well as stay true to their mission of helping Black people by funding cultural work through economic means. Shindana, in return, produced 13,000 dolls and made approximately $1,000 a day in sales in its first year (about $7,400 in 2019).[19]

In a December 1976 interview with *Jet* magazine, then-president Robert Bobo explained that Shindana's mission was to make dolls "ethnically correct with Black features" available to Black consumers, rather than, like other companies, make "black versions of a white doll."[20] While similar to R. H. Boyd's, Marcus Garvey's, and Sara Lee Creech's missions to create Negro dolls for Negro children that were anthropologically correct or representatives of a particular Black aesthetic, Shindana's ideal of creating "ethnically correct" dolls with "Black features" communicates an understanding of "correctness" that goes beyond the attempts of previous doll companies. Ethnically correct, in this sense, meant that the "correctness" of each doll was judged by the ideals and ideologies of Black ethnic identity, rather than a lofty or even idealistic ethnic representation or cohesiveness. Bobo's comment acknowledges that the design of each doll had to meet the acceptance of Black people, while also prominently displaying the features of Black people. This provided a much more diverse possibility for doll design than previous Black dolls, while also limiting the concerns about aesthetics or features to the concerns of Black people solely. Bobo's comment also illustrates Shindana's intentional approach to the development, naming, and marketing of its dolls, which were designed and sewn by mostly Black women in the Watts community while Black men comprised almost the entire workforce of the doll factory. Although Shindana's executives had the uplift of Black communities in mind during the production and marketing of dolls, the commodification of blackness or "cultural heritage" Shindana harnessed, articulated, and promulgated illustrates how Black producers, too, were complicit in the turn to commodify difference. Even the aesthetics of each doll fed into the project of racial uplift, unity, and positive representation that the founders of Operation Bootstrap subscribed to themselves.

After receiving a $200,000 gift from Mattel (about $1.44 million in 2019), and loans from Chase Manhattan Bank and the Black-owned Bank of Finance, Shindana Toy Company released their first doll, "Baby Nancy," to department stores in 1969.[21]

The relationship between Mattel's Ruth Handler and Shindana Toy's leaders is unknown because Handler's position at Mattel had become precarious due to financial issues; however, Mattel committed to a two-year backing of Shindana, which included not only financial support (and leveraging to entice other financiers to get involved), but also support from their marketing and sales personnel to help promote Baby Nancy and other Shindana products (which also eventually included board games and action figures based on popular Black icons like Shaft, Flip Wilson, J. J. Evans from *Good Times*, and O. J. Simpson, after the acquisition of a Black-owned board game company). Renowned Mattel designer Carol Spencer explains that Mattel used this time with Shindana to test the market's response to dolls that were "ethnically correct with Black features."[22] Although correspondence with doll collectors and Spencer herself does not explain exactly how Mattel benefitted from the Shindana relationship, Mattel studied the design and marketing of Shindana Toy products to develop and sell the Christie doll as well as subsequent dolls.

Although it is unlikely that Mattel's gifts and offerings duped Shindana executives, based on the history and racial ideologies of their parent organization

(a)   (b)

FIGURE 2.3a and 2.3b. Shindana's 1969 Baby Nancy and
1969 Malaika dolls. Source: Courtesy of the Indianapolis
Children's Museum, Indianapolis, IN.

Operation Bootstrap, the information that Shindana gained about toy production, marketing, and sales differed from the cultural knowledge Mattel executives gained; this exchange seems evident from multiple vantage points. As
benefactors, or at least seemingly benevolent competition (which does not
exist in capitalism, especially in the same industry), Mattel's financial support,
social capital, and manufacturing knowledge gave it access to Shindana's conversations, design and marketing ideas, and employees with which to develop
their own assets. Mattel was able to make Black dolls in their own way through
an ethnography-like participant-observer relationship with Shindana, unlike
previous white doll companies which simply released dolls as they imagined,
in brief consultation with Black celebrities and in white people's image. This
relationship positions designers and developers at Mattel in the 1970s and 1980s
with an "allyship" model: one in which they worked to assist and help Shindana fortify their business acumen, designs, and relationships with retailers,
but ultimately used the information they gained and gathered to produce their

own Black dolls, successfully, and with the support of some Black consumers. Shindana's success at selling Black aestheticized dolls provided the market assurances that Mattel needed to develop and sell its own Black Barbie versions.

Mattel's marketing team was able to research and potentially test their ideas about market responses to darker painted dolls, different hair textures and styles, box colors, doll fashions, and advertising styles through their relationship with Shindana. As evidenced by arguments by Black entrepreneurs and intellectuals some fifty years prior, the most important aspects of creating a Black doll for Black children (with the purpose of racial uplift and improved self-concept) focused on the complexion color and the hair texture or style. The doll's complexion and hair easily attracted or repelled consumers and seemingly bespoke the ideological commitments of the company creating the dolls; there was a distinct difference between P&M Doll Company's 1919 Topsy doll and UNIA Doll Company's 1922 dolls (spearheaded by Henrietta Vinton Davis who wanted to aestheticize Paul Laurence Dunbar's poem, "Little Brown Baby").[23] Like Shindana's Baby Nancy, Malaika, and Disco Wanda, Mattel's Christie was particularly darker than other ethnic dolls on the market. But while Baby Nancy had a kinky afro style, Christie maintained Barbie's signature straight coif. These distinctions illustrate a vacillating ideal of what blackness looked like, but more importantly what aesthetics more authentically portrayed blackness to a consuming public; regardless of whom the dolls were created for, Black entrepreneurs and designers were well aware of the white gaze, which weaponized white consumer dollars.

Because of Shindana's Afrocentric roots and Black Power background, Mattel witnessed the successes and pitfalls of marketing their dolls, action figures, and board games to consumers who wanted to educate their children on Black history as well as Black popular culture including idioms and clothing styles. Shindana worked intentionally to highlight and celebrate Black celebrities like Rodney Allen Rippy, a four-year-old featured in a 1973 commercial for fast-food chain Jack in the Box with a memorable tag line, "It's too big to eat!" from which Shindana decided to make a facsimile doll. Interestingly, Shindana replicated his famous line with a 1974 doll that had a Mattel voice box.[24] Obviously, Mattel was involved in the development and gleaned from the success of the doll. As with the Julia doll, Mattel executives learned from the popularity of Black popular culture to develop products that closely aligned with Black cultural attitudes.

Mattel also studied the value of Black employees in the development and marketing of ethnic dolls. Tuesday Conner, a former Shindana employee, along with her mother Doris and older sister Lynne, remembers seeing Baby Nancy for the first time when her mother was asked to make clothes for her: "Mom [Doris Conner] worked with Operation Bootstrap, which helped to get people on their feet and start their own business. Bootstrap gave Mom a factory and sewing machines, and she taught people to sew. We got a contract to make Baby Nancy clothes and many of the cloth [dolls] like J.J. dolls, Lil Souls, Rodney Allen Rippy, and Flip Wilson. Mom helped to create a better-selling doll by creating new clothes for Shindana."[25] Through their interactions, Mattel was able to witness firsthand the community-centered and Black-centric business model of Shindana and Operation Bootstrap. By supporting the Conner family, for example, Shindana created a lifetime of success for Tuesday, who went on to sew clothes for celebrities like Jennifer Holiday and Chaka Khan for over fifty years. While Mattel could not replicate this relationship to the community, since Bootstrap was an outgrowth of it, it could extrapolate the importance of Black women employees in the building and the success of consumer products geared toward Black people.

In a 1969 interview, Shindana's sales manager Herman Thompson further explained this point. When asked about "special problems" facing Shindana, Thompson argues that Black dolls require a different strategy of sales than those typically used by white toy salesmen. He says, "I feel as though that our approach can be more effective than a Mattel approach for an example. It is our aim to become allied with other Black manufacturers perhaps who are having the same problem that we're having so far as distribution is concerned."[26] His comments reflect that while Shindana may have been successful in creating jobs within their community, creating a product that aligns with its ideals, and moving its product from production floor to American homes, there may have been issues with getting the dolls into the hands of Black children. This raises some key problems in the framing of dolls and doll play as the arbiters of creating better self-concept for Black children. As Elizabeth Chin points out, what becomes of Black children who never play with (or who do not want) Black dolls?[27]

When the Shindana Toy Company ceased operation in 1978 due to rising production costs, Mattel (alongside a few minority-owned toy companies) guided Shindana's customers to its products.[28] By the late 1970s, changes in cultural attitudes about people of color allowed for other businesses to get started and many used Shindana as a model for developing their own companies. My focus, however, stays with Mattel, which already owned a lion's share of the doll market and expanded its offerings with the first Black doll named Barbie released in 1980; Kitty Black Perkins—a Black woman hired in the mid-1970s at Mattel—designed the doll.

Black Women Are Dynamite:
Black Barbie Comes to Mattel

A native of South Carolina, Louvenia "Kitty" Black Perkins was hired in 1976 to join Mattel's Barbie team.[29] Trained as a clothing designer, Black Perkins was familiar with creating fashionable items for women and was drawn to Barbie, even though she did not own a doll as a child. It is unclear whether Black Perkins worked with Shindana Toy Company executives like other Mattel representatives; however, she worked under the tutelage of Carol Spencer who helped develop Julia and Malibu Christie, and knew about the work with Shindana. Black Perkins spearheaded her first big project in 1980, further developing a popular Black aesthetic that extrapolated from not only Mattel's relationship

(a)

(b)

FIGURE 2.4a and 2.4b. Mattel's 1980 Black Barbie (front and back). Source: Courtesy of the Indianapolis Children's Museum, Indianapolis, IN.

with Shindana, but also Mattel's earlier attempts to create a Black doll with Colored Francie (1967), Julia (1968), and Malibu Christie (1969).

Named "Black Barbie," Black Perkins's design took cues from Black popular culture in fashion, hair, and accessories. Additionally, her name "Black Barbie" signified the cultural emergence of "Black" as an identifying label—replacing "Negro" and "Colored" in the cultural self-definition of African-descended people in the United States. Black Barbie was painted three shades lighter than Mattel's earlier attempts, but her hair was in a distinctly afro-style. Black Perkins seemingly built on Shindana's popular afro-wearing dolls and she even accessorized Black Barbie with a "stylish haircomb/pick" and choice of hoop or dangle earrings to match her "disco" outfit. The box details how to "fluff her hair with the pick" when playing with Black Barbie and includes an illustration of these instructions for those unfamiliar with the practice. Short of a satin bonnet, Mattel is clear to name, communicate, and illustrate how to play with this new addition to the Barbie line, further explaining the difference in play that she represented.

Black Perkins and the Mattel marketing team pointedly reminded buyers on the box that Black Barbie can fit all of Barbie's fashions and has a circle of friends that includes "Hispanic Barbie"—another ethnic doll that Mattel had created around the same time.[30] This statement reassures buyers that Black Barbie does not replace Barbie, but rather is a "fun" addition to Barbie play since like earlier Black dolls her proportions allow for the seamless swapping of clothes between dolls. Yet, the instructions do not explicitly communicate that while her clothes could be swapped with any of Barbie's or her friends' clothes, Black Barbie's hair and the idioms used to describe her, and the overall box aesthetic, illustrated the "real" differences. The introduction of a Black doll, in many ways, cannot shift the hegemonic ideal of Barbie as always white and usually blonde (especially twenty-one years after Barbie reached the market), but it speaks to a growing intention on Mattel's part to directly influence and commodify the epistemological knowledge of Black people.

An important aspect of Black Barbie's marketing is the tagline on the front of the box. Although it is pink, like her plastic foremother Christie's, Black Barbie's box is adorned with the words "She's black! She's beautiful! She's dynamite!" under her name. Like her "disco" jumpsuit, afro-styled hair, and "stylish pick," Black Barbie's tagline connects Black Perkins's vision for the doll with specifically Black popular trends in television and music. Although James Brown's popular song "I'm Black and I'm Proud" came out in the late 1960s and J. J. Evans's refrain "Dy-No-Mite" died with the end of *Good Times* in 1979, Black Perkins and Mattel executives' use of similar language infused the cultural resonances of blackness that post–Civil Rights Era-aged parents and children were familiar with and would recognize on the doll's packaging.

Black Barbie's description in 1980 attempts to harness the symbolic power of the pro-Black movement that permeated communities in the United States and globally in the 1960s and 1970s. In *Liberated Threads*, Tanisha Ford explains that Black women used aesthetics like afro-styled hair and Afrocentric clothing to "re-aestheticize the black body" in response to "social and physical violence and as a source of pleasure."[31] Ford clarifies that Black women (women who would have been peers of Kitty Black Perkins) used aesthetics like clothes and hair to claim their bodies in an expression of radical freedom. The afro style, too, became commercialized when wigs and hairpieces were sold across the globe to give women this aesthetic. Witnessing this shift in the cultural significance of the afro style, Black Perkins knew that this particular hairdo on Black Barbie would resonate with Black women and girls who styled their hair in this way, too. Black Perkins was able to construct an ideological bridge to Black women and girl consumers through deliberately using the images, sounds, and aesthetics that resonate within Black communities as well as the ideologies that undergird our ideals, a practice I call harnessing Black symbolic power. Black Perkins intentionally used this radical-turned-commercial language of blackness and beauty to market her doll to consumer demographics in the United States who were not only familiar with the idiom and cultural significance, but also who desired a material aesthetic that taught racial pride. Similar to Shindana executives' decisions, Black Perkins's decisions are based in a move to market aesthetic forms of blackness to Black people across the globe as well as in a desire to promote greater representation of blackness in material culture.

The "disco" clothing and the word "dynamite" in the description bespeak a cultural knowledge of Black vernacular that Black Perkins and her team used as well. Echoing the Shindana Toy Company's use of the character J. J. Evans's popularity in the late 1960s, Black Perkins astutely tried to tap into the symbolic resonances of Black vernacular idioms to map Black Barbie alongside other popular Black characters in the US cultural imagination. What is most interesting—about the use of these Black vernacular idioms as well as the visual scripting of blackness that Black Barbie receives from Mattel—is the historical dissonance. Despite the knowledge that Mattel has already curated Black aesthetics in their design of Colored Francie, Julia, and Malibu Christie, their ability to produce Black Barbie in 1980 is contingent upon Black vernacular and historical connections that predate the doll. Rather than a group of Mattel executives who were unfamiliar with Black popular culture, Black Barbie's aesthetics more heavily indicate that she was indeed a creation of Kitty Black

Perkins, who came of age during the late 1960s and 1970s; Black Perkins used embodied objectification to design Black Barbie.

Raised in and a product of desegregation, southern Black community organizing and resistance, multiple assassinations of major civil rights figures, and substantive shifts in the representations of Black people in popular culture, Kitty Black Perkins infused her own experience into the creation of Black Barbie. Her "symbolic habitus"—a term I coin as an adaptation of Pierre Bourdieu's theorizing of symbolic power and habitus to explain the amalgam of socialization one receives from popular culture, historical events, and familial lessons—shaped her approach to her job at Mattel, especially after Mattel's relationship with Shindana. Of interest, too, is the fact that Black Perkins did not own a doll as a child—meaning that her ideas for the symbolic visual possibilities for Black Barbie were shaped more by her other cultural experiences than nostalgic memories of Barbie or other doll play. This furthers my argument about Black women's relationship to consumption and consumer products from chapter 1; Black women like Kitty Black Perkins used embodied objectification to make dolls for the Black girl she was and for Black girls she imagined would play with the doll. The ideological relationship between Black women—the bridge between producers and consumers that hail consumers through their identification with a product—then, forms the basis for which ideals, idioms, and perspectives about blackness, womanhood, and beauty are taught through play. In the creation process, Black women cultural producers use embodied objectification as a process through which they utilize their experiences to aestheticize a product, to make it perceptibly Black and therefore able to hail Black consumers. Embodied objectification explains how Kitty Black Perkins's childhood experiences affected her design decisions for Black Barbie and illustrates the ways that Black women cultural producers in the business of using Black symbolic power for consumer products create work within the space between memory and imagination, addressing both the lack of representation they see in the present and the pleasure in play they experienced in the past. The ideological relationship between Black women as producers and consumers exists at this symbolic level of their experiences and their ability to harness their epistemological knowledge so that Black women and girl consumers will identify with those products enough to purchase them.

Black Perkins, in many ways, activated her symbolic habitus to inform the embodied objectification that made Black Barbie come alive. On the shelf, Black Barbie hailed Black girls and women, while also beckoning Mattel executives and enthusiasts to acknowledge the beauty of Black vernacular traditions alongside the history and popularity of the "original" Barbie. By Black Perkins imbuing plastic with the cultural idioms and aesthetics of Black womanhood—not the arbitrary or stereotypical, but information based on her experiences and those of her historical and contemporary community—she made Black Barbie a symbol of the aesthetics of Black women.

In the creation of a niche Barbie market, Black Perkins centered Black women's culture, inserting Barbie not only in Black children's play, but also in Black women's discourses. For example, Black Barbie predated the first Black woman crowned Miss America, twenty-year-old Vanessa Williams, by three years, yet visually mapped similar aesthetic terrains of beauty, afro-styling (albeit a somewhat straightened version compared to Angela Davis's iconic afro), and reimagining previously solely white cultural spaces. Black Barbie's aesthetic bridged Black cultural knowledge and discourses from the Civil Rights, Black Power, and Black Arts Movements with the integrationist strivings of people like Williams. Black Barbie assisted in readying the US cultural landscape for more Black firsts on television and in popular culture that we saw in the late 1980s and 1990s. Literally and symbolically, Black Perkins's first doll design—Black + Barbie—asked consumers to consider new possibilities for who Barbie could and would be but also which spaces Black people, and specifically Black women, could occupy. Like the Black hair industry entrepreneurs from chapter 1, Black Perkins was able to align Black cultural discourse with a product that called forth Black women's ideals about the body, about beauty, and about the products they would support for themselves and their children. The consumptive practice of creating and consuming Black Barbie bridged the ideological relationship between Black women.

While Black Perkins was interested in the aesthetic expansion of blackness in the doll industry on the one hand, she also actively participated in the aesthetic reification of blackness on the other. Her choices to shape the consumption of Black aesthetics through material cultural production were, as Ann duCille puts it, the "concurrent racing and erasing" of Black heterogeneity for "mass-produced sameness."[32] Black Perkins's choices were complexly progressive and regressive at the same time.

Black Women Are Marvelous: The Shani Dolls

Kitty Black Perkins's ability to shape the US cultural imaginary through the consumption of Black aesthetics in doll form was not exclusive to Black Barbie in 1980. Alongside two other Black women—Mattel production manager Deborah Mitchell and psychological consultant Darlene Powell-Hopson (now Powell Garlington)—Black Perkins continued to shape US acceptance of aestheticized

FIGURE 2.5. Mattel's 1991 Shani (Shani doll line). Source: Courtesy of the Indianapolis Children's Museum, Indianapolis, IN.

blackness into the early 1990s with new dolls.[33] After several successful designs, Mattel gave her more leeway with the design and development for Barbie, culminating in her pitch for a doll more reflective of the Black women she loved and with whom she identified. In 1991, Black Perkins designed a new line, "Shani."

Like early twentieth-century Black designers, Black Perkins was interested in developing dolls that would assist Black children in developing a strong self-concept. The Clark Doll Test fortified the idea that play could prompt Black children's negative or positive self-esteem. From 1939 to 1947, in New York City and Clarendon, SC, Drs. Mamie and Kenneth Clark conducted the well-known Clark Doll Test. Based on Mamie Clark's dissertation research, the studies measured "children's racial awareness." Clark asked 253 Black children between the ages of three and seven to choose between one Black doll and one white doll in a series of questions: "give me the doll that . . . (1) you like to play with or the doll you like best? (2) is the nice doll? (3) looks bad? (4) is a nice color? (5) looks like a white child? (6) looks like a colored child? (7) looks like a Negro child? (8) looks like you?"[34] If, the argument went, Black children played with dolls

that looked like them, they would be able to imagine themselves as successful, beautiful, and professional people and stave off negative emotions about
their color promoted by racist stereotypes. These ideals of the importance of
play, specifically with dolls, mirrored Ruth Handler's original idea about the
personification of Barbie as a womanly model with whom girls could identify
that Mattel had marketed in the 1950s. The marrying of these two ideals—of
habitus formation for those who played with dolls and the importance for
Black children to play with dolls that looked like them—substantiated Black
Perkins's development of the Shani doll line.

Like other psychologists since the *Brown v. Board of Education of Topeka* case,
in which the NAACP defense team used the Clarks' findings in its argument
before the Supreme Court, Dr. Darlene Powell-Hopson completed her own
version of the doll study in the late 1980s. Powell-Hopson's findings expanded
the Clarks' results of some fifty years before. She asked 105 Black preschoolers
and 50 white preschoolers about their preferences and then intervened in the
process by modeling choosing the Black doll; this intervention, that Powell-
Hopson called "social learning theory," greatly changed the initial result of
the study, which supposedly illustrated that Black children associated blackness with grossly negative ideas such as dirtiness, ugliness, and criminality
through modeling.[35] Powell-Hopson argued that children should have Black
dolls and should be taught about Martin Luther King Jr., Harriet Tubman,
George Washington Carver, Malcolm X, and Jesse Jackson to help create racial
pride.[36] Although the Clarks' studies had become controversial within psychology and law for their flawed study design, psychologists like Powell-Hopson
continued to affirm their results and argued for the need for intervention in
children's play for the benefit of Black children's self-esteem.[37]

With Powell-Hopson's 1985 study (which was featured on the front page of
the *New York Times* and was the basis for her best-selling book *Different and
Wonderful*) and the ideological belief in uplift through identification in play,
Black Perkins and Deborah Mitchell sought to create dolls that would shift
negative associations through attention to phenotypic aesthetics like hair, nose
shape, hip size, and plastic paint color.[38] After approaching Powell-Hopson to
become a psychological consultant, and enlisting a Black woman–owned marketing firm, Mattel moved forward with production with the belief that these
dolls would greatly expand their Black consumer base.

For the first time at Mattel, Black dolls were stylized with supposedly different molds than white dolls. Black Perkins, Mitchell, and Powell-Hopson
argued that Shani dolls had fuller lips, wider hips and noses, and different textures of hair than the "original" Barbie; these changes were directly reflective of

Powell-Hopson's doll study and the need for Black children to see themselves in play.[39] Like Shindana some twenty years earlier, Black Perkins, Mitchell, and Powell-Hopson worked to make "brother and sister dolls" through aesthetically Black indicators. They believed that the attention to symbolic representations of blackness would impact the ways that Black children would feel about their cultural heritages and skin complexions. These three Black women, two of whom were employed by Mattel directly, tried to harness the symbolic power of racialized ideologies in US cultural discourse to affect the habitus of Black children—more specifically, Black girls. As Black cultural producers, they bridged intraracial community discourses to produce consumer products that aestheticized their own experiences and stereotyped their bodies. Black women specifically chose aspects of the body like hair, nose shape, and the contours of a Black woman's body as an extension, in some ways, of scientific racism and ways Black people have embraced ideas that Black people were phenotypically different than white people.

In naming her new project, Kitty Black Perkins seems to have been inspired again by Shindana to name her dolls. Shindana used Swahili in its company name and Afrocentric aesthetics in the names and clothing of its dolls. The popularization of Kwanzaa and the use of African languages (specifically Swahili and Yoruba) in the late 1980s and 1990s as a connection to the Black Power past of the 1960s and 1970s as well as a pan-African ideology inspired the Shani line. According to Black Perkins, "shani" means marvelous in Swahili. The three dolls in the Shani line—named Shani, Asha (which means life in Swahili), and Nichelle (not Swahili and probably named after the famed 1960s *Star Trek* actress)—were different shades of brown and were marketed as reflecting the diversity of the African American community in hair texture, clothes, hues, and facial features. In response to the doll collection, Ann duCille remarked, "in the eyes and the advertising of Mattel ... Shani and her friends are the most authentic black female thing the mainstream toy market has yet produced."[40] Because of Black Perkins, Mitchell, and Powell-Hopson's influence in the dolls' creation, Mattel believed that it had successfully achieved aestheticized blackness. The use of Swahili in the production of these dolls aesthetically connected the essentialist Afrocentric ideal of diaspora through language with the material existence of brown plastic dolls; the dolls were *made* Black through the inclusion of Black political and aesthetic ideals as understood by Black women. The rollout of these dolls, and their overall success as far as Mattel and the three Black women who created the dolls were concerned, should not only reflect the so-called authenticity they had achieved in the Shani line, but also the Black community.

duCille further illustrates the authenticity Mattel via Black Perkins, Mitchell, and Powell-Hopson tried to achieve when they released the dolls in 1991. At the February 1991 International Toy Fair, the dolls were released at a Mattel gala that included "a tribute to black designers and an appearance by En Vogue singing the Negro National Anthem, 'Lift Every Voice and Sing.'"[41] By using the popular R&B group of Black women En Vogue at the height of their popularity to sing the Negro National Anthem—a song written by brothers James Weldon Johnson and John Rosamond Johnson that was historically taught to children as an educational tool about Black history and legacy in hopes of creating citizens invested in Black uplift—Mattel positioned the Shani dolls as an extension and evolution of the historical Black narrative of overcoming struggle for equality, recognition, and (at times assimilationist) capitalist success in the United States.[42] While the International Toy Fair had occurred every February since 1904, it has coincided since 1976 with the now nationally recognized Black History Month. The tribute to Black designers at the fair performed an ideological commitment to Black uplift and to remembering Black pasts.[43] The gala performances and tributes connected to symbolic genealogies of blackness—visual, sonic/aural, aesthetic, and historical—in ways that not only hailed Black people attending, but further ideologically connected the Shani dolls (as well as the Black women who created them) to Black discourses, pasts, and presents. Shani, Asha, and Nichelle were presented as conduits and connectors to Black people—with music, history, and Black celebrities that normally would not be present at a toy convention. Black Perkins and Mitchell symbolically positioned En Vogue to entertain based on the ways that they believed blackness could be connected aurally. The performance of blackness through Black history, Black celebrity, and Black music squarely positioned Shani dolls within Black popular culture, and yet, this performative release of the doll in 1991 further instantiated ideals and perceptions of blackness that were apparent in the ideological underpinnings of the doll and in popular culture at large.[44] These dolls courted the US cultural imagination through the targeted commodification of aestheticized blackness, in layered and multifaceted ways, as performed and substantiated by Black women.

Shani's 1991 commercial doubled down on Mattel's attempt to connect to Black consumers. Against a black-and-white cityscape, three girls (two Black girls and one faceless, seemingly white girl who has no lines) highlight Shani, Asha, and Nichelle. The two Black girls smile and look admiringly at the dolls while a jazzy song overlays the scene repeatedly cooing Shani's name. A call and response song begins in which vocalists sing "Oooooh Shani is here/Shani Shani/you walk and smile/Shani Shani/you got style/so hot/we love all the looks you got/jewelry that fresh wear it anywhere/and you got all that gorgeous hair." The culmination of the song comes at the end of the commercial when the main Black girl twirls Shani and remarks, "You're everything I want to be."[45] The Black girl's final statement, "you're everything I want to be" almost exactly mirrors the ending of Barbie's first 1959 commercial's ending explored earlier in this chapter: "Someday, like you, I'm gonna be, until then I know just what I'll do—Barbie, beautiful Barbie—I'll make believe I'm you." The Shani commercial goes even further, however, to cater specifically to Black girls and women. The vocality and song style as well as the prominent featuring of Black girls in the commercial illustrate Mattel's target audience and the ways they have tried to hail Black people through the television. The city backdrop and the jazzy song, too, illustrate Mattel's attempts to signify on ideas about Black culture that reify blackness as synonymous with urbanity and certain musical styles. In the 1959 commercial, a woman sings about "making believe" a girl is Barbie while the 1991 commercial features a Black girl saying her Black doll is "everything" she wants to be. The ideological connection to a doll here is even more intense because this is not make-believe or Barbie play: the Black doll *is* who the Black girl wants to embody and become. Unlike the 1959 Barbie ad, in which a doll was what girls used to fantasize about their adult lives, the 1991 ad shows that the Black doll becomes the standard and idol for Black girls; rather than being a mechanism to figure out one's aspiration, Shani was constructed *as* the aspiration. The doll stands in for actual Black women that a Black girl would see and want to become or emulate, furthering the embodied objectification from Black Perkins and Black women consumers to Black Perkins and Black girls directly.

Through the articulation of the dolls using Swahili, the reification of blackness as urban and musical, as well as other aspects of Black cultural heritage, Black Perkins and Mitchell (who led the Mattel production and marketing team for Shani) worked with a Black woman-owned marketing firm to make this presentation of a Black doll—not authentic as a doll—authentic as a Black cultural artifact.[46] The assemblage or (to use the Black vernacular idea of remixing) sampling of Black cultural aesthetics, in this case, was supposed to not only challenge the symbolic power of whiteness in the ways that Barbie had been presented, but also reify the dolls within Black popular culture. Powell-Hopson notes, too, that the marketing firm sent her on a ten-city tour to conduct workshops with Black organizations such as book clubs and Jack and Jill groups.[47] Her workshops in cities with large Black populations and through historically rooted Black organizations run by middle-class and wealthy Black women asked participants about their first experiences with race, which usually brought about conversations on trauma and reconciliation. As a psychologist and as a consultant for Mattel's Shani dolls, Powell-Hopson used these workshops to discuss the dolls and their ability to create high self-esteem and positive racial development based on her research. These workshops, then, became another point of entrée for middle-class Black women consumers who would know and identify with the Black cultural politics around dolls and racial development (and also have the financial means to buy dolls) that have stirred cultural conversations since the early twentieth century.

The various modes of "blackening" the dolls—through workshops, aesthetic changes, and the team of Black women working to make the dolls, marketing, and social reach of the dolls acceptable to Black people—would accost Black people with the ways blackness was being aestheticized with these Barbie dolls; the use of Black histories, music, and legacies to which they were attached would hail Black people as consumers. As Paul Gilroy explains, however, blackness, particularly in the production, expansion, and consumption of popular culture, must always contend with the idea of authenticity.[48] Naturally, there is no such thing as an authentic blackness; however, Black people as cultural producers and consumers often actively debate what aspects of culture are representative of a Black experience through debating the inclusion and exclusion of people and ideas within Black history, Black music, and Black culture. In the case of the Shani dolls, Black consumers' ideas of authenticity conflicted with how Mattel (and more pointedly, Kitty Black Perkins) described the dolls as "authentically Black" because of their various "complexions," "vibrant colors," and not-quite-straight hair (Black Perkins decided to create a crimped hairstyle on Shani, Asha, and Nichelle to produce a more textured look than traditional Barbie's straight coif).[49] Black consumers rejected these attempts to appropriate and market "signifiers of blackness" that were part of Mattel's mission for what duCille calls "quick fix" multiculturalism.[50]

As aestheticized blackness became a commodity through attempts like this one to align consumptive products with those marginalized in society (considered niche markets), Black consumers readily have and continue to negotiate the authentic representation of themselves in the popular sphere. Despite the $19.99 purchase price (the equivalent of $38 in 2019) for Shani and her friends and the Black sartorial fanfare with which the dolls were released, Black consumers were not convinced that the Shani dolls truly represented Black communities. Some consumers complained that the dolls were "not Black enough" because they still had long hair, were relatively thin, and promoted the ideal as other Barbies did that "if I don't look like this I won't be accepted," but Powell-Hopson argues that the dolls show that "society values black people as much as white people."[51] Powell-Hopson's commentary on the doll's potential to produce high self-esteem in African American girls seemed to completely miss the concerns of Black (mostly women) consumers who instead saw the dolls as still too much like their white counterpart, Barbie. Historically, these concerns were not new to the production of Black dolls; however, the idea that a doll could or could not be "black enough" acknowledges the desire for an authentic performance of Black culture, even if any authentic representation of blackness is arbitrary because it is built on homogenizing the myriad lived experiences and shifting subjectivities of Black people.[52] Black consumers know this, and yet, their critique speaks to both a desire to see themselves reflected in popular culture, particularly in contrast to historical misrepresentations created through the eyes of white producers and consumers, as well as some discomfort with how corporate entities have commodified difference over time to sell stereotypical representations of blackness back to Black people.

These tensions over Black representation as well as Mattel's own unwillingness to support the dolls led to their eventual demise as well as Kitty Black Perkins's exit from Mattel. Before she left, however, she was instrumental in mentoring and championing Mattel's next Black woman designer, Stacey McBride-Irby, who also tried her hand at making authentic Black dolls.

Mapping Blackness (Again) at Mattel: So In Style dolls

After working at a children's clothing company and taking a fashion design computer class, Stacey McBride-Irby cold-called Kitty Black Perkins and said she needed a job. Thankfully, Black Perkins was hiring. McBride-Irby joined Mattel in 1996 as an assistant to Black Perkins and the two of them formed a mentorship relationship that taught McBride-Irby the work and beauty of toy design for Mattel, featuring Barbie dolls specifically.[53] With the help of Black Perkins, McBride-Irby designed her first doll in 1996, the Blossom Beauty Barbie; the doll came in both Black and white versions accompanied by a similarly racialized fairy who sprinkled glitter and changed Barbie's floral skirt into a bed of flowers. After the success of Blossom Beauty Barbie, McBride-Irby was promoted to a design position, transitioning out of her apprenticeship role under Kitty Black Perkins. By then Black Perkins's Shani dolls had essentially disappeared from the Mattel doll lineup; Shani's boyfriend Jamal was incorporated in the main Barbie line as Steven and there was no more money or design time committed to the Shani doll collection. Mattel later incorporated a miniature Black doll named Shani into its 1998 Polly Pocket "Fashion Polly!" line.[54]

Stacey McBride-Irby worked with Mattel from 1996 to 2011 and remembers the secondary status of all Black dolls. In our June 2019 interview, McBride-Irby described the design environment on the Barbie team as built on design competitions that highlighted those who could be the loudest, not necessarily the best designer. She noted, "Black Barbie was secondary; we always designed Barbie first, then the marketing team would say they need a Black Barbie like that as well."[55] Her comments illustrate a culture of design that maintained the thin, blonde, and blue-eyed Barbie as the sole focus and design aesthetic within Mattel; it also explains the corporate environment with which Black Perkins and McBride-Irby, as Black women, engaged daily even if they both had ideas and aspirations to create Black dolls for Black children.

In August 2008, Mattel released a special edition collector's doll that commemorated the centennial celebration of the first historically Black sorority, Alpha Kappa Alpha Sorority, Incorporated (AKA).[56] The AKA Sorority Barbie doll was the first of its kind to acknowledge and celebrate Black Greek-lettered organizations and children's play.[57] Furthering Black women's consumption habits of Black dolls within the Mattel Barbie world, AKA Sorority Barbie revitalized the early 1990s fanfare that connected Mattel to Black history, culture, and aesthetics via Black women. Stacey McBride-Irby was the person who designed the doll in conjunction with representatives from AKA; although not a member of the sorority herself, McBride-Irby cherished the opportunity to develop a doll that specifically featured and was marketed to Black women.[58] McBride-Irby explained that while only a collector's item (and therefore not mass-produced like other dolls), the AKA Sorority Barbie sparked her desire to develop "a doll that would be good for Black women."[59] Especially in light of the rising fame of Barack Obama, who had become the presidential candidate for the Democratic Party and whose wife Michelle had been invited to become an honorary member in AKA, as well as buzz surrounding Disney's first animated story of a Black princess in *The Princess and the Frog*, McBride-Irby created a pitch for a doll that would connect these ideas, capture the collective energy and hopefulness of Black people at the time, and highlight the interests and experiences of Black girls like her daughter, who had just turned six years old.[60] McBride-Irby's experience of developing a doll that was imbued with the history, culture, and sartorial presentation of Black sorority women fomented an ideological relationship between producer and consumer; her inspiration, beyond Barack Obama and Princess Tiana, was the possibility of creating for herself, the women she understood as peers, her daughter, and the children she imagined as playmates for her daughter.

Mattel agreed to revisit the idea of culturally aestheticized and so-called affirming dolls with Stacey McBride-Irby at the helm in September 2009. Like the Shani line, Stacey McBride-Irby's So In Style (SIS) dolls—Grace, Trichelle, and Kara—were a triptych made to reflect the diversity of African Americans.

McBride-Irby maps the emergence of the So In Style dolls within Barbie's original history in this way: Grace was Barbie's best friend in Malibu before moving to Chicago where she befriended Trichelle and Kara. Not only does McBride-Irby connect her dolls with the lineage of Mattel's Black dolls, but she articulates the dolls' cultural heritage in an urban environment that is consistently read as a Black city with a rich history of Black success, music, and cultural influence. As home to the formidable Black newspaper the *Chicago Defender*; famous Black intellectuals, writers, artists, and cultural producers like Lorraine Hansberry, Charles White Jr., Nichelle Nichols, Don Cornelius, Quincy Jones, Redd Foxx, Shonda Rhimes, Bernie Mac, Oprah Winfrey, Jesse Jackson, and Michelle Obama; and the political home of then-presidential hopeful Barack Obama, Chicago became the homeplace of the So In Style doll brand intentionally. In line with the popularity of the Obama family, McBride-Irby migrated the dolls from the (white) Barbie homeplace of rich, white, and beachy Malibu to the Black cultural mecca of Chicago while also connecting them to the lineage of Mattel's brown-painted dolls in Malibu; rhetorically, McBride-Irby makes Grace the descendant of Mattel's 1969 sun-kissed Malibu Christie. As a

(a) (b)

FIGURE 2.6a and 2.6b. Mattel's 2009 So In Style Kara and Kiana (front and back). Source: Courtesy of the Indianapolis Children's Museum, Indianapolis, IN; Courtesy of Stacey McBride-Irby.

Barbie lover and collector from an early age, Stacey McBride-Irby was aware of the history of Barbie as well as the cultural influence of Chicago. As a form of embodied objectification, the So In Style dolls combined McBride-Irby's love of doll culture, fashion, and play; her desire to create for the girl she was and her daughter; and the contemporary cultural discourses surrounding Barack Obama and the history of Black people in Chicago.

Grace, Trichelle, and Kara—like Shani, Asha, and Nichelle—were purported to have wider noses, curlier hair, and different "complexions." Paired with "little sisters" Courtney, Janessa, and Kiana, the SIS dolls were created for both older and younger girls to play together and help them aspire to activities like playing music, creating art, and cheerleading that McBride-Irby considered positive. All the dolls had long hair that could be curled with water and a curling iron that was included in each box; the lone male doll, Grace's high school lab partner-turned-boyfriend Darren, had a short buzz cut.[61] In late 2009, Stacey McBride-Irby also spearheaded a partnership with Baby Phat and RocaWear—urban style brands led by supermodel Kimora Lee Simmons and rapper Jay-Z respectively—to license their popular styles for dolls' clothes. Reaping the benefits of Black cultural signification, the So In Style dolls' association with Baby Phat in particular reformulated the imaginary lavish lifestyle of Barbie with that of Korean–African American Kimora Lee Simmons. Businesswoman, model, and author of *Fabulosity*, Simmons in the late 2000s represented a beautiful, successful, and aspirational lifestyle to which Black girls could aspire through So In Style doll play.[62]

Alongside the Baby Phat and RocaWear fashion significations, McBride-Irby and Mattel used Black vernacular phrases like "chillin'" as well as a cartoon of McBride-Irby on the back of the box to lure Black girl consumers. McBride-Irby's cartoon was paired with a commentary called "Meet the Designer" that introduced consumers to the designer and her inspirations behind the dolls; the box read, "As a Barbie doll designer for more than 10 years, I want African-American girls to know that dolls can represent their career aspirations, hobbies, and ethnic backgrounds. Barbie inspired me to realize my dream of becoming a designer, and I want my dolls to inspire girls to play, create, and live out their dreams."[63] In the tradition of Black doll designers and producers, McBride-Irby uses embodied objectification to create an ideological relationship between herself and the consumers she hopes to target with her dolls. Using her own history and relationship with Mattel, and the ideas she had about the kinds of products she hoped would inspire her daughter, McBride-Irby attempted to harness the representational value of her face and narrative to win over Black buyers. As Kitty Black Perkins did with the Shani line, Mattel used the association of Black cultural idioms, sartorial cultural aesthetics (and their respective relevance to the growing popularity of hip-hop culture) via Baby Phat and RocaWear, and aspirational cultural discourses via McBride-Irby's own success story to market SIS dolls at Black Entertainment Television (BET) events and inside *Ebony* magazine.

Although the So In Style (SIS) dolls saw success in the US market, they too were faced with critiques from Black consumers about the lack of diversity in the dolls' looks. Citing the 1939 Mamie and Kenneth Clark doll tests (which were re-created by Darlene Powell-Hopson in 1985 and used to inform Shani's creation), consumers argued that the dolls were not as representative as they should be of Black culture because they lacked the "unmistakably Afrocentric" features that Black girls have and instead affirmed European beauty standards.[64] Mattel later released other dolls, Chandra and Marisa respectively, to represent darker complexions and Afro-Latina ethnicities, addressing consumers' comments about the lack of diversity in doll "complexions" and the need to accurately and authentically portray Black people.

A Black male designer, Stephen Sumner, who was hired under Stacey McBride-Irby's leadership and worked intermittently at Mattel, notes that the So In Style dolls fell to a fate similar to the Shani dolls before them.[65] After Stacey McBride-Irby's departure—in part due to lack of support from the marketing team and an overall cultural attitude at Mattel that maintained the importance of white Barbie over all other doll products—the So In Style dolls gave way to an even more diverse line of dolls called Fashionistas that even today present myriad hairstyles (including big afros, shaved undercuts, and blue curls), clothing, and career choices. Despite Mattel's reluctance over the past sixty years to produce Black Barbie collections as well as the major decline in global doll sales, the company has seen record-breaking success with the release of novelty collectible Barbie dolls based on Black celebrities like Ava DuVernay, Maya Angelou, Rosa Parks, and tennis star Naomi Osaka; the 2016 introduction of new Barbie body types that include petite, curvy, and tall Barbie; and the 2019 release of "Creatable World" dolls (not Barbies) that present gender-neutral options for doll play.

Confluence in Selling
Twenty-first-Century Blackness

In this chapter, I have examined how Mattel has attempted since 1968 to aestheticize blackness for consumption in the United States with their first Black dolls, Julia and Malibu Christie. Both Julia, based on actress Diahann Carroll, and Malibu Christie had the same doll bodies and aesthetics as Mattel's white dolls. However, as Mattel's consumer relationship to Black communities grew—through its relationship with Black-owned Shindana Toy Company and by hiring Black women in its design, production, and marketing teams—the dolls reflected a greater variety of characteristics of Black communities in the United States. Kitty Black Perkins, in particular, provided much of Mattel's knowledge about Black popular culture from her own experience as well as led to the hiring of more Black designers like Stacey McBride-Irby and Stephen Sumner and a push for more diverse dolls at Mattel.

If, as she has admitted, twenty-first-century Black women cultural producers like Stacey McBride-Irby understand that their aesthetic choices have an impact on the symbolic habitus of Black girls across the diaspora, how then can we understand their continued affirmation and maintenance of white supremacist and patriarchal performances of femininity? I maintain that both McBride-Irby and her forebearers in the doll industry recognize the importance of maintaining allegiances to "mainstream" consumers and audiences because they understand the symbolic power of whiteness and white beauty aesthetics in the United States. In many ways, these consumers dictate what products major corporations like Mattel will manufacture despite the success of smaller companies like Shindana. Moreover, from Malibu Christie to Rosa Parks Barbie, Black women cultural producers' use of long, straight hair and thinner body types (alongside their inclusion of darker skin complexions, wider noses, and wider hips) illustrates the aesthetic tensions within Black cultural discourses about representation. Despite the desire to create products that speak directly to Black girls and women—"brother and sister dolls for brothers and sisters"—Black women cultural producers must still contend with the ideological resonances of "positive representation" and racial uplift in their production; according to bell hooks, "the acknowledged Other [in this case the Black dolls that have been ushered into the Mattel landscape] must assume recognizable forms" because consumer culture teaches us as consumers how to interact with the Other.[66] Their aesthetic choices communicate that even though contemporary discourses dictate that anything is sellable in our society, there are some symbols of beauty, femininity, and sexuality that will sell better than others.

However, Black Perkins, McBride-Irby, and other Black women cultural producers infuse their work for all audiences with the same Black cultural productions, traditions, and idioms that Shindana Toy Company's success illustrated were important for Black communities to become loyal consumers of "Black" material products. They showed that the introduction and maintenance of Black cultural traditions in their work not only resonated with Black communities, but also saw large dividends from white consumers as well. In this way, these Black women cultural producers were able to concentrate the Black symbolic power of dolls to shift the doll industry by centering the memory of and pleasure in Black girlhood play. Their decisions to claim beauty, femininity, and poise alongside fashion, cultural vernacular, and afro-styled hair shifted the cultural imagination of Black womanhood to include America's most beloved doll.

Like others after her, Kitty Black Perkins decided to aestheticize blackness through hair, clothing, Black vernacular, and music; these choices shaped not only the symbolic power of Barbie within Black communities, but also the way that consumers more broadly understood the relationship between Barbie, American femininity, and blackness. Stacey McBride-Irby's So In Style dolls marked a shift in the popularity of Black dolls because of their alignment with another cultural product that was becoming a global phenomenon: hip-hop (via urban streetwear and colloquialisms). As we will see in the next chapter, the alliance between Black cultural products in different industries not only shifts the cultural imagination about Black women, beauty, and the possibilities of representation, but also guarantees a cultural phenomenon that changes how Black girls see themselves in popular culture.

CHAPTER 3

From Bootstraps to Glass Slippers

Black Women's Uplift
in Disney's Princess Canon

Since the early 1900s, Black people manifested the ways that consumption provided opportunities for equal respect in the United States. As a marker of their modern subjectivity, Black people worked to illustrate themselves as part of the American polity through consumption. Black women, in particular, became invested as producers and consumers in the sartorial aspects of consumption as a visual (and political) repudiation of narratives that construed their complexions, butts, lips, and hair as monstrous and undesirable.[1] As an extension of the ways Black women cultural producers narrated the ability for Black women to participate in the production and consumption of US culture I explore the aesthetic and narrative representational choices for Black Cinderellas that these cultural producers made in two distinct yet interrelated cases: Disney/ABC's made-for-television *Rodgers & Hammerstein's Cinderella* (1997) and Disney's *The Princess and the Frog* (2009). Reshaping quintessentially American fairytales that purport faith in individual progress through hard work and the ability to shift one's economic and social circumstances overnight, I center the stories of Black Cinderellas—and the Black women who created them—as a late twentieth- and early twenty-first-century evolution of Black uplift narratives. These stories align Black people's struggle for autonomy and economic independence with US princess narratives. I question how and why the Cinderella story lends itself to fantasies specific to Black women's experiences as well as which visual choices Black women make as producers of these narratives to communicate Black women's beauty and industriousness.

As I locate visual, narrative, and ideological connections between Black Cinderella stories as cultural products in the late 1990s and early 2000s, I also highlight the narrative choices that further instantiate the importance of Black people's participation in the commodification of blackness in corporate environments. As in previous chapters, I explore the nexus of the connections between Black women's cultural productions; corporate interests; US discourses on race and beauty; and the ideological relationship between Black women cultural producers and consumers through what I call embodied objectification—the process through which Black women infuse consumptive products with the histories, knowledges, and aesthetics that encapsulate their cultural heritage to hail consumers. I extend those discourses to include two films that Disney used specifically to build relationships with Black consumers. Created, funded, personified, and voiced by Black women, these popular princess films invite further questioning of how fantastical narrative imagination, blackness, coyly referenced (hetero)sexuality, and beauty standards in popular culture mold the images and ideas that Black girls connected with in the late twentieth and early twenty-first centuries.

The relationship between visuality and the American Dream is imbedded in the emergence and narrative structure of Cinderella as Black. While the story of Cinderella has proliferated globally as a story about a poor (or even enslaved) girl who is unjustly persecuted after the death of her father and then "rewarded" with the love of and marriage to a king, the particularities of Cinderella in the Western world have bound Cinderella's misfortune to her family and her reward to a handsome prince who notices her with the help of a fairy godmother. The story, regardless of its cultural location, presents the possibility for a massive shift in personal circumstance due to magical intervention.

A distinctly feminine struggle resulting in the end of unjust treatment and servile labor, the story of Cinderella—a girl whose own name bespeaks her color (ashen) and station in life—specifically maps onto US ideals of hard work leading to good fortune. Yet, the presentation of Cinderella as a Black woman in the US context conflates ideas of unjust persecution and misfortune with individual hard work, beauty, and magic. I argue that this shift in context and meaning is due to the relationship of Black people to modern subjectivity through histories of oppression. I examine Black women's harnessing of Black symbolic power for Cinderella stories through the construction of Black US struggles for equality as "rags-to-riches" narratives and how they become part of the cultural products of Black women who want to illustrate themselves as beautiful as part and parcel of modern subjectivity through princess narratives. I consider how we might understand the purposeful inclusion of Black women in princess narratives as producers, actors, and consumers. Black women's roles in the creation of Black Cinderellas redirected the narrative of rags-to-riches with the help of a handsome prince to the ability for Black women to act as their own change agents, creating their own opportunities for success and self-fulfillment.

Extending the relationship between Black producers and consumers I have explained in the last two chapters, here I contextualize Black women's role in the tradition of Black Cinderellas as visual markers of their war on ideological narratives that present Black women as undesirable. The merging of Black striving narratives and the fairytale story of Cinderella illustrates a strong identification with and correlation between Black historical rags-to-riches narratives and the popularity of Cinderella's story in the United States generally. Further, I trace how these Cinderella stories capitalize on both the symbolic power of Disney's original Cinderella story as well as Black people's attachments to modern subjectivity through Cinderella as a visual example of their shift from an oppressed past to modern, worthy-of-respect subjects. I conclude with a discussion of how these images both affirm and deconstruct traditional Cinderellas as only white and blonde. Together, the images of Black girl princesses I explore form a narrative that critiques and rewrites the ideological belief that whiteness is a prerequisite for royal status, especially at Disney. Alongside the not-so-fictional Black princess Megan Markle who spurned global awe and disdain in 2018, these stories say, "it's possible" for a Black girl to be desired, to be a princess, and to be herself, while also navigating the historical stereotypes of Black women.

Black Uplift Breadcrumbs: Popular Culture, Consumption, and Black Citizenship

Popular culture in the United States has and continues to craft narrative imaginative spaces that privilege stories of underdogs overcoming seemingly insurmountable social obstacles and political or economic strife, the Horatio Alger myth. Early colonial Protestant preachers like John Winthrop saw the so-called new land of the Americas as the Jerusalem to which God was sending his people, establishing US attachments to the Protestant work ethic and faith-fueled prosperity. Sacvan Bercovitch points out that many historical documents were inflected with Protestant jeremiads in which the founding fathers "confine[d] the concept of revolution to American progress, American progress to God's New Israel, and God's New Israel to people of their own kind."[2] American progress became synonymous with the success of wealthy Judeo-Christian Europeans who used indentured servitude, enslavement, and proximity to the status of church clergy to create the capitalist system on which the US contemporarily operates. The fantasy of the American Dream is built on the belief in a god or system that favors certain people, and that favor is illustrated through one's ability to participate in consumptive practices to prove one's citizenship. The spirit of America is therefore built on a cultural consensus about progress and the need to remain "one nation under God" to receive providential favor.[3] For this reason, the highly individualistic Judeo-Christian idea that steadfast faith in oneself can result in unparalleled accomplishments is recycled in everything from car commercials to films about sport and cultural heroes. Popular culture, and its pervasive recycling of faith-based capitalist values, acts as the main conduit for the narrative ideologies that privilege "underdogs" or hard-working individuals as the keys to collective progress. These ideologies transform the stories of individuals into stories that instill a greater symbolic civic faith in the downtrodden's ability to rise despite active discrimination, systemic laws, and pervasive attitudes that secure their place at the bottom of the economic ladder. Specifically for Black people in the United States, the infusion of Judeo-Christian ideals of faith despite circumstance and hope for a better future while one toils—which Kate Bowler calls "prosperity gospel"—formed the basis for many cultural attitudes that infuse American cultural products.[4]

Ann Petry's famous 1946 novel, *The Street*, provides an example of Black narrative imagination that captures the correlative faith in prosperity and therefore consumption. The novel follows the story of Lutie Johnson as she struggles to understand her place in society as a Black working-class, single mother. Lutie wholeheartedly subscribes to the belief "that anybody could be rich if he wanted to and worked hard enough and figured it out carefully enough."[5] Throughout the novel, however, Lutie is confronted with racialized, gendered, and classed discrimination that hinders her ability to achieve the American Dream and is consistently reminded of the ways that she will never measure up to others who are doing well. Lutie's narrative arc reiterates the ways that Black people, especially Black women, cannot always be prosperous in American capitalist structures of success. The attachment to this idea, however, is built on its prevalence within many of the narrative ideologies of the United States.

The ways that people in the United States approach Black history, too, illustrate the belief in Black people's seemingly superhuman ability to accomplish modernity, success, and freedom despite societal barriers; even Black superheroes—like Storm and Black Lightning—are imagined as everyday Black people whose "Otherness" is based on harnessing powers from a genetic mutation, rather than some alien origin.[6] Blackness alone becomes a superlative quality that can hurtle Black people past centuries of constant and dehumanizing oppression, securing their place as full—meaning economically favored—citizens within the American polity. Alongside white supremacist violence that actively stalks Black lived experiences, Koritha Mitchell calls this propulsion to create, strive, and achieve "a deep sense of success and belonging," Black folk's "homemade citizenship."[7]

For Black people, these narratives manifest the connections between the historical demonization and enslavement of Black bodies and any individual's struggle with racism, sexism, and economic poverty. The establishment of the Smithsonian's National Museum of African American History and Culture, for example, at the end of the presidency of Barack Obama was spun as a *culmination* of the struggle for recognition and acceptance for Black people rather than the result of many Black people's decades-long organizing, fundraising, and petitioning to create the museum.[8] The narrative arc of the Blacksonian, as it is sometimes colloquially called, too follows a superlative rags-to-riches construction in which the election of Barack Obama was the goalpost for the inclusion of Black people in the US cultural landscape.

Yet the cultural beliefs that undergird the museum and its narrative arc follow in the footsteps of the late nineteenth- and early twentieth-century ideological uplift oratory and economic habits of Black intellectuals. Nannie Helen Burroughs, for example, explained that one of the most important things that "the Negro must do" in the early 1900s was buy a home.[9] She believed that the foundational pieces of life—like buying a home—would make Black people acceptable in society and create financial stability. As a way to minimize racism and discrimination, as Burroughs, Anna Julia Cooper, and others argued, Black people must illustrate their ability to participate fully in the intellectual and economic work of the United States, and show their participation in society through their ability to consume.[10] Davarian Baldwin explains that at the turn of the twentieth century, many Black people saw freedom enacted through the ability to consume and produce in the marketplace, a partial embrace of liberalism to assert themselves as citizens: "the overt desire for autonomous black cultural production through economic control, and specifically through consumer strategies, was arguably the most salient aspect of Chicago's New Negro consciousness" because Black people saw that a "symbiotic relationship" between consumers and producers was needed to truly be free.[11] The symbiotic relationship between Black producers and consumers was directly tied to the development of a modern Black consciousness in which both individuals and collectives could make themselves citizens through the ability to create and consume products—especially those created with Black people in mind.

As more Black people moved to larger cities, seeking economic advancement through business ownership and civic society membership, the belief that a "modern" Black subjectivity required some adherence to capitalism spread. Through a faith that consumption could and would make Black people respectable to the white American public, Black people became active in capitalist endeavors. In short, consumption *could* make Black people fully human (even while their dehumanization was the basis of modern, global capitalism). This relationship to consumption was particularly important because of Black people's (newly acquired) ownership of their bodies, labor, and property. The right to consume in the United States is seemingly protected under the law and therefore constituted Black people as citizens who had to be protected. Jasmine Cobb explains how even enslaved Black people used pictures to visually connect themselves with citizenship and therefore making themselves modern, protected individuals; Black people were "not just creating distance between freedom and slavery's meditation of Blackness . . . they were reimagining and reconstructing Black visuality" through "staged intelligence and literacy."[12] Black people staged daguerreotype images to construct themselves as modern and therefore capitalist subjects.

For Black women, in particular, their recognition as women occurred through the growing relationship between consumption, ownership, and respectability. As modern subjects, Black women were able to claim not only their right to consume, but also their right to control their bodies as protected and as beautiful.[13] For example, both Katherine Williams Irvin, editor of the *Half-Century Magazine,* and *Sunday Chicago Bee*'s editor Olive Diggs created the intellectual space for Black women's interests and political insights to exist on the front page of the Black press. As proprietors of New Negro womanhood through the curation of Black women's opinions and concerns in their respective publications, Williams Irvin and Diggs articulated a "respectable" Black womanhood as a counterbalance to "Mammy" and "Jezebel" stereotypes.[14] Their work within the Black newspaper and magazine industry overlapped culturally and ideologically with the haircare products Black women entrepreneurs like Annie Turnbo Malone and Madame C. J. Walker created as well as the speeches, pamphlets, poems, and books Black women like Sojourner Truth, Ida B. Wells-Barnett, Zora Neale Hurston, and others wrote to illustrate Black women's ability to create and consume as modern subjects. Black women in multiple industries and over the course of the twentieth century labored to illustrate their own industriousness as well as Black people's collective potential to achieve the American Dream. Citizenship, modernity, and blackness were built together around Black uplift through the production of themselves and consumption of various goods and services. Black people used visuality as a means to illustrate their ability to produce and consume, a key element of progress within the US capitalist structure. In the latter part of the twentieth century, with new opportunities to produce and therefore control nationally (and at times globally) circulated images of Black women, Black women cultural producers turned to projecting Black uplift in more fantastical ways.

Colorblind Magic:
Black Cinderella Debuts at Disney

There have been many iterations of Black Cinderella narratives (e.g., the picture book *Mufaro's Beautiful Daughters* and Broadway Cinderella plays with Black actresses), but my research focuses on the aesthetic and narrative representation of Black Cinderellas in two cases: the made-for-television Disney/ABC special *Rodgers & Hammerstein's Cinderella* (1997) and Disney's *The Princess and the Frog* (2009). Principally, I focus on these versions because of their popularity since they were released and the controversy surrounding the films' ability to represent and imagine Black girls as princesses. Additionally, Disney's purchase of ABC in 1995 produced a televisual empire that allowed the corporation to connect television, film, theme parks, and merchandise to their princess pantheon.[15] Disney's empire has been built on strategic fantasy-making, which typically reiterates specific racial, cultural, and gendered performances. Since popular culture is already constituted by fantasy and desire, much like narratives of the American Dream, Disney's particular narratives of race and gender push popular culture to extremes.[16] Disney obscures societal and cultural specificities for the so-called love of imagination, like Mattel, whose empire is also built on fantasy-making for children and the nostalgia of parents. Whereas Mattel argues that the company's products provide a platform (in Barbie play) for children to imagine themselves, Disney *proscribes* imagination, through its films, network television shows, and subsequent material objects. Disney imagines possibilities for children, rather than allowing them to craft narratives of their own. Those possibilities, as D. Soyini Madison reminds us, are always white, rich, and heterosexual, within which Disney princesses function as romantic upward mobility success stories.[17]

The difference between material product and visual product—dolls that Black girls can assemble and disassemble as they wish versus images that Disney uses to imagine narratives *for* girls—is important to distinguish. Because of Mattel's hesitancy to prescribe a life for Barbie—whether Black or otherwise characterized—children and adults participate in queering Barbie's presentation, narrating her experiences and life through the very act of play.[18] This shifting authorship of Barbie's narrative illuminates the ways that Barbie as a material product differs from Disney's Cinderella as a visual one. Peggy Orenstein and Karen Wohlwend agree that Disney's princess narratives communicate particular messages about identity that perhaps are not as present in material objects.[19] Moreover, Disney's hypercapitalist enterprise for selling princess narratives, through the extreme merchandizing of princess paraphernalia "blurs the line between play and reality, allowing children to live in-character."[20] Children can live an entirely Cinderella-themed lifestyle through the consumption of Disney's bedsheets, Tupperware, lunchboxes (full of princess cereal and fruit snacks), princess apparel (tiara included), bookbags, costume jewelry, makeup, and fuzzy slippers. Orenstein finds that around age seven, children learn that material objects determine their gender identity; therefore, Disney (and Mattel's) encroachment into even earlier moments of childhood—through the infantilizing of teenage princesses into young girls in films and play—tries to secure strict consumer allegiance from very early on.[21] Both companies have embedded themselves in US constructions of childhood so much so that there are few other possibilities. For this reason, Disney is the exemplar in the relationship between Black producers and consumers, particularly in the command of children's imaginations in a capitalist structure.

Disney is in the business of harnessing the symbolic power of its films to create lifelong consumers on multiple platforms; similar to Mattel's Black Barbie endeavors that have impacted Black girls across generations, Disney's Black Cinderellas have become a feature of Black girlhood over the past thirty years. These iterations—1997 and 2009—ultimately illustrate that Black women can do more than wish on a star to change their lives; they can choose their destinies and make it happen on their own with hard work. Unlike the traditional Cinderella fairytale, which frames a prince as the resolution of Cinderella's conflict with her stepfamily, these versions display Black women taking initiative and, in many ways, creating their own destinies (with a good-looking non-Black/American man as the icing on top). In these iterations, Black women defy the lazy stereotypes and insurmountable odds that permeate US popular culture by being *recognized* as hardworking, beautiful, and therefore, marriageable. However, Black Cinderellas continue to reify "rags-to-riches" ideologies through their struggle and a bit of "good" magic (read: luck) that drastically changes their circumstances within a few days.

Although the historical beliefs about blackness compete with ideas that a Black woman could be a princess (or a fairy godmother), these Black Cinderellas shift the imaginative space available for Black women and girls. As fantastical tales, these Black Cinderella productions envision Black women as beautiful and worthy of any suitor, which in many ways disrupts "scientific evidence" of Black women's inability to find a mate that has proliferated in US discourse since Daniel Moynihan's report on the Black community in 1955. Tamara Winfrey Harris describes the so-called crisis of Black relationships precipitated by Moynihan that feeds current statistics—the US Census in 2010 reported that 46 percent of Black women were unmarried as if the success of Black marriages rests solely on Black women's shoulders.[22] As Black women cultural producers enact these narratives to protest the lack of representation of Black women and girls visually, they also defy statistics and cultural attitudes that continually put Black women at the bottom of the hierarchies of desire.

Black women cultural producers position Black women in these fairytales as resistant agents, visually scripting the affirmation of Black cultural and idiomatic traditions while also confirming the importance of princess uplift narratives. Their work, too, affirms the importance of US white heteronormative fantasies of success, in which a girl's fantastical future must include a man to confirm her beauty and importance. In this way, Black women cultural producers affirm Black allegiances to US capitalism and the strivings in which Black people have participated to be included as modern subjects.

Treat Me Like a Person:
Black Cinderella Makes Her Television Debut

Disney's network relationship with ABC (and with Mattel) materializes the ways that visual culture creates and maintains consumers through fantastical worlds. Disney's *Wonderful World of Disney*—which released the Rodgers & Hammerstein's musical version of Cinderella—recouped much of Disney's film magic for primetime television; originally slated for CBS but homeless after shifts in leadership there, *Cinderella* was seen by then-chairman of Disney, Michael Eisner, as the best way to relaunch the *Wonderful World of Disney* brand.[23] In the late 1980s and early 1990s, specifically for Black consumers, Disney and Mattel made the "multicultural turn" to "identity politics" despite national backlash. Discussing British multicultural propaganda to obscure cultural racism, Rajeev Balasubramanyam explains, "a multicultural society refers to a society with black or brown people in it"; therefore, "multiculturalism refers to propaganda that tell us that . . . a multicultural society, is not racist, or rather that the state and corporations are not-racist and so the society is moving in this direction."[24] "Multiculturalism" is then a post-1980s dogwhistle for Black and Brown assimilation, a necessary marketing method to lure new consumers and benefit from the great economic potential of nonwhite communities in the United States (and find new markets or laborers in other global markets).

Five years after Kitty Black Perkins developed and released Mattel's Shani dolls with their own Afrocentric welcome party, Disney/ABC debuted their made-for-television *Cinderella* (1997). This fairytale premiered during prime-time on Sunday, November 2, 1997, with Robert Iscove as director.[25] This film reflected a multicultural shift in television programming and expanded ideas of compatibility across racial and ethnic barriers, garnering 60 million viewers and seven Emmy nominations. As the only Black woman on a team of producers, Debra Martin Chase controlled the multicultural agenda within the production of the television film for the *Wonderful World of Disney*, an important launching of the sub-brand that would specifically garner new consumers through television. Whitney Houston, who starred as Fairy Godmother, and Martin Chase had worked together previously on *The Preacher's Wife* (1996), a film from Houston's production company, Brown House Productions. After the success of *Cinderella* (1997), they continued to produce girl-led or "niche" films like *The Princess Diaries, The Princess Diaries 2*, and *Sparkle* together. Martin Chase had a longstanding deal with Disney to produce these and other films that capitalized on teenage girls as the main actresses.[26] Newly popular starlet Brandy Norwood starred as Cinderella, while Whoopi Goldberg was cast as Queen Constantina. This adaptation highlights a multicultural cast, yet Black women are prominent; Fairy Godmother, mother of the prince, Cinderella, and stepsister Minerva were all recognizable Black women, especially in Black cultural productions: Houston had an amazing career as a singer and had started acting; Goldberg saw stardom with the *Sister Act* franchise, highlighting her acting and singing; Brandy's show *Moesha* and budding musical career after a successful first album made her a valuable choice for Cinderella; Natalie Desselle also had a budding acting career in popular Black films *Set It Off, B*A*P*S*, and *How to Be a Player*. Executive producer Martin Chase explains that she hoped this *Cinderella* "reinforces the art of dreaming—having a vision and understand[ing] that everyone has the power within to make that vision come true."[27] In her statement, Martin Chase shifts the "Disneyfication" of blackness to reinforce the "art of dreaming" that Disney perpetuates in all of its films and multicultural inclusion.[28] She and Whitney Houston also visually constructed *Cinderella* as distinctly Black through Black vernacular idioms, multitextured clothing patterns, and interracial couples, and memorably the Whitney Houston and Brandy Norwood song "Impossible" that headlines the film.

In interviews for the twentieth anniversary of the film's release, the writers, actors, and production team remember the energy with which each person understood the film. Originally, Houston was supposed to be Cinderella, capitalizing on her popularity in music and acting at the time. Martin Chase and Houston were distinctly invested in crafting a multicultural narrative of Cinderella with a Black lead whose robust personality would carry the film, and Disney executives believed Houston transcended any issues they might have by casting a Black woman as Cinderella: "because Whitney was so huge at that time; to a lot of executives she was popular entertainment as opposed to being defined by her race."[29] This erasure of Black identity and cultural upbringing is typical for many Black performers who experience mainstream fandom. In US cultural and political spaces, the tensions between blackness and multiculturalism—the ideology that bespeaks inclusion while obscuring anti-Black attitudes and behaviors—become palpable when someone like Houston, whose performances and aesthetics are rooted in a Black Christian experience, reaches stardom in which her particularities are erased in favor of a multicultural inclusiveness and therefore universalism that can be identified with whiteness and by white people. In the twenty-first century, this rhetorical replacement of blackness with multiculturalism has shifted to postracial discourse wherein race is not notable and therefore representable (and where the mere mention of race is considered racist and un-American). Janell Hobson argues that racialized and gendered meanings become attached to bodies, rather than specific racial groups, as evidence of racial progress, thereby inviting so-called Others "to dismiss their own lived experiences of sexism, racism, classism, and imperialism in exchange for the mediated vision of 'progress' advanced in social and political representations."[30] Multiculturalism, and postraciality or colorblindness, especially in Hollywood, encourage diversity as simply phenotypic disparities based in ocular recognitions of difference rather than robust and strategic understandings of race, ethnicity, and identity formation.[31]

In this vein, Martin Chase and others made sure to balance the diverse representation of the cast, struggling to make sure this Cinderella kept its multicultural flair. Norwood was hand-picked by Houston, who felt she had aged out of playing Cinderella, while the rest of the cast was built around these two Black women actresses and the voices they would bring to the musical. Martin Chase recounts the importance of Black women specifically in front of and behind the camera when she says, "I got into this business to change images and break down stereotypes. When I grew up I never saw myself on screen."[32] Her comment not only undergirds the specific work of blackness in the made-for-television film, but also reinforces the ideological relationship between production and consumption that was important in the making of the film; and, as evidenced by the joyous social media celebrations when Disney announced the film would be added to its streaming platform in February 2021, *Cinderella* continues to connect to Black girls and women because the film majorly shifts the narrative to match ideological beliefs to which many adhere.

A conversation between Cinderella and the Prince reinforces that this Cinderella will be different than previous princess narratives: after the Prince suggests that he would like to get to know Cinderella—"What would a man have to do to find himself in your good graces?"—she challenges his confidence and questions his knowledge of how a girl should be treated. The Prince says, "Like a princess, I suppose," while Cinderella responds: "No, like a person—with kindness and respect." The Prince responds, "You're not like most girls, are you?" highlighting how this narrative (and this Cinderella) is differentiated from other princess and even Cinderella narratives. This Cinderella is "not like most girls," so audiences should expect a change in the narrative plot. Beyond typical romantic cliché, this character's desire to be treated "like a person—with kindness and respect" is more related to the lives of Black women than princess narratives because royalty is always understood as distinct and superior to common people; this Cinderella establishes a desire for consideration rather than possession. While Rebecca Wanzo suggests recognizing "the pitfalls inherent in doing black versions of generic narratives. Escaping from black history is challenging for the knowledgeable reader, and if the reader is not knowledgeable, that can produce even more disturbing results," I contend that the construction of respect and dignity of personhood in *Cinderella* is salient because of Black history.[33] It is distinctly because of Black history that Cinderella's seemingly cavalier statement resonates within Black strivings narratives of uplift despite the multicultural façade of the film. Both Black women and princesses were inherently objects to be owned and used as props garnering upward mobility and status for others. This Cinderella's distinction implies a lean toward gender equality since we know that men treat other men of a similar or higher caliber with kindness and respect. As the poor girl who amuses herself among the cinders, the daughter without a father, the Black girl mistreated and overlooked, she is perceived to be "not like most girls" as are many Black women and girls in the United States, and yet her only desire is to be treated "like a person." This desire for recognition of her humanity not only bespeaks cultural undertones of Black striving narratives and respectability, but also foreshadows how other Black Cinderellas I will mention later situate themselves within princess narratives.

Although this *Cinderella* does display typical plot formations (such as an evil stepmother, a prince who wants to find a wife, and a fairy godmother), it is distinctly Black. Its blackness is intrinsically connected to the fact that visually, Black women characters (Cinderella, Fairy Godmother, and Queen Constantina) propel the narrative forward. They ultimately become aligned in a trifecta of fantasy in the castle by the end of the film with Norwood and Goldberg becoming "family" and Houston hovering over the whole scene. These three women shape the narrative, punctuated by the song "Impossible," which features sonic connections to Black communities' desire for change and prosperity. These aspects of the film are not accidental, especially since Disney's 1950 animated *Cinderella* as well as Rodgers & Hammerstein's 1957 and 1965 television film versions of the musical (all based on Charles Perrault's story) have no people of color at all; Black women in this film as producers and actresses shape how the narrative reflects and develops Black possibilities for change through Black cultural traditions of music and desire for beating impossible odds, rather than further substantiating Black women's historical positions as servants and wise-cracking wet nurses.

While the plot progression and characters are salient to the film's "magic," the song "Impossible," twenty seconds into the feature, is the conduit through which the entire film and, more importantly, the project of multiculturalism Disney attempts to establish with *Cinderella* occurs when Whitney Houston (and indeed it is Houston rather than the Fairy Godmother since we do not yet

FIGURE 3.1. *Cinderella* opening shot, Whitney Houston as the Fairy Godmother. Source: *Cinderella* (1997), Photo by the author.

know anything about the film) is superimposed on a deep indigo background in a confetto of gold, green, and red. Slowly punctuating each word, Houston sings, "Impossible, for a plain yellow pumpkin to become a golden carriage/Impossible, for a plain country bumpkin and a prince to join in marriage." Speaking plainly, she continues, "a slipper made of glass is just a shoe and dreamers never make the dream come true. Impossible." She disappears in a flurry similar to the one with which she entered and the words "*THE WONDERFUL WORLD OF DISNEY and WHITNEY HOUSTON present*" replace her. This positioning of Houston and the song in the film, before the production team, actors' names, and brand are announced, is not coincidental; the so-called multiculturalism of the film is built upon harnessing Houston's own mainstream recognition and success, while also signaling to Black (women) consumers. In cultural and entertainment spaces, multiculturalism as a concept stands in for codifying Black expressive traditions, Black people, and Black sartorial practices for white viewing audiences, therefore narrowing Black representational opportunities to ones that are recognizable to white people, while also hailing Black consumers who will know, identify with, and celebrate these opportunities as Black symbolic power.

After meeting Cinderella at home, the song continues with the Fairy Godmother singing to Cinderella and us, "But the world is full of zanies and fools/ who don't believe in sensible rules,/and won't believe what sensible people say./And because these daft and dewy-eyed dopes keep building up impossible hopes/Impossible things are happening every day!" These lines of the song bespeak her lesson to Cinderella about how to go from dreaming to action. The lyrics illustrate a collective dissonance between dreamers and doers that ultimately frames the resolution between Cinderella and the Prince as well as the dissolution of Cinderella's family unit. As a dreamer, Cinderella's desires are directly in conflict with her treatment and social status, but she returns to them as a "daft and dewy-eyed dope." The song reminds her, as well as the audience, that impossible things are happening every day, but not by themselves; we must *do* rather than waiting on things to happen.

Because the song "Impossible" is about deconstructing what is conceived as impossible and making it happen with what is already available, Black women's roles in this *Cinderella* are imperative. For example, Whitney Houston is the first sight on screen, making the Fairy Godmother a central role in the fictional tale. Her introduction features Black vocal traditions and aesthetics; her popularity at the time (and forevermore) resonates even without having any context for who she is in the film. Later, she also invokes Black idioms and expressions with verbal inflections like "honey," eye and neck rolls, and facial expressions.

She tells Cinderella, "If you want to get out, you have to do it yourself, honey," which mirrors the discounting of hopes and dreams in the song and reflects similar cultural lessons that Black people, especially Black women, spread in their communities. When she introduces herself to Cinderella (and the audience), the Fairy Godmother says: "I'm your fairy godmother, honey," "you got a problem with that? 'Cause if you'd rather have some old [read: white] lady in a tutu sprinkling fairy dust in here. . . ." Her inflection and her mention of another type of fairy godmother again reminds the audience that this is not the typical Cinderella story; Houston is not the dowdy old "bibbidi bobbidi boo" white woman familiar from Disney's previous Cinderella stories. The Fairy Godmother is not here to just sprinkle magic dust and give Cinderella what she wants. In fact, Fairy Godmother's power comes from her fingers—from her inner essence—rather than a magic wand; when asked how she "did" that after making a fire and closing the door without moving, she says "practice" rather than with magic or a spell. In this way, the Fairy Godmother does not just change Cinderella's situation with magic, but inspires in her an ideological shift—one that heralds the importance of going beyond wishing and believing to create change. Her song "Impossible" pushes the idea that Cinderella should go do something—so much so that Cinderella preaches the same idea to the Prince, causing him to defy his parents and search for his beloved on his own after losing her at the ball. Whitney Houston as both producer and Fairy Godmother positions herself as a formidable force in the ways that Cinderella's narrative develops, aligning her own ideological (and Christian faith-based) position in life with the underlying lessons of the film.

After being questioned by the Queen and King about her family and stature, Cinderella escapes to the garden for a brief conversation with her Fairy Godmother. Bristling from the questions, Cinderella requests to go home. Fairy Godmother says, "Oh, so you're just giving up?," pushing Cinderella not to abandon the plan that she desperately wanted. Cinderella replies, "I'm not what they think I am" and the Fairy Godmother reminds her "All they're thinking is that you're the most beautiful girl at the ball, and you are." The Prince finds her in the garden and admits he wasn't interested in attending the ball either: "Don't you think it's a little medieval, everyone circling around as if I were some prized bull they were trying to rope in?" Both the Fairy Godmother's reassurances and the Prince's mentioning of the "medieval" pageantry of the ball remind the audience and Cinderella that this is not a typical Cinderella film. In medieval times, none of the characters the audience has grown to adore would be present. Similarly, if family and societal stature mattered, Cinderella would have no chance beyond hopes and dreams. However, the "magic" of this story is built within the project of multiculturalism—we are reminded that the true magic of this narrative is in the diversity of people as well as in the ideological shift from believing in the Disney-perpetuated importance of magic and dreams to the Black striving narrative structure of dreams backed up with action. Additionally, the Fairy Godmother's challenge to Cinderella's desire to leave the ball echoes the lessons young Black girls learn about facing difficulty. By staying faithful to the process, one learns, "impossible things are happening every day." The Prince launches his kingdom-wide search for her and successfully replaces her slipper with her lost glass shoe, and Cinderella sings, "It's possible, for a plain yellow pumpkin to become a golden carriage/ It's possible, for a plain country bumpkin and a prince to join in marriage." Together, Cinderella/Godmother sing: "It's possible!"

Much like the coalition of Black women that helped Mattel develop the Shani dolls in 1990, Whitney Houston and Debra Martin Chase actively shaped the ways that *Cinderella* was cast and therefore aestheticized. Both women had worked on successful films prior to this production and understood the ways that blackness could be inflected to entice audiences of color, while also maintaining the traditional Cinderella storyline that white audiences love. Because this production did not receive the Afrocentric introduction to the world that the Shani dolls did six years earlier, *Cinderella* even more so represents the multiculturalism that corporations like Disney, Mattel, and even Coca-Cola and McDonald's sought to use to inspire loyalty from ethnic audiences to their brands. Culturally, the inclusion of Black and Latino populations in television shows and movies mirrored their rise in representation in commercials and advertising; more Black and Latino artists producing more complex melodies for jingles on television and radio represented this change, too. Like the way Mattel used its relationship with Shindana and Kitty Black Perkins to expand its brand, Disney learned through this production that Black women understood the aesthetic choices necessary to broaden Disney's princess fanbase in Black communities. To have a successful production and a successful launch of the larger *Wonderful World of Disney* sub-brand, Disney learned it had to employ Black women and appreciate their cultural traditions as instructive in Black women's work.

However, consumers were keenly aware of the film's shift toward diversity, and its difference from past Disney or Cinderella films. Both the royal family and Cinderella's stepfamily were strangely inclusive. A running joke still, more than twenty years after the film's premiere, is how a Black woman (Whoopi Goldberg as Queen Constantina) and a white man (Victor Garber as King Maximillian) could produce an Asian prince (Paolo Montalban), or how a white mother (Bernadette Peters as Stepmother) could have both a white and a Black daughter (Veanne Cox and Natalie Desselle); Jason Alexander recalls that "blind casting" came to a hilarious moment in the film when his character Lionel is "trying the slippers on all the girls in the kingdom. Cinderella was clearly African-American—that was the whole point—but . . . in the long run, it didn't matter. That's how we knew the world really worked. Because by the time the audience got to that point in the movie, they weren't asking those questions."[34]

FIGURE 3.2. Cinderella and the royal family.
Source: Courtesy of Photofest.

Kristen Warner argues that this "quantifiable diversity" vacates how roles are written "racially neutral e.g. white" rather than creating "culturally specific roles for people of color," yet the popularity of this casting process continues today with television's most beloved shows, such as Shonda Rhimes's *Grey's Anatomy*.[35] While described as colorblind casting, however, *Cinderella* seemed to cast with particular actors in mind. Because Whitney Houston had been specifically chosen as the centerpiece and showrunner for the film, all the other writers and producers worked specifically to create a diverse group of characters. This color-specific casting was illustrated even in the background characters, who displayed their own multiethnic community that somehow made the plausibility of the narrative dissolve into the film. Perhaps the work of Disney's magic or the culpability of 1990s audiences, Black girl consumers coming of age when the film was released recall their love of the film because it showcased "a girl like me" as beautiful, desirable, and the center of the narrative.

Black actress Keke Palmer was cast as Cinderella for the 2014 Broadway adaptation of *Rodgers & Hammerstein's Cinderella* and she notes, "the reason I am able to do this is definitely because Brandy did it on TV," recognizing the imaginative possibilities the 1997 film created within the viewing public.[36] Palmer also proclaimed a globalizing narrative that connects to the overall theme of the 1997 film, but also to the larger Black striving narrative underwritten by Martin Chase and Houston in the film: "In me doing this, it shows everybody that everything is possible."[37] Palmer's comments reflect both the underlying ideological relationship that Black women cultural producers and consumers have as well as the ways that relationship is extracted within global capitalist markets for "everybody." The false promise of colorblind casting actually only provides opportunities for certain actors, like Palmer, to take on a role like Norwood before her. Between the 1997 *Cinderella* cast, especially Brandy Norwood as Cinderella, and Keke Palmer as a consumer (she was four when the film was released), the idea of Black women's place in these narratives—as the featured character rather than as an extra—was solidified. The Fairy Godmother's lessons to Cinderella—dreaming and wishing alone will not change your circumstances; within you is the power to do anything you want to do—resonated with ideas Black women had heard and Black girls had been told. As an "interpretive community," a community in which collective meaning and importance are shaped, Black women and girls as producers and consumers recognized and identified with the lesson that wishing was not enough to change one's circumstance; they learned to save themselves because of their own positionality and how histories of racism and sexism dictate Black women and girls must do more than wish to accomplish anything.[38]

Although the film ends traditionally with the Prince marrying Cinderella, he actually finds her as she is hitting the road alone. Rather than waiting to be rescued by her white knight, Cinderella has already decided to leave because she "deserved to be loved." Cinderella's interaction with the Fairy Godmother, then, was not for an evening or one dance with the Prince. Reminiscent of one of Houston's greatest hits, "The Greatest Love of All," Fairy Godmother's insistence that Cinderella "find the music within" and go beyond simply wishing and dreaming to change her circumstance became the basis for a transformation of her character and her outlook on life. Fairy Godmother underscores the necessity of escaping a bad circumstance even when it goes against promises made to others such as recently deceased loved ones because "this can't be what [your father] had in mind." Cinderella's realization and subsequent exit from her stepmother's house codifies a lesson to Black girls and women like her: a person, even a Black female one, is worthy of love and dignity, and should leave if that love is not felt. This lesson is one that can be extrapolated to all audiences watching the film, a directive that makes the girl power moment of the 1990s palpable; Fairy Godmother parrots the idea that one must set one's own terms.

While the film is heralded as the "first interracial television production" of *Cinderella* that is "colorblind," and shows "a normal mix of people," the multicultural mission of the film is grounded in the performances of "blackness" throughout.[39] Disney's 1997 *Cinderella* is created and shaped by the representation of Black women from popular Black shows and films in every important narrative role as well as the use of Black idioms and cultural vernacular; song choices, jewel-toned aesthetics, and background instruments; and lessons known and recognized by Black women and girls. Cinderella's braided hair, beautiful gown, and fairytale ending showed Black girls coming of age in 1997 that nothing is impossible—impossible things are happening every day!

Historical, Geographic, and Contextual Blackness: The Magic of a New Orleans Princess

Twelve years after Brandy Norwood embodied the Cinderella fairytale on television, Disney's "first black princess" emerged in movie theaters. Set in Jazz Age New Orleans, Disney's *The Princess and the Frog* (2009) was said to be the first Black princess added to Disney's princess pantheon; inspired by novelist E. D. Baker's *The Frog Princess*—an adaptation of the Brothers Grimm's *The Frog Prince*—*The Princess and the Frog* follows the story of Tiana, a hard-working Black woman who is intent on starting her own restaurant, and her eventual relationship with and marriage to the fun-loving and philandering Prince of Maldonia, Naveen. While Naveen's fictitious kingdom is only a cruise away from New Orleans, Tiana's life and experiences form the basis of the conflict throughout the film; her major lesson hinges on her "fairy godmother" Mama Odie's song to "dig a little deeper" to find out who she is beyond hard work, which will unlock her purpose and peace.

Anika Noni Rose voices Princess Tiana, a Black woman who becomes a princess through marrying a prince-turned-frog. The child of a hard-working serviceman father (Terence Howard) and seamstress mother (Oprah Winfrey), Tiana was taught that hard work and believing in her dreams could get her the things she wanted. In an early scene of her as a child, she tells her father about a fairytale book owned by her white friend Charlotte, and the importance of the evening star in that narrative: "Charlotte's fairytale book said if you make a wish on an evening star, it's sure to come true." Her father replies, "You wish and dream with all your little heart. But you remember, Tiana, that that old star can only take you part of the way. You gotta help it along with some hard work of your own and, then, you can do anything you set your mind to. Just promise your daddy one thing: that you'll never ever lose sight of what's really important." Mirroring the Fairy Godmother's words to Cinderella, Tiana's father tells her that traditional fairytale narratives are not enough for a Black girl child like her; hard work is as integral to success as wishing and dreaming. Tiana's paternal lesson too mimics much of the American Dream that circulates in US popular culture: lots of hard work and faith in goals, coupled with luck, can give you everything your heart desires if you are Black.

After her father dies while serving in the military, Tiana's dreams of owning a restaurant become her sole focus; to honor her father's legacy and love of cooking for others, Tiana subscribes to the American Dream as experienced by many Black people—constantly working to save more. Despite working multiple waitressing jobs, however, Tiana is seemingly turned away from her dream at every corner—her Black friends and employers critique her self-sacrificing spirit; her mother bemoans her lack of grandchildren and reminds Tiana of her biological clock; and her best friend Charlotte, the daughter of a wealthy white sugar baron, is so preoccupied with marrying a prince herself that Tiana is left to her own devices most of the film. Tiana is characterized as industrious and hard-working like her father, yet completely self-sacrificing so that she may have her own restaurant called "Tiana's Place."

Although Tiana, unlike the fairytale Cinderella, has a loving family, her story is ultimately a Cinderella story through the ways that Disney depicts the landscape and geography, her fashion aesthetic, her relationship to Charlotte,

FIGURE 3.3. Tiana's Place. Source: *The Princess and the Frog* (2009), Photo by the author.

and the resolution of her narrative. Conceptualized with the idea of a Black princess in mind, and knowingly constructing all of the characters with attention to Black cultural traditions, culinary knowledge, histories, and music, *The Princess and the Frog* presents the first Black princess within the Disney pantheon. Unlike rekindling a traditional Cinderella story around the casting of a Black singer/actress like Whitney Houston, the Disney production team started with blackness at the center of how this princess would be introduced to the world. However, the film starts with introducing two Black women's voices, disembodied to illustrate a fairytale beginning: Anika Noni Rose's voice welcomes the audience to the magical land as she sings: "The evening star is shining bright/so make a wish and hold on tight/there's magic in the air tonight/and anything can happen." The audience is beckoned into a towerlike window where pink curtains alert you to whom you might be meeting. Oprah Winfrey's voice begins recounting a story, where a frog is begging a princess for a kiss to undo a wicked witch's spell. While Anika Noni Rose's voice may not be distinctive to many audiences, Oprah Winfrey's voice—even reading a children's story—is immediately recognizable. The combination of geography, Tiana's fashions, her relationships with white people, and the distinct racial differences throughout the film bespeaks a palpable tension between Disney magic and Black cultural traditions. These two voices and the first few scenes not only construct the sing-song and wish-driven narrative that is reminiscent of Disney's popular animated princess stories, but also attempt to lure Black girl and women consumers' attention, much like the precredit use of Whitney Houston's voice in *Cinderella*.

Set in New Orleans between 1910 and 1940, *The Princess and the Frog* was released just four years after Hurricane Katrina exposed the racial and economic disparities undergirding the fun-loving and harmonious cultural imagination that surrounds the geographic location. In many ways, Disney's remapping of New Orleans serves to reassert the importance of its Mardi Gras culture (accentuated by the promotion of beignets, gumbo, and masquerade in the film) over the images of catastrophe and deprivation the media used to describe the hurricane's aftermath; after Katrina, many of the businesses and cultural outlets, too, in New Orleans underwrote media campaigns to reshape the national imagination of its landscape and its racial problems. The use of the bayou, likewise, highlights the geographic blackness of the film—especially where "backwoods" white men catch escaped-people-turned-frogs and a house deep in the woods serves as refuge from the hunters.[40]

Disney writers were careful to obscure racial dynamics in a fantastical pre-Katrina New Orleans by overlaying images that display socioeconomic status with ideas of thrift and magic, further illustrating their "imagineering" of social and economic realities. Disney's imagineering of New Orleans as the setting for a twenty-first-century Black princess—the first in its princess pantheon based in the United States—is consistent with the physical and cultural gentrification of predominantly Black areas and cities that wish to harness blackness as "cool," while divorcing the political, social, and spatial elision of Black people from the space.[41] For example, as Tiana and her mother travel from her employer's neighborhood, the images of white families with mansions, pedicured lawns, and poodles is passed over in a dreamlike state until Tiana arrives home. As if under a spell too, Tiana leaves the plush pink bedroom of a wealthy white girl on a streetcar to the Black side of town where families like hers have small shotgun houses, no sidewalks or lawns, and little to eat, but share everything they have with others around them. The shift from mansions to shotgun houses is unremarked upon, as if the magic that occurs later is not specifically tied to the physical space of the mansion as a white space. The opening scene illustrates this dichotomy and foreshadows Tiana's "funny" and unfortunate frog transformation later on: Tiana's mother, Eudora, is a seamstress for a wealthy white family whose daughter, Charlotte, loves fairytales and Cinderella stories; all of her dresses are pink and all of her storybook characters are white. While Charlotte is dressed as a duchess (or perhaps a dunce) with a puffy pink dress and matching cone-shaped headdress, Tiana wears a green sheath dress with a small crown foreshadowing her becoming a frog-turned-princess (rather than

FIGURE 3.4. Tiana and Charlotte. Source: *The Princess and the Frog* (2009), Photo by the author.

princess-turned-frog) while Charlotte only has the trappings of royalty with dresses and grand furniture.

A conversation between the girls foreshadows their future fates as well: disgusted by the storybook princess's agreement to kiss the frog, Tiana says with all the vocal intonation and head and body movements of a young Black girl, "There is no way in this whole wide world, I would ever ever ever, I mean never, kiss a frog. Yuck!" Charlotte replies, "Is that so?" as she dresses up her feline companion in a knitted frog costume and shoves him toward "Tia." She says, "I would do it. I would kiss a frog. I would kiss a hundred frogs if I could marry a prince and be a princess." Throughout the film, Charlotte's obsession with marrying a prince is positioned as outlandish and juvenile.[42] Her dunce cap then represents a faux-feminist commentary that her desire is foolish and she should instead be more like Tiana, who is disgusted by the idea of kissing a frog prince. The girlhood scene also reinforces the gendered racial dichotomies that present Black women as hyperindependent and focused on economic independence rather than love like their white women peers. And yet the racialized dynamics of their friendship align Tiana's status and value in relationship to Charlotte's; as Kimberly R. Moffitt argues, their friendship presents the ideology that "Black women's bodies exist only when placed in contrast to whiteness, or specifically White female bodies."[43]

Later, at the Mardi Gras masquerade ball, when Tiana and Charlotte have grown up, Charlotte wears an enormous pink ball gown to win the affections

FIGURE 3.5. Queen and serf. Source: *The Princess and the Frog* (2009), Photo by the author.

FIGURE 3.6. Faux Princess Tiana. Source: *The Princess and the Frog* (2009), Photo by the author.

of Prince Naveen while Tiana is in a yellow and brown serf outfit, serving white ball attendees her "man-catching" beignets. After she is told by the Fenner Bros. realtors that a "little woman of your background . . . [is] better off where ya at" even after they have taken her initial down payment for the restaurant location, her dreams are crushed (and her dress splashed with food). Charlotte helps her upstairs to change into a blue dress and a crown much like Brandy's brown-rags-to-blue-gown transformation in *Cinderella* (1997). Charlotte reminisces after seeing Tiana's outfit change, placing a crown atop her head: "Seems like only yesterday we were both little girls dreaming our fairytale dreams, and tonight they're finally coming true." This statement not only shows how different Charlotte and Tiana are experiencing the evening—Charlotte is waltzing with Prince Naveen while Tiana's dreams are destroyed (and money stolen, since it is unclear if her deposit was returned). But it also glosses over the larger difficulty that Tiana experiences every day trying to fund her restaurant dreams while Charlotte merely needs to "wish harder" for hers. Charlotte's wistful statement illuminates the irony that Cinderella was in a blue dress as an aesthetic marker of reaching her dream, while Tiana is in blue at the expense of hers.

Some critics have noted that originally Disney had purported to name their first Black princess "Maddy" with the occupation of a chambermaid; however, consultation with Black mothers at the behest of Oprah Winfrey (voicing Tiana's mother in the film) made the narrative changes that became integral to the film's plot.[44] Enlisting Oprah Winfrey as a cultural consultant to host focus groups with Black mothers not only illustrates Disney's understanding of the relationship between Black cultural producers like Winfrey and Black women consumers, but also how Black women (like Oprah Winfrey as Eudora, Jenifer Lewis as Mama Odie, and Anika Noni Rose as Tiana) constitute another trifecta of cultural producers (like the trio in Cinderela) that make *The Princess and the Frog* a "Black" production, despite the directors and writers being white men. Like the aesthetic choices that Black women at Mattel instituted to make their Barbie dolls more aesthetically pleasing to Black women audiences, as well as Debra Martin Chase and Whitney Houston's decisions to make the Fairy Godmother's hair curly and Cinderella's hair into long braids, Disney's developers drew Tiana's childhood hair curly (she has afro puffs) and her skin distinctly browner than previous princesses. Tiana also uses facial expressions and vernacular idioms that differentiate her from other princesses, yet connect her to Whitney Houston in *Cinderella* and Black cultural traditions. As the voice-actor, Anika Noni Rose's own personhood became the basis for Tiana's facial expressions, attitude, and even left-handedness; the animators consulted heavily with Rose to make the first Black princess feel genuine to Black women and Black girl viewers, including the kind of details, intonation, and ideological values that Black women and girls would recognize as like their own.[45] With the exception of one white friend—made through her mother's employment, which echoes the role that enslaved and free Black girls played as playmates for white children while their mothers handled the house—Tiana is situated in a Black enclave that privileges the sights, sounds, religious undertones, and foods of Black culture.

Tiana's restaurant, additionally, plays into historical connections of Black bodies and waterways without commentary. Her desired restaurant location is an old sugar mill with water access and she falls in love with Prince Naveen then later marries him in the bayou. Unlike traditional Cinderella versions, which position marriage to a prince as a way out of hard labor, Tiana's vision still centers on work—which Kimberly R. Moffitt and Heather E. Harris show solidifies the ideological connection between Black women and girl audience spectators and the characterization Tiana embodies.[46] Even in her dreams, she is working—although she is dressed in all white as if she is married to her restaurant. And, although she serves a multicultural crowd, all of her staff are Black (similar to how the only Black attendees at Charlotte's ball were the musicians and Tiana, all of whom were working). While she is able to envision her life changing to include her dream, she (through Disney's writers) is unable to see a world where racial hierarchies of power, capitalism, and privilege change.

Unlike Cinderella, whose perspective is changed almost immediately after meeting her Fairy Godmother, Tiana seems stuck in her struggle to open a restaurant regardless of how often her friends, mother, or "godmother" beg her to consider other ways of being. While her mother asks for grandkids, Tiana restates her dismissal of other ambitions; she starts her song "Almost There" by speaking, "Mama, I don't have time for dancing," then singing, "That's just gonna have to wait a while/ain't got time for messing around/and it's not my style." She notes how the geography and "good times roll" sentiment of New Orleans "can slow you down/people taking the easy way," but she reminds her mother (and us) in the chorus, that she's "almost there/people down here think I'm crazy but I don't care." In the faith-based Black striving narrative fashion, her song speaks of her father's passing and holding down two jobs to save for her restaurant as "trials and tribulations" and his advice to her to wish, but work hard since "fairy tales can come true/you gotta make 'em happen/it all depends on you." Despite her mother's reminder that her father had everything he needed in the love of his family, Tiana's view is that her father's unfulfilled dreams can eventually come true only through her own success in an old sugar mill turned stylish restaurant. The impossibility of Tiana's vision, and demise of the confident security she has in her own industriousness, is underscored when the door closes after her final "almost there" declaration; the banister that once held her jacket and hat falls in a cloud of old sugar dust. Her dream will not happen the way she envisions.

Like Cinderella, Tiana has a "Fairy Godmother" in the form of Mama Odie who will save her from her mucus-coated state as a frog. The main antagonist, Dr. Facilier or Shadowman (Keith David), represents dark (yes, Black) magic, while Mama Odie represents the good that can be done with magic. Like Fairy Godmother Whitney Houston, though, Mama Odie forces Tiana and her frog prince to recognize the power that they have in their own right. In some ways, the narrative is supposed to be about Tiana reaching her dreams, but the different inflections of magic or uses of "black magic" take center stage. The Shadowman's magic is based on desire, greed, fear, and obscuring the truth with "Friends on the Other Side" represented by dark creatures, while the song "Dig a Little Deeper" characterizes Mama Odie's magic—an enhancement of what you already have on the inside and a call to Black/African spiritual traditions that harness the power of one's ancestors to buttress their access to and demonstrations of respectability.[47] Beyond the figurative struggle between darkness and light (and its likeness to every fight, biblical or otherwise) within the narrative, the film culminates in a battle between Shadowman and Mama Odie's bayou representative, a lightning bug named Ray, who uses his brightly lit rear to kill Shadowman's friends; like Cinderella's Fairy Godmother, Ray is able to harness magical abilities through his inner essence rather than a spell. According to Mama Odie, your own "magic" can help you "find out who you really are" and "what you need." Your own magic steers you to what you need and is like sunshine, which refracts the darkness created by centering desire and greed. Mirroring the lessons Cinderella learns in 1997 from her Fairy Godmother, Tiana is taught to think deeply about who she is and what she deserves; Tiana, though, is a bit more stubborn when it comes to shifting her focus and life philosophies.

This poignant struggle throughout the film emphasizes the tensions between Disney magic (i.e., wishing on a star) and the Shadowman's mystical magic; centering desire, in contrast to hard work and determination, always ends badly in *The Princess and the Frog*. For example, when Tiana indulges in dreaming like Charlotte by wishing on an evening star on Charlotte's bedroom balcony, she becomes a frog. By wearing Charlotte's clothes and wishing while on her balcony—connoting to me a succumbing to white wealthy epistemologies, after losing hope in her own ingenuity and focus based in Black cultural traditions and knowledge—Tiana finally surrenders to Charlotte's fairytale dreaming and is seemingly punished for it. After wishing on the "evening star" to help her accomplish her dream, she doubles down on Charlotte's fairytale lifestyle by kissing a frog (whom we learn is Naveen). Rather than turning him into a prince as in *The Frog Prince* story, Tiana turns into a frog. Tiana's shift from realistic to magical dreaming illustrates that indulging in magic—based in desire like that displayed in the Shadowman's "voodoo emporium"—results in getting further away from her dream and herself. Once Tiana abandons her self-assuredness in her own ingenuity, every character she meets (Frog Prince Naveen and the trumpet-playing gator, Louis—another gesture to Black cultural traditions and the jazz great Louis Armstrong) is also motivated by dreams, things they wished for but resigned themselves to not getting.

Eventually, Tiana must embrace her froggy form (punctuated by her shouted remark, "it's not slime, it's mucus") to return to her former self. The wedding in the bayou with creatures as witnesses maintains the use of animals from traditional stories like Snow White and Cinderella—furthering Disney's inclusion of Tiana in the princess pantheon—while the second wedding in New Orleans as humans again shows Tiana dressed identically to the dress she wore in her vision earlier in the film. Visually, this wedding replaces her previous vision's marriage to her restaurant. The color green marks her new life—the merging of frog knowledge and her experiences as a young Black woman into money, access, and respectability—after becoming a princess. Like her previous vision, she and Prince Naveen continue to work because, as she notes in the last line of the film, mirroring her stance in "Almost There," "dreams do come true in New Orleans." This narrative reinscribes the American Dream narrative for Black people: if they only work hard enough, they can achieve their dreams too.

FIGURE 3.7. Wish Upon an Evening Star.
Source: Courtesy of Photofest.

However, the advice for Black women is double-edged; they must work hard to achieve their dreams, seemingly forsaking all other ambitions or desires and not waiting for a wish to do the work, but Black women must also be fun. Frog Prince Naveen tells Tiana while walking to Mama Odie's home, "You know, waitress, I have finally figured out what's wrong with you . . . you do not know how to have fun." Called a "killjoy" and "stick-in-the-mud," after working two jobs her whole life, Tiana is not just aesthetically based on Black women. Her experience, while glossed over in typical Disneyfication fashion, is fueled by Black women's embodied objectification; the success stories of Anika Noni Rose, Oprah Winfrey, and Jenifer Lewis (as well as other popular narratives describing Black women's labor and desirability) are embedded in Tiana's struggle and her triumph. As exemplified by Tiana's journey, Black women are taught to trust the same system that makes it difficult for us to be successful (and desirable) in the first place. Yet, we should do it with a smile.

Lessons from Glass Slippers, Star Wishes, and Black Cultural Traditions

Both *Cinderella* (1997) and *The Princess and the Frog* (2009) are narratives that position Black women as hyperproductive and therefore deserving of their good fortune; as the American Dream dictates, Cinderella and Tiana worked diligently and were therefore rewarded for their steadfast faith. Both women, too, are sedulous in their particular situations because of their dead fathers' wishes: Cinderella's father asked that she stay with her abusive stepmother because he wanted them to be a family, while Tiana's father reminded her to match her dreams with hard work but not forget about the importance of family. (Fairy God)Mothers in both cases remind these Black girls to dream big and find love that reflects their dreams. The salience of these films rests not only in seeing princesses depicted as women steeped in Black cultural and vernacular traditions, providing a shift in the US cultural imagination of princess narratives—especially those constructed by Disney—but also, in how they represent some descriptive resolution to Black girls without fathers, even while recognizing the ways that fathers' attitudes and behaviors may still impact them. Because Black women voiced and embodied these princesses, and Black cultural traditions were employed in the musical, geographic, and narrative arcs of both narratives, the reoccurrence of hyperproductivity in these Black princesses' experiences is not just coincidental. The construction of Black women as industrious maintains the characterization that the US cultural imagination recognizes and is comfortable with based on histories of

Black women's labor and narratives about "strong Black women."[48] Insightfully, these characterizations also communicate the ways that some Black women, the persons who grafted their experiences with labor and love to provide the details of the films, wish to present themselves, their lives and experiences, to the consuming public.

The fact that Black women participated and engaged as producers, actors, and character models to shape these narratives that maintain characterizations of Black women as both beautiful and industrious elucidates the ways that Black women appreciate and even highlight the "strong Black woman" stereotype. Debra Martin Chase, Whitney Houston, Whoopi Goldberg, Brandy Norwood, Anika Noni Rose, Oprah Winfrey, and Jenifer Lewis are some of the most influential Black women in Hollywood and therefore are some of the most influential Black women to serve as models for how US (and even global) consumers understand the Black girls and women they encounter in daily life. As singers, comedians, and producers—women in the business of entertainment—these women and the roles they portray frame much of the US understanding of the lived experiences of Black women because of audience belief in mimesis as reality. Mimesis—or the imitation of real life in cultural products—shapes the ways that representations of Black people in popular culture are always believed to be real. In this way, these narratives problematically become hyperconstitutive of Black women as highly productive, industrious people whereas the narratives of beauty, self-determination, and the love of blackness are downplayed. These narratives, too, tell Black girls and women whom they should wish to become, reinforcing conceptualizations of blackness as tied directly to what labor can produce in a capitalist structure and that will still ask where is your joy, as you work constantly.

Despite the dependence of Black women cultural producers on these particular characterizations of Black women (based in the history of Black striving narratives and acceptance of the American Dream) in films made for children's consumption, Cinderella and The Princess and the Frog present possibilities for Black women and girls to see themselves outside of the norm of Hollywood representation while capitulating to narratives that bind our blackness and desirability to our labor and attractiveness to men. In addition to showing other audiences ways that they can connect with Black people and their experiences, both films highlight and celebrate Black cultural traditions and knowledges with which Black girls and women connect. At The Princess and the Frog's DVD premiere in 2010, actress Audra McDonald and her nine-year-old daughter Zoe Madeline Donovan gushed about being able to share the special moment together and relating to Mama Odie's advice to Tiana, much like Keke Palmer heralded Brandy's performance in *Cinderella*. McDonald too noted that her experience with her daughter was accented by seeing a large group of Black women in their forties, fifties, and sixties attending the film together.[49] Illustrated by this intergenerational connection and exchange, Black women are hailed by the ideological work of Black women cultural producers, connecting their life experiences with the ones reified on Disney's big screen. The ideological bridge Black women cultural producers build between themselves and Black girl and women consumers even through the façade of multiculturalism in consumer markets not only produces the conditions where Black princesses reshape Disney's own claims of diversity, but also those in which Black women and girls become the consumers of their own narratives. In this way, Disney's glass slippers and wishes erase the systemic mistreatment and dehumanization of Black women like Cinderella and Tiana in favor of highlighting the dream-filled honoring of industriousness and Black cultural aesthetics.

Commodifying Black Women's Experiences for Glass-Slipper Wishes

Cinderella stories are important to the construction and propagation of the American Dream because of the ways that US popular culture uses them to socialize people into the Protestant belief that steadfast work results in overcoming odds. Traditionally, Cinderella's value only becomes apparent when the Prince chooses her as his wife, whereas the examples throughout this chapter illustrate how the inclusion of Black women in Cinderella narratives changes the story. Rather than simply casting Black characters in fairytale princess narratives, Black women cultural producers crafted alternatives by becoming agents of their own cultural narratives; they used their experiences and knowledge of Black symbolic power to provide so-called authentic lessons to all consumers. Under the umbrella of Disney films, Debra Martin Chase and Whitney Houston, specifically, produced new ways to narrate an "underdog" story for Black girls. Although Black women cultural producers sought to provide encouragement to Black girls via Cinderella and Tiana to dream big and chase their dreams, they maintained the importance of a heterosexual relationship via a prince as the answer for Cinderella's woes and Tiana's hyperfocus.

Alongside the rise of multiculturalism as a marker of the commodification of race in popular culture, *Cinderella* (1997) and *The Princess and the Frog* (2009) illustrate how Black women as cultural producers shape the imaginative space available for Black girls within popular princess narratives as well as the ideological relationships that Black women and girls have to each other. Dorothy Hurley explains that children learn "cultural information about themselves, others, and the relative status of group membership" through the images they are exposed to in cultural texts like television shows and children's books.[50] For Black girls and women, viewing lessons and singing songs under the auspices of Disney's multicultural mission related to their own experiences both undergird and expand the imaginative possibilities within which they learn about themselves. How those lessons and songs are then utilized by non-Black consumers and viewers, then, is the basis of the next chapter.

CHAPTER 4

A Black Barbie's Moment

Nicki Minaj and the Struggle for Cultural Dominance

Nicki Minaj was the only mainstream Black woman hip-hop artist from 2009 to 2018. In that time, she represented a substantial amalgam of Black Barbie's fictive creation and plasticity, Black Cinderella's hopeful industriousness, Black women's creativity through embodied objectification, Black strivings narratives as portrayed through hip-hop culture, and US cultural attitudes about Black beauty, Black female bodies, sexuality, and authenticity. Praised for her diversity of musical talents, campy style, playful performances of bisexual prowess, and appropriation of traditionally hyperfeminine and white representations of womanhood, Nicki Minaj personifies embodied objectification and the ways that Black women's investment in the tenuous ideological relationship between themselves as producers and consumers is not isolated from the global capitalist market of consumption.[1]

Previous chapters have focused on how Black women utilize their own lived experiences and knowledges to produce consumptive products. This chapter considers how Black women's embodied objectification still operates within a white supremacist capitalist structure that enacts dehumanization and labor exploitation through appropriation. I argue that while Black women's embodied objectification works to shift stereotypical representations in popular culture and empower Black girls and other Black women to do the same, the "meme"-ification of their bodies, creative projects, and relational connections continues to work against their aims; centered in others' images and products,

Black women serve as relational figures that connect otherwise benign ideas with a system of racialized representation. Black women become the markers for multiculturalism and diversity, the embodiment of all things nonnormative, and therefore able to hail the individuals and communities that continue to be rejected from mainstream representation. Using Nicki Minaj's music, music videos, performances, and interviews as a prominent popular example, I illustrate how Black women's embodied objectification utilizes the ideological connection to Black consumers in their own creative process, which is then commandeered and thus altered in the global popular consumer market, especially by white performers. Black women cultural producers' ability to connect with others in their communities is inverted and puppeteered to communicate another cultural producers' proximity to urban edginess, to Black communities, or to diverse populations in general. By framing Minaj's embodied objectification and utilization of prominent white icons like Barbie and Cinderella as well as how others have used her likeness to sell their own products or comment on US political positioning, I question how and why certain representations of Black women—while oppositional and perhaps even revolutionary for us—continue to be used to serve particular imaginative purposes that demonize and dehumanize Black women writ large.

Barbie Bitch!: The Construction of Hip-Hop's Barbie

When Nicki Minaj emerged in 2009 on the popular stage, a more authentic Black doll and the first Disney-stamped Black princess created by Black women for Black girls and women had just been released. Stacey McBride-Irby's attempts to create a doll that was aesthetically Black showed the complexion, hair, facial features, and body shape of a Black woman alongside Oprah Winfrey—and Jenifer Lewis—infused fantastical lessons of a Black princess born of magic and fairytales in New Orleans—as well as parents' and children's disapproval of their commodification of Black cultural knowledge and aesthetics—provided the possibility for a Black woman from the Bronx (by way of Trinidad) to situate herself as Black Barbie within mainstream popular culture. Minaj's own Barbie aesthetic harnesses the historical, fashion, and material culture of Barbie that Black women cultural producers strategically shifted in 1980, 1990, and 2009. Although Minaj's persona was informed by the Barbie aesthetics previous Black and white women cultural producers created, her appropriation ultimately tries to sublimate Barbie to the persona of Nicki Minaj. In other words, Minaj used Barbie aesthetics to market her own performance for capitalist gain, while also desiring to impart cultural knowledge and confidence to Black girls. In many ways, Minaj's choice to be both Barbie and "bitch" in her 2009 album, *Pink Friday*, highlights the relationship to blackness and beauty that many Black girls experience at early ages. Minaj's association with the Barbie image—directly through wearing a Barbie chain and calling herself Barbie as well as indirectly through reliance on aesthetic parallels—and therefore the genealogy of Black Barbie dolls—allowed Black girls to see themselves as not only beautiful, but as Barbie too. Jennifer Dawn Whitney contends that Nicki Minaj's use of the "plasticity" of Barbie in her music puts "forth a playful alternative to the static Black doll representations imaged by Mattel"—another opportunity for Black girls to realize their place within American culture as beautiful and diverse full humans.[2]

While Minaj's campy performances eventually were accepted as mainstream representations, her initial presentations adopted white hyperfeminine icons like Wonder Woman, Marilyn Monroe, and Barbie to align herself with a feminine presentation already acceptable and adored in US popular culture. Nicki Minaj's first mixtape *Beam Me Up Scotty* became available online in the wake of Stacey McBride-Irby's So In Style dolls release in 2009. Like McBride-Irby's dolls that were aestheticized to perform a girly hip-hop aesthetic via Baby Phat

FIGURE 4.1. Beam Me Up Nicki. Source: Nicki Minaj Instagram, Photo by the author.

and their iconic leader Kimora Lee, *Beam Me Up Scotty* and subsequent performances showed Minaj as the quintessential "bad bitch"—a Black woman who is ultrafeminine, yet willing to take control and handle any personal or professional business without hesitation. The mixtape cover features Minaj in a Wonder Woman outfit with the light of a spaceship projecting behind her—displaying Minaj as both a white American cultural icon and an otherworldly Black woman with a bright pink afterglow.

Like other hip-hop artists who use the names and imagery of infamous US icons (e.g., Scarface and Noreaga), Minaj's merger with iconic Wonder Woman imagery attempts to liken her to the power and importance of the icon, while highlighting the particular aspect that makes her different—her blackness. Blackness in this sense is constructed as abject or Other; an "out-of-this-world" experience of selfhood that is only constructed through the lived experiences of Black people—Black subjectivity. Marlo David connects similar outer-space-like representations of blackness by Black women musical artists to the concept of Afrofuturism—the artistic representations of blackness as futuristic or otherworldly.[3] As a Black woman rapper when women rappers were not receiving mainstream attention, Minaj's sophisticated rhymes, multivocal personas, and ultrafeminine aesthetic stuck out as distinctly otherworldly in the masculine ethos of hip-hop music and culture when she debuted. After landing within the culture, Minaj shifted her aesthetic to perform something much more familiar and even beloved in American culture.

In almost all of her cameos in 2009 and 2010, Minaj merged her previous Afrofuturist style with a new articulation of Barbie. Minaj's pink hair and Barbie aesthetic became iconic in these earlier performances and symbolically transitioned her from an outsider in hip-hop culture to a major player. Minaj embodied her favorite ad-lib "Barbie bitch" in many colorful wigs—most principally, pink, blonde, and two-toned black-and-pink wigs—so much so that girls at parties I attended during the time competed for who looked most like her based on their ability to replicate her wigs.

When she signed with Lil Wayne's label, Young Money/Cash Money Records (a subsidiary of Universal Music Group), in late 2009, she was gifted a platinum chain with "Barbie" emblazoned on it with white diamonds—firmly cementing the symbolic slippage between herself and Barbie and her place in mainstream hip-hop culture. While Lil Kim before her had used Barbie aesthetics in various lyrics or visual performances, Minaj was (and continues to be) recognized as hip-hop's (Black) Barbie because of the ubiquity of her Barbie performances.

As a student of theater and performance, Nicki Minaj notes multiple influences on her perspective on performance and fashion, including Cyndi Lauper

FIGURE 4.2. Harajuku Barbie Nicki.
Source: Courtesy of AP Images.

and Japanese Harajuku culture.[4] In many ways, Minaj merged and layered these cultural influences with her appreciation and appropriation of Barbie fashion, in what Seth Cosimini calls an "embodied bricolage"; she, like other popular artists, took inspiration from popular musicians and styles during her coming of age to inform her aesthetic.[5] However, Minaj's revisioning of campy visuality produced a specific sartorial expression, which Uri McMillan calls "nicki-aesthetics," for Black femmes, "reconfigur[ing] camp as a female-centered practice" where hip-hop and camp collide.[6] Minaj's attention to blackness and femaleness became a bricolage through playfulness and satire, knowing the ways that Black women's bodies and queerness had been used in hip-hop culture (and beyond) as sites of exclusion but also the ways that all things feminine, especially Barbie, have been "antithetical to women of color" as Shoniqua Roach contends.[7] On the receiving end of the ideological relationship between Black women and girls as producers and consumers and Black Perkins's embodied objectification, Minaj reframed the antithetical connections between blackness and Barbie and infused her own cultural productions with the aesthetics created by Black women combined with other popular aesthetics.

Many of her most popular outfits are reminiscent of Barbie fashion by Black women designers like Kitty Black Perkins in the 1980s and 1990s. For example, Mattel's 1990 Flight Time Barbie (designed by Black Perkins), which characterizes Barbie as a pilot in a pink suit and pilot's hat, is almost entirely replicated in Nicki Minaj's outfit for her perfume's release party in 2012 and the perfume bottle itself. Likewise, her entire first studio album, *Pink Friday*, replicated not only the baby pink aesthetic typical of Barbie, but Minaj's eyes, legs, and arms were doll-like in every image.

FIGURE 4.3. Flight Time Nicki.
Source: Courtesy of AP Images.

FIGURE 4.4. Pink Friday 1, Pink Friday 2, Pink Friday 3.
Source: Nicki Minaj Pink Friday.

While the photographs included with the CD accentuated her eyes and limbs to mirror doll-like proportions, her poses simulated a satiric approach to being a doll. The images named Pink Friday 1, 2, and 3 (figure 4.4) show Minaj in positions almost antithetical to the ultra-pink doll aesthetic. In Pink Friday 1 (figure 4.4a), she draws from both King Kong and ballerina aesthetics. The pink tulle cascading around her legs connotes grace and dainty femininity. Yet, her legs, arms, and face communicate an imposition of her body into the pink, tranquil landscape. Pink Friday 2 and Pink Friday 3 (figure 4.4b and c) echo this juxtaposition—and yet magnify how she may aesthetically seem demure and playful, while her face and body correspond to the "crazy" or "monstrous" hip-hop bravado that Nicki Minaj claims in her music. A merging of aesthetics typical of US white femininity and the ways Black women are presented as monstrous or larger than human, Minaj's Kong ballerina seems to insert this new Black Barbie as a collator of US cultural imagery of "the feminine" and an almost laughable response to it. Perhaps the most interesting aspect of Minaj's re-presentation of Barbie aesthetics in the album artwork for *Pink Friday* was the combination of Afrocentric and Barbie aesthetics in a large poster included with the album. The poster unfolds to reveal Minaj as an Afrocentric Barbie doll (see Figure 4.5).

Rather than the layers of pink that characterized the other images, Minaj's colorful outfit and body language re-create African cloth and dance that is already circulating in Black popular traditions. Like the Shani doll, Minaj used complex colors and patterns to signify on the Black fashion traditions that designers made popular in the 1980s and 1990s, subtly calling to consumers who would recognize and notice the nonnormative characterization of Barbie she presents in *Pink Friday*. Minaj draws on some of the more essentialist elements of previous Black Barbie, which both subverts and reifies those tropes. She displays an otherworldly approach to Barbie iconography—a Barbie steeped in Black cultural aesthetics that not only signifies to Black women and girl consumers, but also playfully dispossesses Barbie of the stoic plasticity that made her difficult to imagine beyond white and blonde.

The aesthetic play that Minaj enacts in her *Pink Friday* cover combines the background and her clothes with her body. Nicki Minaj's Barbie also embraces a latent sexuality that Mattel's dolls try to avoid. Magnifying Ruth Handler's initial desire to educate girls about their bodies with Barbie, Nicki Minaj's performances of Barbie remind girls that their bodies are beautiful and important aspects of who they are. By elongating her body and performing satiric poses, Minaj remarks upon the stringent norm of Barbie as white, thin, and fixed or, more accurately, plastic. Because, as Whitney points out, Barbie has "a certain blankness that enables interpretive versatility," Minaj is able to critique, affirm, and resituate Barbie's importance in the American cultural landscape through her *Pink Friday* cover and performances.[8] An act that follows Danielle Fuentes Morgan's argument that the satiric is not only an intrinsic part of contemporary Black cultural production, but also that it works by "problematiz[ing] the existing social sphere by highlighting its absurdity—both the reality of racialization

FIGURE 4.5. Pink Friday Afrocentric. Source: Nicki Minaj
Pink Friday album.

and the mythology of a 'post-racial' that suggest race is now irrelevant—and its reification through the continued centrality and substantiation of white supremacy."[9] Minaj's claiming, use, and critique of Barbie is therefore in line with Black satirical traditions. Minaj affirms Barbie's importance by using her as an inspiration, and yet critiques Barbie's own plasticity through satire.

In many ways, Minaj's performances disturb the pristine, hyperfeminine pedestal on which Barbie is perched and the cultural landscape that recognizes Barbie more than any other brand globally.[10] Marrying Black cultural traditions, Black women's so-called abnormal body proportions, and Barbie's legacy, Minaj forces her fans and critics to consider the possibility of a Black woman as Barbie, and therefore the ways that Black women's bodies and sexuality have been displayed to the American public. Sabrina Strings connects the confluence of whiteness, thinness, and Protestant godliness as markers of moral and societal importance in direct opposition to "black fatness" as early as the sixteenth century; Black women in the twenty-first century, then, are directly linked to a global and transcultural depiction of them as lowly and servile yet well apportioned.[11] Working against the hardening of these cultural attitudes and constructions in the twenty-first-century United States, Nicki Minaj's *Pink Friday* album and artwork become an opportunity to trouble the narrow asexual (yet implicitly heterosexual) legacy of Barbie, while acknowledging the Black women and Black dolls (and even white women like Cyndi Lauper) who have tried to provide alternative representations of femininity for girls.

Nicki Minaj's long legs, doll eyes, and pink clothing in *Pink Friday* insert her in an aesthetic lineage to Mattel's brown-painted dolls, including Christie, Julia, Black Barbie, Shani, and the SIS dolls. In her interview with *VIBE* magazine about her music and perfume line, Minaj remarks, "As a little girl growing up in the Southside Jamaica Queens, if anyone would've told me I'd have my own perfume one day, and be able to inspire young black girls everywhere, to go into Macy's or Nordstrom and see their face staring back at them—I wouldn't believe them."[12] An example of embodied objectification, Minaj explains her own disbelief in her ability to infuse cultural products with her likeness and therefore connect to Black girls when they encounter them. Sharon Raynor explains how this ideological relationship between Black Barbie aesthetics and personal identity development in this way: "My first black Barbie reminds me so much of myself now: innovative, fashionable, friendly, and living on the edge."[13] Although retrospectively able to identify the ways she has mirrored the doll she played with—a direct connection to the marketing desires of Black Barbie—Raynor's statement illustrates the ways in which Kitty Black Perkins's, Stacey McBride-Irby's, and even Nicki Minaj's choices can actively engage with Black girl self-making through an ideological relationship made through consumption. Nicki Minaj's choices to wear multicolored wigs, comment on and display high-fashion labels in her music, and prominently display her derriere in skintight jumpsuits, skirts, and dresses all rescript visual narratives of Barbie, American femininity, and blackness, specifically through the ways Black girls and women interpret her presentation. She participates in what Jillian Hernandez calls an "aesthetic of excess," an ostentatious display of self-fashioning by Black and Latina women like Minaj who make themselves "hypervisible" to create such styles of abundance in concert with their "racial, ethnic, and gendered culture, and the desire to utilize the body creatively, admire [their] self image, and potentially attract the gazes of others."[14] This indulgent self-expression is, as Hernandez notes, in sartorial conversation with others within the community, a performance of legibility even as outsiders may interpret it as fake and classless.

If, as Minaj has admitted in her own creative process, twenty-first-century Black women cultural producers understand that their aesthetic choices have an impact on the identity development of Black girls across the diaspora through consumptive practices and play, and if they desire to help Black girls and women accept themselves as beautiful, how then can we understand her continued affirmation and maintenance of white supremacist and patriarchal performances of femininity? The answer, I maintain, is that Minaj recognizes the importance of maintaining allegiances to "mainstream" consumers and audiences because of the symbolic importance of whiteness and white beauty aesthetics in the United States. In many ways, these consumers dictate what products major corporations like Mattel will manufacture despite the success of companies like Shindana or Stacey McBride-Irby's So In Style dolls. Moreover, from Malibu Christie to Nicki Minaj, Black women cultural producers' use of long, straight hair and thinner body types (alongside darker skin, wider noses, and wider hips) illustrates the aesthetic tensions within Black cultural discourses about representation.

Despite the desire to create products that speak directly to Black girls and women—like Shindana's "brother and sister dolls for brothers and sisters"—Black women cultural producers must still contend with the ideological resonances of white supremacy in their production; according to bell hooks, "the acknowledged Other must assume recognizable forms" since "consumer culture promises to show the way" to interact with the Other.[15] In this way, there are only a certain number of available representations for Black women to occupy in popular culture—as a recognizable representation and therefore a commodity—and those representations as well as where and how consumers can purchase them exemplifies how people interpersonally should interact. Black women cultural producers' aesthetic choices communicate that even though capitalist discourses dictate that anything is sellable in our society, there are some symbols of beauty, femininity, and sexuality that will sell better than others because of how they occupy (and even perhaps narrowly expand) the set of already recognizable and, at times, relatable representations.

However, Black Perkins, McBride-Irby, and Minaj all infuse their work for all audiences with the same Black cultural intertextuality—heritage, traditions, and idioms—that earlier successes illustrated were important for Black communities to become loyal consumers of "Black" material products. The introduction and maintenance of Black cultural traditions in their work not only resonated with Black communities, but also saw large dividends from white consumers as well. These Black women cultural producers were able to concentrate the symbolic power of aestheticized dolls to affect the lived experiences or habitus of Black girls. Their decisions to claim beauty, femininity, and poise alongside fashion, bravado, and afro-styled hair shifted the cultural imagination of Black womanhood to include America's most beloved doll, Barbie.

Nicki Minaj, in particular, occupies multiple and varied "recognizable forms" of Black women's representation in consumer culture and therefore harnesses multiple commodified forms of blackness simultaneously and asynchronously. For example, as she highlights and participates in the form of Black woman as Barbie, as I have shown, she is also active in the form of Black woman as Cinderella.

Black Cinderella and Fairy Godmother: Nicki's "Moment 4 Life"

Born in sites of Black musical ingenuity, urban poverty, and youthful exuberance of the 1970s, hip-hop as a genre is an avenue through which Black people express their joy, love, and discontent. While specific to the socioeconomic circumstances of the moment, hip-hop mirrors other Black cultural traditions that interpret consumption and materialism as markers of modern subjectivity. Now the most popular global musical genre because of the ways that other marginalized people can and do identify (or disidentify) with narratives of struggle and otherness, hip-hop artists bespeak a commitment to naming protest and trauma as well as collective expressions of pleasure. This purposeful, and economically successful, expression has allowed for artists like Shawn "Jay-Z" Carter and Sean "Diddy" Combs to create business empires. From corner boys to billionaires, Carter and Combs represent a recognizable form of hip-hop that is believed to be more authentic when it exemplifies Black striving narratives.[16] Many artists, therefore, build their careers on the authenticity of their upbringing and eventual success—usually including poverty, drugs, gangs, altercations with the police, and sexual encounters; the closer to one's lived experience, the more authentic the story. Despite the undercurrent in musical content where artists push back against the idea that they have changed after receiving mainstream recognition (especially when they discount other artists who become mainstream from a place of privilege), many artists understand that recognition changes their financial and cultural impact; like many Black entrepreneurs at the turn of the twentieth century who sought material gain through affiliation with larger (usually white) corporations, Black artists know that recognition by a major label can improve their financial circumstances. They can then reach success—as modern and therefore consuming subjects—represented by artists participating in high-fashion campaigns and popular displays of wealth like MTV *Cribs* (a show, syndicated in 2008, where cameras were allowed to follow artists around their plush residences) or the Met Gala. Their stories are, quintessentially, Cinderella stories.[17]

While she had articulated her authenticity through her proximity to other content themes within hip-hop music such as sexual prowess or expensive cars and clothes, Nicki Minaj specifically added the Cinderella persona to her hyperpink Barbie aesthetic in the fall of 2010. Capitalizing on her Barbie status as well as the well-established reference of rappers as rags-to-riches successes, Minaj relayed her own Cinderella story in her music video, "Moment 4 Life" (on her first studio album, *Pink Friday*). Although similar symbolically to Barbie because of ideological similarities as a white, thin, blonde, and fictive woman that others use to play out their own idealized subjectivities, Minaj's princess aesthetics—which specifically adapted Cinderella narratives—steer more toward large tulle ballgowns, tiaras, and glitter, and general decadence as a reward for hardship endured.

Minaj's narrative privileges the rags-to-riches arc of Cinderella's life because it replicates the rise of artists in the music industry, especially hip-hop artists. Hip-hop as a genre, too, reiterates the narrative importance of steadfast faith in one's own ability and hyperproductivity until artists become the hip-hop bravado version of Cinderella. The story of hip-hop that privileges what we might call "hood to mansion" narratives sustains the importance of mainstream recognition and notoriety to have "made it"; Nicki Minaj's presentation as Cinderella visually marks this shift in her career. She harnesses the symbolic resonance of Cinderella to represent her career and her belief that, like the other Black princesses I have described in chapter 3, her hyperproductivity as an artist will result in the life that she wants—with or without a male partner. However, at the same time, she critiques the limited gendered notions of power within the Cinderella narrative to present an alternative to traditional heteronormative iterations of success, especially for Black women.

The "Moment 4 Life" video opens with an image of a storybook and harps playing, signifying a fairytale experience. Old English–styled lettering in the storybook reads:

> Once upon a time there lived a king named Nicki. One day, while sitting on her throne, she received an enchanting visit from her fairy Godmother. She would remember that moment for life.[18]

Unlike previous Cinderellas, Minaj is positioned as already royalty; using "king" and gendered pronouns "she" and "her" communicates that Minaj is both masculine and feminine—she is all the royalty there is. With a blast of pink dust, the video transitions to Minaj in a bright blue gown seated at a large white mirror and vanity, brushing her hair (a recognizable black bob style with bangs she popularized earlier in her career). Unlike other Cinderella stories, where the narrative illustrates the mistreatment and squalor Cinderella experiences, "Moment 4 Life" starts in a castle with Minaj positioned as king. King Nicki is startled by her "Fairy Godmother" (also played by Minaj) appearing in a pink ball gown, white wings, and large crown tucked into her blonde beehive.

After a less than sweet interaction between King Nicki and Fairy Godmother "Martha," which ends in Minaj calling her godmother a bitch—a marker of the hip-hop-enhanced rewriting of the traditional story—Minaj is given bedazzled red-bottomed Christian Louboutin pumps, representative of a capitalist marker of feminine beauty and exorbitance. These high-heeled shoes, replacing Cinderella's traditional glass slippers, represent King Nicki's transformation into Cinderella. Additionally, her interaction with her Godmother (as herself) conveys the doppelgänger mirroring that occurs between this narrative and the traditional Cinderella fairytale. This mirroring of Minaj as King/Cinderella and as Fairy Godmother represents Minaj's desire to be both producer and recipient of her success. As Fairy Godmother, she has the ability to change her circumstances with the wave of a wand; as King/Cinderella, she must only ask to reap all the benefits of success.

Throughout the video, Minaj as King/Cinderella is shown in only two outfits: the blue ballgown with black bangs and a gold headpiece, reminiscent of Cinderella, and a yellowish-brown tulle bodysuit with a bright pink wig that

FIGURE 4.6. Nicki's Fairy Godmother. Source: Nicki Minaj "Moment 4 Life," Photo by the author.

aesthetically connects her earlier representations on the colloquial "come up" with Tiana's dress at Charlotte's party before losing her dream in *The Princess and the Frog*. Represented in these ways, Minaj's fairytale advances the tradition of Black princesses.

However, at the end of the video when Minaj and the Canadian rapper Drake (whose career has mirrored Minaj's in a quick rise to stardom, although not the same rags-to-riches story) have been ushered into a wedding ceremony thanks to Fairy Godmother Martha. The wedding symbolism is codified with a tux for Drake and a white dress, pink wig, and bouquet for Minaj, the clock strikes twelve as they lean in for a kiss, and the video starts over with Minaj in her room

(a)

(b)

FIGURE 4.7a and 4.7b. Brown and Blue "Moment 4 Life" dress.
Source: Nicki Minaj "Moment 4 Life," Photos by the author.

in the blue ballgown. This resolution illustrates that although Minaj desires to be partnered, she is already King and simply wants to share her moment at the top with someone else; Drake, although standing next to her, seems more representative of both of them marrying "the game" as hip-hop artists and as labelmates. Although there are two chairs for royalty earlier in the video, Drake is never seen enthroned with Minaj because Minaj is King, Cinderella, and Fairy Godmother. She does not require a prince, as in *Cinderella* (1997) or *The Princess and the Frog* (2009), to change her situation. Her only desire is exemplified throughout the video when she meets Drake in her palace and later symbolically marries him—representing a heterosexual coupling to her current perfect moment. But because this coupling is never represented by Drake taking the King's chair, consummation, or even them riding off in matching colors like other Cinderellas, men's representational function in Minaj's "Moment 4 Life" is simply a pro forma placement to the final outcome of her fairytale. The fairytale she wishes for is the one she already owns—represented in the fact that the palace is already hers. She is already living in her moment, with all the things she wants except for a partner.

As King, Cinderella, and the Fairy Godmother in "Moment 4 Life," Nicki Minaj illustrates a shift in the symbolic representations of princesses generally, and Black princesses in particular. The music video creates imaginative space for Black girls to see themselves as agentive in creating and curating their destinies as imperfect, yet content human beings. Black girls can control which fantasies are important and which ones become real. Through their own merit and "magic," Black girls are able to shape their futures with or without the heterosexual imperative for marriage.[19] In this way, marriage does not "save" Cinderella from her situation—it merely enhances the joy she already experiences there. "Moment 4 Life" elucidates self-determination as dream creation and provides a "pinkprint" for those watching, therefore shaping their internalization and identification with Minaj's narrative. Minaj's use of princess narratives shapes new symbolic possibilities for Black girls through her attention to the aesthetic choices she makes—ones that Black girls and women will ideologically connect with—and the overlap with other visual representations of Black princesses.

The major lessons in *Cinderella* and *The Princess and the Frog* promoted Black girl desirability in an interracial coupling, a Black girl's ability to dream and succeed, and the enduring hope that success will occur if she works hard enough. Both narratives in *Cinderella* and *The Princess and the Frog* engaged the idea that anything is possible if a Black girl works hard enough and knows the right people (in the form of a fairy godmother, a non-Black prince, or a rich white person like Charlotte). In the absence of her father, Cinderella's Fairy

Godmother tells her that she can dream, but has to work to achieve it. Tiana's father communicated the same narrative to his daughter. Therefore, Cinderella and Tiana both represent Black girls who took the traditional Black strivings narrative route to success; and at the end of their strivings, they were "rewarded" with a non-Black prince. Contrasted with Minaj's princess moment, these stories culminate with a prince who can manifest a shift in Cinderella's/Tiana's life rather than simply a return to the decadent life already achieved by Minaj.

Although Black women produced the images in *Cinderella* and *The Princess and the Frog* that communicated the ways Black girls could find love and success through traditional Black striving narratives, Nicki Minaj's "Moment 4 Life" illustrates how, as producers, Black girls could create their own success and reap the benefits as well. They are not required to have a fairy godmother, prince, or white friend because they can craft their success narratives themselves based on what they desire and therefore stand in the metaphorical gap for themselves. While Minaj's prince is present throughout the video, her story does not end with a heteronormative "happily ever after" like Cinderella or Tiana (although the presence of Drake does present the desire for a heterosexual coupling). Nicki Minaj's narrative ends where it started—she tosses the bouquet into the camera, which signals her beckoning the audience to follow her lead. She goes back to her room, alone, where her dreaming began.

From Embodied Objectification to Appropriated Object: Minaj and Social Media Consumption

Harnessing Barbie and Cinderella early in her career, Minaj intentionally escalated her popular reception by using images, ideas, and attitudes that the public recognized and could therefore align themselves with as consumers. Whereas her use of Barbie and Cinderella specifically attached Black cultural traditions and idioms to signifiers that white publics could also recognize, her transition to stardom by her third studio album meant that the ideological relationship between her and Black women and girls as producers and consumers began to shift. In this context, Minaj's intentionality to connect to Black consumers with Black cultural attitudes, idioms, and bravado was pushed beyond an intraracial ideological relationship. She worked to shape public perceptions of Black women (alongside other popular Black women personas like Michelle Obama, Beyoncé, and Serena Williams), but also coaxed the support of non-Black consumers to identify with her—what is popularly understood as "crossover." As she became a globally recognized artist, the "in-group" connection that was signified on and used to curry favor with Black consumers, especially Black women, was then available to all consumers—some of which knew nothing of the cultural specificity with which Minaj performed. Like many performers who transition to mainstream or crossover status, Nicki Minaj's music, performances, and embodiment became the discussion and concern of people much beyond her community or the Black girls she hoped would see her in Macy's. Her embodied objectification was also then made available to non-Black consumers, precipitating specifically white consumers and producers to identify with and then harness her newly accomplished cultural dominance for their own popularity.

Upon the release of her third studio album, *The Pinkprint* (along with her subsequent music videos and internet presence), in 2014, Minaj moves away from harnessing the cultural power of Barbie and Cinderella to sell her albums, and begins to promulgate more complicated ideas of race and domination shied away from in the United States despite reoccurring discourses and images in popular culture. Her performance of a "Hottentot" in the "Anaconda" music video and later its appropriation in a Third Reich–esque militarism in the "Only" lyric video by singer-songwriter Jeffrey Osborne, respectively, further engages US history with Black women's bodies and domination enacted through violence.[20] Because memetic culture is built on re-creating, imitating, promulgating an idea or a behavior, usually through stark juxtaposition, the rest of this chapter explores which of Nicki Minaj's images are used for memetic hilarity and in what ways. The response to Minaj's "Anaconda" music video and then the "Only" lyric video illustrates the ways that in the twenty-first century, Black women's bodies are still relegated to particular narratives that the US public understands and, therefore, celebrates. Minaj's decisions to "Hottentot" herself and play with white popular perceptions that sexualize Black bodies, and the later appropriation of her body with Nazi imagery, were based in challenging histories of Black women's objectification, and yet, the memes that followed maintain the symbolic subjugation of Black women for white enjoyment.[21] Embodied objectification and signifying move beyond popular music videos so that the same cultural spaces that Black women have created to fortify Black girls and women's symbolic habitus are recolonized. In short, I use social media memetic culture to understand how the US popular sphere recapitulates the harm that Black women's cultural productions have sought to challenge.

These ideas are particularly important because Minaj's performances seem to have become more centered on the experiences and histories of publicly recognized Black women, even while others seem to find her performances more easily representative of larger US cultural attitudes and behaviors. Framing Minaj as a Black woman cultural producer, what does it mean for a pop culture icon to expound upon ideas like these that are not wholesome and beautiful but no less representative of the American popular imagination? How can and do Black women as cultural producers use and appropriate unwholesome imagery to articulate powerful stories about Black womanhood and affect the public perception and reception of Black girls? Although Nicki Minaj's own attitudes and decisions about her image are unclear, Minaj's videos and subsequent memetic digital reproductions on Twitter and Instagram epitomize how objectionable images can also help shape ideas of sexuality and power—two imaginative spaces in which Black women and girls are constantly illegible.

Memetic culture is the collective use of images to digitally narrate a situation. Memes are usually humorous because the images are taken out of their original context and used to explain a different situation. We know this process in advertising as bricolage and even product placement.[22] On social media, the number of people (or rather IP addresses) that circulate a video, an article, or an image constitutes its popularity. Usually, the spreading of these items—their virality—is based in shock value. In a discussion of virality and imperialist logics, Lisa Nakamura explains that the memetic quality of images is based on centuries-old racist logic that "depict[s] the black body in abject and bizarre poses and situations . . . [and] that spreads using user and audience labor."[23] Nakamura points out that the memetic power of images or rather the desire for the image to be shared and replicated with new captions and contexts is based in the peculiar and spectacular; this desire to replicate a bizarre image provides its viral value. In other words, the more bizarre, the more likely the image will be circulated for consumptive enjoyment. This symbolic power not only illustrates what images become popular in the US cultural context, but also which bodies constitute US cultural ideologies of bizarre and abject.

Nakamura explains that "the internet is not simply a place of free and agentive self-composition or self-presentation where memes are consumed, produced, and unreflectively enjoyed. It is not just a source of memetic power, the power to amuse or garner 'likes' from friends sharing a social networking service or image boards."[24] This means the internet—including the memetic power of social media—is embedded in logics of racial and gendered violence that predate enslavement and yet have "infected" the ways in which we engage each other online through symbolic power. Following Whitney Phillips's coining of "lulz" as a "derivation of lol or laughing out loud," Ryan Milner calls the use of irony and critique in images and text like those I describe the "logic of lulz": a digital circulatory system that perpetuates the proliferation of racist and misogynist cultural attitudes by users creating their own version of stock images for "lulz."[25] In many ways, viral images on platforms like Instagram are caustic reminders of the discourses of postracial and postfeminist America in the twenty-first century that are successfully fortified and proliferated in political, economic, and legal spheres. In short, the images we find the most appalling, entertaining, and problematic are loaded with viral potential because their abjection is based in cultural attitudes that already constitute our lives in the everyday; Minaj's use of memetic culture and the ways that others have claimed her body through memes typify this system of digital appropriation.

Black Ass Goes Viral: Nicki Minaj's "Anaconda"

Nicki Minaj's music video "Anaconda" opens with birds chirping, lush green trees, and a grass "hut," reminiscent of Tarzan's tree house. Nicki Minaj is clad in black, high-cut boxer briefs and a gold choker and bra connected by chains dangling across her breast. Four women dancers are dressed in all-black suits; they start dancing as Sir Mix-A-Lot's voice—a sample from his popular 1991 song, "Baby Got Back"—plays from a pineapple record player. Historically and culturally around the world, pineapples signal a friendly welcoming; Minaj's pineapple beckons us to refresh our view of Sir Mix-A-Lot's song and welcome a new take on an intraracial conversation about Black women's bodies.

Minaj's voice interrupts Mix-A-Lot's declaration that his "anaconda don't want none" and begins to impart her sexual exploits: she gladly recounts her male partners, Troy and Michael; mentions their ability to provide both material wealth ("bought me Alexander McQueen, he was keeping me stylish") and sexual pleasure ("he toss my salad like his name romaine"); and reminds us that, although they may be enjoying her physical attributes, any pleasure received is based on her body receiving pleasure first, both sexually and materially. "Anaconda," in this way, lyrically and visually speaks back to Mix-A-Lot; Minaj gives a voice and power to Black women who never voice acceptance or opposition within Sir Mix-A-Lot's song (except for "me so horny" at the beginning and "yeah" at the end) despite their gyrations. Minaj also speaks back to the white gaze articulated by the white women at the beginning of Sir Mix-A-Lot's video, who voice their disgust with Black women's round derrieres and their blackness. Minaj's song responds through Minaj's repeated phrase, "Oh my god. Look at her butt," and her critique of "skinny bitches" later in the song. These two comments mirror her critique of the celebration of white women like *Sports Illustrated* cover models, much like Sir Mix-A-Lot derides the "Cosmotypgian" in his video; Minaj argues that fashion models' derrieres are considered "angelic" and "acceptable" while hers is demonized.[26] Minaj does not explicitly invoke race in her musical celebration of Black women's bodies; because she is situated within twenty-first-century capitalist discourses as a producer and consumer of culture, Minaj recognizes the possibilities of forfeiting her mainstream fans if she does. However, her re-voicing "look at her butt" in a way that celebrates Black women's bodies presents postracially coded language that denotes the spectacle of looking and also the politics of racial visuality. This type of negotiation for Black women in the public eye requires an adept understanding of race, positionality, and audiences—a tactic Ralina Joseph calls "strategic ambiguity," or "a way of pushing back . . . through a coded resistance to postracial ideologies" by "foregrounding crossover appeal, courting multiple publics, speaking in coded language, and smoothing and soothing fears of difference as simply an incidental sidenote."[27] While Black women like Michelle Obama use strategic ambiguity to navigate away from controversial topics with coded language, Nicki Minaj seemingly revels in the opportunity to create controversy even as she pairs similarly coded phrases with bravado.

Nicki Minaj and her entire career have been based in ideas of the spectacle. Much like popular Black women performers before her, such as Josephine Baker and Tina Turner, Minaj's highly sexualized performances utilize already available ideas of Black women's bodies, sexual prowess and promiscuity, and the spectacularity of Black butts and breasts.[28] Early twentieth-century race science studies that proved the depravity of Black bodies still heavily influence the contemporary American visual imagination, especially for Black women. What Nicole Fleetwood calls the "excess flesh" of Black women's bodies "naturally" disrupts visual images, making them hypersexualized; Fleetwood maintains that women like Josephine Baker, Pam Grier, and Serena Williams are able to use excess flesh to their advantage, insomuch as using excess flesh signals "historical attempts to regulate black female bodies" while also acknowledging "black women's resistance of the persistence of visibility."[29] Through a version of Black feminist sexual politics which I describe as "anaconda feminism" later, Nicki Minaj is ultimately challenging what "constitutes positive or productive representation of blackness, by refusing the binary of negative and positive."[30] Minaj's performances collapse binary assumptions about blackness, womanhood, and sexuality, constituting alternative ways to explore these ideas for Black women and girls.

Nicki Minaj's unabashed display of physical assets, and lyrical celebration of women like her, recast Sir Mix-A-Lot's original song and video as almost PG-13. For many people, the unabashed display of Minaj and her dancers' assets was a bit much. The cutoff shorts she wore in the video, accompanied by various versions of butt percolations, gyrations, and an all-out "twerktease" on Drake at the end of the video, highlighted her sumptuous behind and encouraged me to shake my own. Thanks to the nearly twenty million views within the first twenty-four hours of "Anaconda"'s release, Nicki Minaj's derriere became the most watched item online. Her video's popularity signaled not only a musical return to the celebration of larger body proportions but also a transition in hip-hop's celebration of Black women's bodies; in this case, Black women were shaking and celebrating their own bodies for their own eyes. Men—symbolized by Drake—too could look at this bodily celebration but not touch. A woman's authorship of these types of images illustrates the ways that one's own gaze represents embodied pleasure (akin to a politics of self-pleasure in adrienne maree brown's "pleasure activism"), while also signaling the ways that the gaze of another cannot be precluded in a neoliberal context like the United States.[31]

Exploring Black women's performances of racial mythologies in hard-core pornography provides a lens to interrogate Minaj's embodied pleasure. Minaj engages how women can produce and consume sexualized performances as pleasure. Murali Balaji contends that Black women "appear in music videos as sexual commodities . . . as affirmations of male rapper's hypersexualized manhood or as sexual 'accents' for a female performer who is seeking to assert her dominance."[32] However, Black women rappers and dancers in "Anaconda" and other videos illustrate pleasure in their own bodily sexuality rather than as subsidiaries to the male gaze or sexual desire. In an industry where Black women's bodies are used constantly as props to substantiate rappers' celebrity and success, Minaj's performance of embodied pleasure nuances traditional commentary of "video vixens."

Jennifer Nash argues that ecstasy is a construct that speaks "both to the possibilities of female pleasures within a phallic economy and to the possibilities of black female pleasures within a white-dominated representational economy."[33] By investigating the ways that Black women experience pleasure in "embodied racialization," Nash wishes to locate Black female pleasures in the same spaces in which racial logics constrain how their bodies are and can be used. Using "racialized pornography as a tool for shifting the black feminist theoretical archive away from the production and enforcement of a 'protectionist' reading of representation" allows for a consideration of "complex and unnerving pleasures" for Black women.[34] The unearthing of "complex and unnerving pleasures" is particularly poignant in the twenty-first century, when Black women performers produce representations that take up the historical demonization of Black female bodies in addition to their own desires for fulfillment and joy.

I consider the ways in which Nicki Minaj might find pleasure in the conjuring of wholesome white "avatars" like Barbie and Cinderella as well as unwholesome ones like the Hottentot Venus and Third Reich militarism because of neoliberal and postracial discourses in the United States—and as Nash points out, Black feminist responses to Black women's representation as always exploitative.[35] Whether Minaj considered these ideas in her production of these images is unknown; however, how the symbolic power resident in Minaj's avatar compiling all of these images—an example of the bricolage of iconography I mentioned earlier—within her career speaks to the pleasure of Black girl sexuality, especially when histories of sexual violence are fully considered. The focus here is on the possibilities for interpretation, reception, and consumption of Black women's cultural production as well as its redeployment through memetic culture.

Nicki Minaj's "Anaconda" song, video, and cover art can provide a platform for ways to consider how Black girls can understand their sexuality in our current cultural environment. Minaj displays what I call "anaconda feminism" or an extension of the hip-hop feminism that previous Black women rappers have portrayed. By sampling Sir Mix-A-Lot's "Baby Got Back"—a song that privileges Black masculine virility based in the desire for women's butts—Minaj extends and "brings wreck" to the idea that Black women's sexuality is only important in the context of Black men's desires.[36] "Anaconda feminism," like hip-hop feminism, brings together the seemingly contradictory spaces in which Black women in hip-hop exist. Nicki Minaj's version of Black feminist politics privileges Black women's experiences, including those of pleasure with penises and in the gaze of others, yet not requiring their inclusion. Anaconda feminism is steeped in genealogies of Black feminists who sought the inclusion of pleasure politics in the theorizing of Black women's experiences for the sake of understanding Black women's pleasure on its own terms. Minaj's performance transitions Black women from objects to subjects by controlling the ways in which men's "anacondas"—meaning their desires, masculine energies, and gaze—exist in the space where we twerk. For me, the "anaconda" is a metaphor for desire, energy, and gaze, but also for embodied pleasure. Although this desire, energy, and gaze is not always masculine, it is important to include the ways that some women—like Minaj in "Anaconda"—enjoy a captive, desiring audience. The term "anaconda feminism" signals a sexual consciousness or sexuality-embracing feminism that centers the pleasure and politics of Black women.

I have found that despite how many may view her body, Nicki Minaj locates her sexual agency in her own display. Unlike Saartje Baartman's historical bodily fragmentation—which continues to haunt us because the symbolic power of her dehumanization illustrates how symbols continue to position Black women's bodies as always already available—Nicki Minaj's unabashed butt display happens on her terms. Minaj is pointed in where her body and eyes meet the camera—she is always watching you as you watch her. Minaj's "Anaconda" promotes the idea that Black women can control who watches, comments on, and penetrates their bodies.

Nicki Minaj ends the video "Anaconda" in a red cutout bathing suit, basking in a lagoon-like pool. Over the beat, she laughs heartily and celebrates "the fat ass bitches in the club," meaning large-proportioned women like her. These shots are juxtaposed with those of her in Janet Jackson "Control"-esque attire displaying the fullness of her buttocks for the audience and her lone male observer in the video—popular Canadian rapper Drake (an interesting figure to include some years after he was the prince in "Moment 4 Life"). Drake is only seen in a profile shot and seated in a darkly-lit room, recalling visual markers of a gentleman's club; but this "club" does not center men's enjoyment or fantasies—it's all about what Minaj decides to perform without any financial exchange or even noticeable reaction from Drake. Although the viewer can see his face from the side, the camera never faces him. Because Minaj's full face and eyes repeatedly meet the camera, I consider this dance a dance for herself more than for who is watching. Minaj leaves the stage, and video, leaving Drake grieved with desire over her "fat ass" and her decision to walk away from the tease she was giving him when he tried to take control of the dance.

Through "anaconda feminism," we can understand Nicki Minaj's dance and defiance of men's desires to control her (represented by Drake, much like in "Moment 4 Life") as a marker of Black feminist sexual politics. Her ability to find joy in her body, celebrate large-proportioned women like herself, and walk away from a sexual encounter she does not desire provides ample cultural space to broach conversations about sexual pleasure, consent, and freedom for Black girls. In a world in which Black women and girls are always already sexualized and therefore "fair game" in the US cultural landscape of sexual desire and violence, we must be ready to challenge these ideas within cultural spaces like Minaj's "Anaconda."

At the same time, Nicki Minaj's social media popularity is based in the racist fascination with Black women's bodies. Centering virality in the concept of blackness as spectacularity, Instagram sharing of Nicki Minaj's "Anaconda" cover illustrates how postmodern logics of colorblind racism and postfeminism sustain the spreading of racist imperialist interpretations and uses of Black women's bodies. Whether meme creators consider themselves fans or not, the use of Nicki Minaj's body for the varying viral images I will describe later in this chapter illustrates the ways that Black women's bodies hold no value in the US cultural imagination. In short, through viral Instagram memes, Nicki Minaj's body becomes a fragmented neoliberal commodity that anyone can claim and use as their own—putting their or characters' heads on her body, making shirts and shower curtains with her picture, inserting her image into famous paintings and popular culture scenes. These instances of memetic creativity use Minaj's body as a joke—a freakishly proportioned mannequin that can cause uproarious laughter when used. Ultimately, these uses of Minaj's body obliterate her face from her body—visually reifying her butt for viral memetic purposes. In the process, they deny Minaj's subjectivity by removing her from the narrative she constructed. Their use of this Black woman's cultural production illustrates the ways that Black women's cultural production, in a neoliberal space, can be used in opposition to the narratives they wish to tell.

Despite the inspiration that could be read from Minaj's performance of Black women's sexual desire and agency in the "Anaconda" video and the subsequent images that surfaced to market it, social media used the infectiousness of the spectacular (i.e., Nicki Minaj's ass) to rebalance the scales of dominance. Thinking specifically of how Minaj's body is used, meme creators purposefully created and populated a "monstrosity" by replacing Nicki Minaj's head with the head of Drake, Miley Cyrus, Lady Gaga, Kermit the Frog, Patrick Star, and Marge Simpson; this illustrates the Frankensteinlike fragmentation and cooptation of Black women's bodies that occur in US consumptive practices. Alexander Weheliye explains the pleasure derived from inflicting violence on bodies based on race distinguishes the full human from the not-quite-human and the nonhuman.[37] Rather than physically inflicting violence as was typical in the enslavement and Jim Crow periods, the pleasure of domination is enacted upon Nicki Minaj's body through her technological decapitation. Her beheading is an example of Christina Sharpe's monstrous intimacies, as "horrors, desires, and positions produced, reproduced, circulated, and transmitted, that are breathed in like air and often unacknowledged to be monstrous."[38] Additionally, the fact that this beheading happened in multiple viral images undergirds the idea that Black women's bodies hold no value on their own; they must be altered until almost unrecognizable to reveal their truly monstrous state.

Miley Cyrus's role in this technological beheading cannot be overstated; as a white female musician who has attempted to "blacken" her pristine Disney girl image, Cyrus has constructed much of her career on Black women's bodies—particularly their backsides. As early as her MTV Video Music Awards performance in August 2013, Cyrus used Black women's butts as prosthetic props. She performed alongside her personal twerk team and smacked a "candy striper" on the rear-end before leaving the backup singers downstage to take her "rightful" place in front of America's viewing public grinding on Robin Thicke. Since that performance, Cyrus has continually excavated images from US Black cultural memory and posted pictures and videos of herself as Lil Kim, Khia (popular for the song "My Neck, My Back"), and as discussed, Nicki Minaj. Cyrus's memetic beheading of Nicki Minaj—in which she replaced Minaj's head with her own—in August 2014 was actually the first meme, becoming popular once Cyrus posted it as her avatar on her Instagram and Twitter accounts. Even if Margaret Hunter and Alheli Cuenca cite Minaj's use of her body as a "body-product" or a "product, in and of itself, to be sold and consumed in the growing entertainment industry" and argue that Minaj encourages this type of "body occupation" on social media as an expression of fandom, the racialized dynamics of Cyrus's appropriation cannot be overemphasized.[39]

Although generally accepting of fans' use of her images, Minaj was particularly perturbed by Cyrus's cooptation of "Anaconda" imagery for "fun" because of Cyrus's history with using Black cultural productions to popularize her own career. Minaj tweeted, "Give me one good reason why Miley made this her twitter avi."[40] Minaj's response on social media and subsequent questioning of Cyrus on stage at the MTV Awards in 2015 with the popular refrain "Miley, what's good?" resisted Cyrus's desire to "eat the Other" to promote herself.[41] Her "funny" or uncanny use of Minaj's body is reminiscent and symbolic of the ritualistic reification of Black women in the United States since enslavement as well as an "evolution in the ways that White people have obsessed over Black culture and used Blackness as a site of entertainment since at least the 1820s when Blackface first appeared in minstrel shows throughout the United States."[42] The symbolic power that Minaj had harnessed through the "Anaconda" video and use of the "Anaconda" image on her Instagram was commandeered to serve as entertainment for Cyrus and her fans; this appropriation of symbolic power reconstituted white supremacy in a neoliberal market that counts all money (inclusive of nonwhite people's bodies) the same. In this way, Cyrus's Instagram reproduction of the "Anaconda" image as a white "Hannaconda" replicated everyday marginalization of Black women's bodies and the cooptation of the hip-hop genre's music and aesthetics in contemporary pop and rock music. Because Black people are overrepresented in the use of social media, Black girls and women witnessed Cyrus's technological hijacking of Minaj's body for enjoyment in the very space they use to find acceptance, community, and feminist confidence.[43] Despite how powerful we may understand Minaj's image to be in popular culture because of its own viral qualities and her public rejection of Cyrus's altered image, we must remember Stuart Hall's words—we cannot escape from representation, and in this case cooptation.

Cyrus's cooptation of Minaj's work illustrated a traditional understanding of cultural appropriation, particularly in terms of popular music and fashion. However, as we have already seen and shall see again, Minaj too appropriates cultural images to promote her own brand and position herself as a powerful, full-bodied, and sexual Black woman. Minaj's use of Barbie, Cinderella, and the sexually objectified Black women in Sir Mix-A-Lot's "Baby Got Back" fed into the discourses that she had been working with and against. However, the use of Third Reich imagery in the "Only" lyric video represented a harnessing of cultural resonances of power and dominance to craft a larger global persona. The fact that these images were not re-created in memes illustrates the very narrow spaces in which Black women's cultural production is celebrated—when on the surface, their production mirrors US cultural attitudes toward Black female bodies.

Appropriated Black Women's Imagery: Nicki Minaj's "Only"

Like the "Anaconda" music video, the "Only" lyric video depicts Minaj as the central figure in a larger ethos of power, sexuality, and control based on her own image. Although the video is a cartoon, her "Anaconda" image is used atop the monument in which she sits, eyeing her empire with smug satisfaction. Released in November 2014 as the second single from *The Pinkprint*, the lyric video—a cartoon world illustrating a military rally, depicting Minaj as dictator in a black leather jumpsuit with black hair and red lipstick—was primarily demonized because of the visual connections to militarism and similarities to

FIGURE 4.8. Goebbels-styled Minaj. Source: Nicki Minaj "Only Lyric Video," Photo by the author.

Nazi imagery, particularly the Joseph Goebbels–styled aesthetic of the video. For most critics, the most objectionable aspects of the video were the visual similarities between the red armbands and banners with a YM (Young Money) symbol cascading down the sides of her monument and Nazi armbands or banners emblazoned with swastikas.

However, I find that a closer look at the lyric video depicts a world where leather-clad Minaj has built an empire. Minaj's Barbz and Kenz are soldiers pledging allegiance to her "big titties, big butt too" and the masculine leaders of Young Money are merely her faith (Drake), military (Chris Brown), and business (Lil Wayne) subordinates. She controls the future of Young Money, and the world beyond it, and has the tools to destroy other artists and cultural discourses that try to dismantle her power, illustrated by the many bombs, tanks, and soldiers. Symbolically, Minaj becomes a world leader worth following,

FIGURE 4.9. Minaj Army. Source: Nicki Minaj "Only Lyric Video,"
Photo taken by the author.

FIGURE 4.10. Young Money swastikas. Photo taken by the author.

doubling down on the ideological value of #Blackgirlmagic built on militaristic dominance.[44]

The lyric video's artist, Jeff Osborne, argues there are many more visual connections to US monuments and militarism throughout the video than the obvious visual resonances of Nazi propaganda on signs, armbands, and the style of the video.[45] Even still, he contends visual and musical artists have been using Nazi imagery to critique US cultures of violence and domination for a long time. He asserts the primacy and emotional resonance of Nazi-like images as a threat to US militarism and therefore a counterpoint to white global power regimes. The fact that Osborne's critique of US militarism inspires a Nazi-esque visual cartoon that centers a large-proportioned and complicated Black woman illustrates the ways in which the US practices of domination, in his view, are at least visually resonant with Nazi practices. The visual producer of this appropriation of Minaj signals a visual reminder—in a post-9/11 historical moment where domination of other cultures is likened closely to American exceptionalism and the American Dream—to understand the ways that Minaj's performances use distasteful visual markers to challenge one-dimensional understandings of US popular culture and cultural beliefs. As aforementioned, the images that are the most viral—both visually and psychologically—in US popular culture represent public attachment to disturbing images of violence, domination, and sex for entertainment. As with Minaj's "Anaconda" cover, the most disturbing images can reconstitute US cultural resonances to alter cultural attitudes and beliefs. Especially in the twenty-first century, consumption is based in the idea of respect, fear, and consuming the distasteful for enjoyment (i.e., shows like *Fear Factor, Bad Girlz Club, The Apprentice*) that Minaj visually tackles in "Only."

Discussing Black women artists who regularly used images deemed unwholesome or controversial like Josephine Baker, Kara Walker, and Carla Williams, Janell Hobson explains that they "interrogate a visual legacy of imperialist iconography" using an "aesthetic of resistance" and/or "oppositional stance" to the histories of demonization of Black beauty, sexuality, and bodies.[46] Similar to "Anaconda" in the ways that Minaj is currying in controversial images, Minaj is able to use visual reminders of violence and domination against minoritized bodies to position Black women as powerful and in control. While Black men are present in her domination of the world as confidantes and soldiers, the world turns on her words; paring the lyrics with the images of militarism, Jeff Osborne presents her lyrics as the marching orders to which everyone must respond. I contend that the video uses an "aesthetic of resistance" not only to challenge cultural attitudes toward power, but also to position Black women as fully embodied dictators. Osborne as a Black man and architect of the lyric video constructs her lyrics and image as a militant superhero, forcing the world into submissive servitude to Minaj's vision.

Described as a superhero who has an "indiscriminate potpourri of power fantasies," Minaj's outfit and candor throughout the lyric video symbolically articulate an alternative outlook for Black women.[47] Using an image that the US replicates through the continued cultural influence of Nazi iconographies of respect and fear, Minaj's "Only" becomes a profound way to understand Black women's sexuality (via a well-endowed leather body suit) and Black women's ability to control their images (as dictatorial producers as well as consumers), particularly through the eyes of others. Nicki Minaj's impact on the public imagination of Black women and sexuality position her empire as one that can control cultural ideas about sex and sexuality in a way that allows for more diversity in its representation. I understand that Minaj's images provide a propaganda that can influence cultural attitudes towards Black women's bodies, reconstituting the ideological relationship between Black girls and women as producers and consumers.

Because "Only" complicates popular and critical responses to Minaj's work, the memetic reproductive value is low. Unlike the proliferation of "Anaconda" memes, there were no memes that re-created Minaj's "Only" imagery. Therefore, despite the image's virality for the purposes of commentary about it, US social media did not respond well to the likening of US cultural political behaviors to those of the Third Reich. Additionally, Minaj's image in the video did not re-create popular symbolic prescriptions of Black women as "video vixens" even if her outfit was reminiscent of Halle Berry's 2004 rendition of *Catwoman* (without the claws or mask). An amalgam of images from dominatrix outfits as well as Halle Berry's performances of Black superheroes Storm (2000, 2003, and 2006) and Catwoman (2004), Minaj disrupted previous symbolic resonances of Black women as only always sexually available. In other words, her performance of a Black superhero demystified some aspects of the cultural space available for Black women in the popular culture sphere. For this reason, then, US social media culture did not find the images to be analogous to the infectious popular images of hypersexualized Black women to re-create for entertainment. Therefore, the video renegotiates the relationship between Minaj and consumers who try to technologically behead Minaj with the racial logic underlying such an act.

Perhaps, also, as an animated appropriation of Minaj—already filtered through the artistic eyes of someone outside of the ideological relationship she directly fosters with consumers of her products—the "Only" lyric video and its representation of a Black woman's dictatorship did not reverberate culturally. There have been very few "positive" representations of Black women as militaristic leaders in US popular culture, particularly because armed Black people, and Black women specifically, are considered dangerous and in need of neutralization. Even the most popular Black women in US culture in the past decade—Michelle Obama, Beyoncé, and Oprah—steer clear of these heavily militarized aesthetics.[48] Therefore, the "Only" video did not fit the reproduction of Black women's bodies that made Minaj's "Anaconda" cover culturally valuable and transferrable.

Because Minaj's empire was interpreted by another artist to create the "Only" imagery, issues of creation and control reflect similar concerns in viral images on social media and how, specifically, her body was used in "Anaconda" Instagram reproductions. For example, while Minaj apologized for the video and even cited the Jewish producer on her team as evidence of her support of Jewish people (rhetorically, akin to "my Black friend" sentiments of white people accused of racism and antiblackness), Jeff Osborne cited the First Amendment and artistic license to support his vision of Minaj's empire.[49] Nevertheless, Minaj's art and body were reinterpreted to create new cultural resonances. This video replicates an attitude and strategy similar to Minaj's original artwork and visual positioning as a cultural producer, which usurps traditional memetic reproductions. For this reason, the "Only" video resonates more symbolically as fanfiction (specifically songfiction or "songfic") than memetic reproduction; this shift in genre, perhaps, allows for larger visual argumentation against hegemonic portrayals of Black women's bodies.

The Plagiarized *Pinkprint*

Contextualizing the cultural uses and resonances in popular culture of Nicki Minaj's images, music, and videos from her 2014 album *The Pinkprint*, this chapter illustrates the ways that twenty-first-century consumers shift their relationship to Black women producers. While Nicki Minaj more substantially dictates an opening of representations of Black women that privileges sexual freedom and social dominance through self-determination and empowerment for Black women and girls, the memetic value of her images has been harnessed by both consumers and other producers to facilitate emotional and political attitudes in US popular culture. These other reproductions use Minaj's body and music, in memes and videos, to stand in for the cultural work that others believe Black women do—sometimes saying and doing things they wish they could.

In "Anaconda" and "Only," Minaj enacts unwholesome images that challenge audiences to consider sexuality, power, and domination in relation to

Black femininity. Minaj's transition from usurping the symbolic power of Barbie and Cinderella to using unwholesome images provides a greater window into possibilities for Black sexual freedom, because all of the images provide a diversity of representation, of experience, and of desire through which Black women and girls can see themselves and their experiences reflected. And yet, Minaj's *The Pinkprint* illuminates how questions of creation, control, and viral value illustrate how Black women's embodied objectification is not and will never be facilitated between Black women and girl producers and consumers in a vacuum; there are others who are always watching.

Coda

The Stakes of Twenty-First-Century Black Creativity

As a Millennial Black woman, I am constantly thinking about how the lessons I learned as a girl in Sisterfriends, as a self-designed Africana Studies major in college, and as a professor of Black women's studies can inform the life I live outside of my work. I talk with fellow Millennial Black women about why the lure of symbolic representation, and symbolic acts overall, is so enticing. For all the reasons I am assertive, entitled, sexually liberated, outspoken on issues of racial injustice and patriarchy, and allow algorithms to determine my watching, listening, and shopping practices, I am also highly susceptible to the ways symbols and symbolism can provoke meaning. For the reasons I jammed out to Spice Girls and protested buying clothes from stores that would not support the life I live and the people I love, I turned to understanding popular culture for the value of symbolic images and how they impact my life.

I learned—in the early months of 2020 when a global pandemic ravaged Black communities in the United States and Europe and worldwide protests for justice against the state-sanctioned murders of Black people forced every organization to produce a statement about whether Black lives mattered alongside images that proved they didn't—that symbolic acts, like elected officials kneeling with kente cloth stoles draped over their necks and protestors dumping monuments to slaveholders into the rivers that once washed the dirt from the bodies of the enslaved, mean everything to the ways the United States (and other nations) understand what we do as a nation and who that nationhood includes.[1] Through the use of Black Barbies and Black actors, statements and ads from organizations like Mattel and Disney—alongside nooses being hung liberally in Black places of worship, work, and entertainment—harnessed Black symbolic power (based in the desire for Black people to see themselves reflected in popular culture) to communicate their commitment to the idea that "Black Lives Matter."[2] Symbolic gestures like those I saw called out to Black people (and those allied with them) about which attitudes, behaviors, statements, and images reflected the values and more importantly, the ideologies that produced the circumstances within which I grew up.

Buy Black: How Black Women Transformed US Pop Culture, then, is not just an exploration of popular culture in which Black women's creativity is centered. It is an examination of the values (read: ideologies) that the United States came to hold dear shortly after the uprisings that are now called the Civil Rights Movement. The world that was created for Black girls like me by the Black women who used corporate environments to reframe discourses of multiculturalism, consumerism, capitalism, feminism, and identity politics occurs at the same symbolic (and therefore ideological) level as the programs for Black uplift, Black children's self-concept, and discourses of girl power that my mother encouraged me to frequent. *Buy Black* calls us to consider which images of Black femininity are created when Black women are integral to the creative process and how these visual narratives interpret and critique other popular images of blackness, femininity, and sexuality. As calls for equal treatment in public spaces converged with capitalist interests for new consumer markets in the 1960s, Black women began to use their positions within larger corporations to renarrate narratives of blackness and femininity as well as incentivize the inclusion of the cultural heritage they loved.

I examine the history of visual and material culture from the beginning of the twentieth century to the present, marking a major shift in broad-based consumer marketing of toys, television shows, and films identified as Black through aesthetic choices in names, hair, skin tone, and clothing. As designers, producers, actors, and icons in large corporations (like Mattel and Disney) that pride themselves on marketing to children, Black women played a pivotal role in the ways that US and global populations consumed Black feminine identity. With the rise of the internet and social media too, these and other corporations sought out Black women as cultural influencers to broaden market appeal. Black women cultural producers utilized these corporate opportunities to share their experiences, fueling consumer practices and constructions of Black women in popular culture; they infused specific products geared toward Black girl and Black women consumers, recapitulating the desires of Black consumers for new niche market creation. From the haircare industry to children's imaginative play with Mattel's dolls and Disney's princesses, Black women have fomented Black women's buying power and the need for corporations and politicians to incorporate Black women's perspectives in their products and ads. As I have shown, Kitty Black Perkins, Stacey McBride-Irby, Debra Martin Chase, Whitney Houston, and Oprah Winfrey foreground contemporary Black women cultural producers' own representation of blackness, femininity, and sexuality and the ideological relationship formed between Black producers and consumers.

As the only mainstream Black women rapper from 2009 to 2018 and an extension of Black women's active participation in the shaping of Black symbolic power at the same time as the twenty-first century's placeholder for racial equality—the installment of Barack, Michelle, Sasha, and Malia Obama as the First Family—took shape, Nicki Minaj's products and personas illustrate the ways that Black women's cultural production can also be commandeered for the purposes of others. Since the 1980s, Black women's collective contributions to shape discourses around race, femininity, consumption, and beauty in material and visual culture to empower Black women and girls have also been used by Black men cultural producers and white cultural producers to insert themselves in similar discourses, or to position Black women as the buffer between themselves and burgeoning ideological relationships to consumers. In the many ways articulated in *Buy Black*, Black women cultural producers and their products have functioned and still function as the spice in the cultural products others create and the virality in images that others circulate.

Therefore, I close this book considering what lies ahead for Black women cultural producers, in an age of symbolic gestures and statements supporting the existence of Black lives. Considering the history of playing with images and ideologies of prominent white popular icons into Black cultural idioms, attitudes, and icons to empower Black girls and women or developing the origins for viral (and sometimes racist) social media content, what are the possibilities for Black women's own cultural production in the twenty-first century? I turn to the discourses surrounding Harriet Tubman's life and legacy in the United States, particularly the argument for her likeness to replace Andrew Jackson on the US twenty-dollar bill and the 2019 Hollywood biopic of her life, to consider the possibilities and problems that Black creatives must contend with in the present moment. I argue that in the creation of products "for us, by us" in the US cultural landscape of borrowing (and theft), Black women cultural producers' best option for the maintenance of the ideological bridge between themselves and Black girl and women consumers is centering our own stories and heroes with the greatest creative differentiation possible. We must work toward the depth of individual specificity as well as the breadth of collective diversity in everything we create.

Free to Be on Money?: Tubman Twenty-Dollar Bill

The Women on 20s organization began a campaign to get a woman on the US twenty-dollar bill in 2012; objecting to Andrew Jackson's representation on the bill, founder Barbara Ortiz Howard argued that women have continually shaped US culture, politics, and economy and therefore should be represented on our money.[3] After popularity on social media soared in 2015, the Women on 20s' campaign received 600,000 votes deciding that Harriet Tubman (winning against Eleanor Roosevelt, Rosa Parks, and other famous women) should be the woman pictured on the twenty.[4] Along with other changes to US currency to better reflect social and political issues that encompass the national narrative, Treasury Secretary Jack Lew (2013–2017) supported the change from Jackson to Tubman, arguing that Tubman represents "the essential story of American democracy."[5] With #DearMrPresident, Ortiz Howard and her organization presented their petition to then-President Barack Obama in hopes of having Tubman's likeness on the twenty-dollar bill for the centennial commemoration of women's suffrage in 2020.

These efforts not only reflect the propensity for multicultural inclusion, steeped in US cultural attitudes about Black people's utility in the telling of American progress narratives; they purport how Black women in particular are rendered within white cultural producers' products to shift US representational possibilities. While Ortiz Howard and her supporters recognize the racialized aspects to their call to remove Jackson from US currency, especially citing Jackson's treatment of Native Americans and Black people, the perceivably democratic support of Tubman representing the US on our currency further corrupts a fuller understanding of Black representation and the ways to acknowledge, celebrate, and honor the contributions of Black people that go beyond mere symbolism. Furthermore, the irony of including a formerly enslaved Black woman—who was considered three-fifths of a person and was herself used as currency—on money that people will use in exchange for goods and services is emblematic of the ways white people as US cultural producers direct initiatives for racial inclusion and multiculturalism more broadly. Harriet Tubman's story is actively included in Black History Month celebrations because it substantiates US cultural narratives that privilege heroic individuals and Black strivings for citizenship as part of the American Dream. Calls to

FIGURE 5.1. Harriet Tubman twenty-dollar bill.
Source: Courtesy of AP Images.

emboss her face on US currency further reify Black women's individual and collective struggle for subjectivity and personhood as nothing more than cultural currency. Said differently, the harnessing of Tubman's legacy by poll voters in the Women on 20s campaign (and reinvigorated by politicians in 2021) bespeaks the cultural cynosure she holds as well as the reification of Black symbolic power present in US popular culture. Tiffany Gill pointedly reminds us that some of the attachment to Tubman and the calls to "put a smile on her" serious countenance that circulated on social media in 2016 were tied to racist and sexist assumptions about Black women, their beauty, and their embodiment in US popular culture.[6] While this particular multicultural performativity does not further financial gains by white corporations, it does illustrate how Black women (especially their bodies and others' perceptions of their bodies) are used to represent US cultural politics or desires to shift popular culture representation as created and curated by white cultural producers.

However, Women on 20s is not the only group interested in using Harriet Tubman to communicate certain ideals of the American Dream based in individual exceptionalism and faith-inspired progress. Black woman cultural producer Kasi Lemmons, like those who have worked for Disney and Mattel, has crafted a multicultural script based on a rendering of Harriet Tubman's embodied objectification in Hollywood. As a Black woman, Lemmons forces us to consider not only the tensions between Black representation and white cultural producers, but also the ways that Black women continue to be complicit in narrating Black stories in service of the American Dream and narratives of progress.

For the Culture: Black Women Producing
Our Own Stories

In the past five years, we have seen numerous Black women shepherd major projects to the silver screen. Black women cultural producers like Shonda Rhimes, Ava DuVernay, Oprah Winfrey, Issa Rae, Lena Waithe, and Kasi Lemmons (alongside Black men such as Ryan Coogler, Tyler Perry, Barry Jenkins, Jordan Peele, Donald Glover, and Boots Riley) have pushed the industry to present more diversity in its representation of Black people. Rhimes, DuVernay, and Winfrey in particular are popular for their ability to showcase Black women as lead characters in stories that resonate without direct mention of race. Rae, Waithe, and Lemmons, however, have worked to engineer a robust, and sometimes biting commentary on race in the United States and the ways that Black women (and men) navigate it; they also have been heavily critiqued for the ways they present so-called authentic Black women on screen.[7] Lemmons, in particular, found her most recent major film, *Harriet* (2019), mired by commentary about accuracy, authenticity, and blackness that mirrored many of the debates about representation that emerge with stories and material objects that are supposed to represent Black women; the same debates I recognized from the early twentieth century about R. H. Boyd's high brown National Negro Doll Company dolls and the UNIA's "duskier" versions. The debates made me consider what happens after Black (women) cultural producers take control of Black women's representation. Now that we have a seat at the table, a foot in the door, and a slice of the pie, what do and will representations of Black women look like? Bringing together social media debates and interviews of Kasi Lemmons and Debra Martin Chase, I assert that Black women cultural producers must shift their ideological relationship to their consumers to embrace the same abundant examples of blackness for which we have argued for a century; their cultural production now requires more than embodied objectification because Black consumers, writ large, want to see more than individual experiences on screen. We are more interested in compelling stories with complicated characters, than the regurgitation of intraracial stereotypes or racist tropes which made cultural producers like Tyler Perry famous.

In the aftermath of the 1990s and 2000s multicultural push for representation and the rise of Black women's role in social media discourse (as well as mass incarceration, police brutality, and Black women's political exigencies) I have charted in *Buy Black*, the stakes of Black women's creativity seem even higher than in generations past. Yet as the reception of Kasi Lemmons's *Harriet* illustrates, we are still concerned with the complexities of authenticity in representation, especially of Black girls and women. Similar to the tensions felt when Nicki Minaj faced a new cultural producer (Cardi B) on the mainstream hip-hop international stage in 2018, what factors will Black girl and women cultural producers need to contend with when Black girl and women consumers desire more options?

Sweet Harriet: The Legend as We Imagined

As a cultural hero and one of the few Black women who is highlighted at yearly Black History Month events, Harriet Tubman looms large in the Black cultural imagination. Representative of the major traumas and triumphs of Black people in the United States, Tubman was both formerly enslaved and a conductor on the Underground Railroad; she felt the worst that the United States (and other colonial countries) had done, and yet also found hope, and was able to extend it to others. A symbol of change and of rebellion, Tubman has been referenced in almost every Black cultural form in addition to US monuments, busts, placards, and awards to recognize both her legacies and also others who supposedly conjure her spirit in their service to the plight of Black people in the United States. Kasi Lemmons's *Harriet*, however, is the first feature-length film about her life.

Produced by Debra Martin Chase, cowritten and directed by Kasi Lemmons, and starring Cynthia Erivo, *Harriet* was in development for seven years. According to Martin Chase, the same producer who worked with Whitney Houston and Brandy Norwood to create the Disney/ABC *Cinderella* (1997) I describe in chapter 3, she struggled to get the film made because of "slave movie fatigue," or the lack of desire for many consumers to see movies that highlight (and sometimes arguably glorify) the dehumanization the system of enslavement wrought upon Black people.[8] Particularly after 12 Years a Slave (2013) with its brutalization of Lupita Nyong'o's character Patsy, many Black consumers decided the depiction of slavery had become too much to bear, despite movies like 12 Years receiving major awards.[9] For many Black consumers, "slave movies" are presented as a moral obligation to remember, a reminder of both what the United States has been but also how change is possible, and that obligation can become even more difficult to witness as they contemporarily became unwilling onlookers to the murder of Black people on nightly television. In the wake of the first Black US presidency and the seemingly overnight reinvigoration of white nationalist organizations, some Black consumers argued that they did not need the reminder of a horrific past.

Martin Chase and Lemmons, however, argued that *Harriet* presents the story of one woman who monumentally shifted the world through her courage and determination—a narrative that should encourage us in this moment. This idea resonates with ideologies of racial uplift that I note are incorporated in most Black cultural narratives from Cinderella films to hip-hop. Lemmons encouraged viewers to resist trauma fatigue because the film was more about freedom than slavery; she contends the film is genre-bending and therefore better characterized as "*12 Years a Slave* meets *Django Unchained* meets *Wonder Woman*."[10] While characterizing any film by using three other films is typical to pitch a project, Lemmons seems to be not only attending to the ways *Harriet* acknowledges the dehumanization of Black people (as in *12 Years a Slave*), but also presenting narratives that highlight a lone individual (like Django or Wonder Woman) turning a system like enslavement on its head with wit and conviction. Lemmons attempted to attach *Harriet* to Black cultural attitudes that encourage the preservation and proliferation of Black historical figures and also US consumers' affinity for stories that present a singular hero, an ideological nod to Protestant work ethic and personal responsibility. Despite these promising ideological undercurrents that relied on US consumers to identify with the titular character, which they hoped would sway audiences, Martin Chase and Lemmons had not anticipated some Black consumers' rejection of Cynthia Erivo, because she is not African American.

Erivo was cast as Harriet Tubman long before the script was settled. Martin Chase saw her perform the character Celie in the Broadway musical *The Color Purple*, and believed that Erivo's voice, stature, and acting abilities would bring the film to life.[11] Lemmons, although aware of recent debates among Black US actors about Black British actors being cast as Black American characters in recent films (e.g., David Oyelowo as Martin Luther King Jr. in *Selma* or Daniel

Kaluuya in *Get Out*), nevertheless considered Erivo's phenotype in her comments about the casting: "I thought, Okay, here's a petite woman who's very strong, who can sing, who's West African . . . I found a lot of similarities."[12] Her size and bodily stature mattered to depicting Tubman as strong, but more importantly, I believe, Erivo's West African features matched the images and beliefs about Tubman and blackness that US historians and popular culture have proliferated. While Cynthia Erivo argued that she worked hard for the role and wanted only to represent Harriet Tubman's story with dignity, her Nigerian heritage and British upbringing gave some US Black consumers pause; pointedly, some called the casting choice of a "non-American, non-descendant of slavery" as disrespectful.[13] The choice to have Erivo present Tubman's likeness and the debates over which kinds of blackness are the best to represent US descendants of enslavement pull from consistent intraracial ideas of who, especially which Black women, will accurately represent the race.

Similar to the early 1900s arguments over the darkness of plastic dolls or the 1990s debates about the blackness of beloved princesses (and their love interests), support of as well as dislike of Erivo's representation of Tubman illustrate the elusive, yet constant concern over Black women's bodies and how their representation will represent the race. Arguments that some scholars have made about postracial ideologies or aesthetics that privilege ambiguity and mixed-race identity must be nuanced to address concerns about the use of Black women who are not African American to represent US imperialist and colonial relationships to enslavement. In this case, and in the case of retelling the stories of a Black US past, the Black women involved must be unreservedly Black in phenotype, in hair texture, and in their mating choices. For Black consumers, and therefore for Black cultural producers, the stakes of creativity rely heavily on the lessons, debates, and ideologies that propelled Black entrepreneurs at the turn of the century; unlike the common phrase, we *are* our ancestors.[14] In many ways, it does not matter how much things have changed in the daily lives of Black people, the concerns about representation in Black narratives, Black histories, and therefore Black futures require some attention to whom those stories will use to represent us. In this way, the symbolic gestures matter.

Notes

Introduction

1. Alexis Harris, "Black Millennial Women as Digital Entrepreneurs"; Fry, Igielnik, and Patten, "How Millennials Today Compare."

2. Hoffower, "5 Things Millennials Are Paying For"; Pew Research Center, "Views on Race in America 2019"; Pew Research Center, "How Millennials Approach Family Life."

3. Hoffower, "15 Ways Millennials Changed the World in the 2010s"; Pew Research Center, "How Millennials Approach Family Life"; Pew Research Center, "Millennials Don't Switch Jobs."

4. Pew Research Center, "How Millennials Approach Family Life."

5. Orr, "Difference That Is Actually Sameness Mass-Reproduced"; Do Rozario, "The Princess and the Magic Kingdom."

6. Banet-Weiser, *AuthenticTM*; Douglas, *Enlightened Sexism*; Rottenberg, "The Rise of Neoliberal Feminism."

7. Crenshaw, "Race, Reform, and Retrenchment," 1332n2. Throughout this project, I purposefully capitalize "Black." Kimberlé Crenshaw contextualizes that capitalizing Black recognizes a heritage and cultural experience that extends. This convention refuses the rhetorical belittling of blackness that occurred with the identifying convention "negro" during enslavement to denote property.

8. Orenstein, *Cinderella Ate My Daughter*, 11; Orenstein, *Schoolgirls*, xvi.

9. Ruth Nicole Brown, *Black Girlhood Celebration*; Love, *Lil Hip Hop's Sistas Speak*; Evans-Winters, *Teaching Black Girls*; Richardson, "Developing Critical Hip Hop Feminist Literacies"; Jones, *Between Good and Ghetto*.

10. Patricia Hill Collins, "New Commodities, New Consumers," 300.

11. Gaunt, *Games Black Girls Play*; Love, *Lil Hip Hop's Sistas Speak*; Lindsey, "'One Time for My Girls'"; Wade, "Indigo Child Runnin' Wild."

12. Chin, *Purchasing Power*; Rand, *Barbie's Queer Accessories*.

13. Eason, Interview.

14. Chapman, *Prove It on Me*; Higginbotham, *Righteous Discontent*; E. Frances White, *Dark Continent of Our Bodies*; Wolcott, *Remaking Respectability*.

15. Cooper, *Beyond Respectability*.

16. Harris-Perry, *Sister Citizen*.

17. Saidiya Hartman, *Wayward Lives*, xv. Ladson-Billings, "Landing on the Wrong Note," provides impeccable context for the *Brown v. Board* decision and its failed implementation.

18. Halliday, "Envisioning Black Girl Futures"; Halliday, "Centering Black Women."

19. Cobb, *Picture Freedom*; Bogle, *Toms, Coons, Mulattos, Mammies, and Bucks*; Jayna Brown, *Babylon Girls*; White and White, *Stylin'*; Rose, *Black Noise*.

20. duCille, "Dyes and Dolls."

21. Richard Henry Boyd, "Negroes Want Negro Dolls," frontpage; Sabrina Lynette Thomas, "Sara Lee," 40.

22. Quoted in Richard Henry Boyd, "Negroes Want Negro Dolls," frontpage; Haidarali, *Brown Beauty*, 68–78.

23. Quoted in Richard Henry Boyd, "Negroes Want Negro Dolls," frontpage.

24. Richard Henry Boyd, "Negroes Want Negro Dolls," 5.

25. Henry Allen Boyd, "When You See a Negro Doll," 6.

26. Haidarali, *Brown Beauty*, 65.

27. Haidarali, *Brown Beauty*, 78–79; Sabrina Lynette Thomas, "Black Dolls as Racial Uplift."

28. Starr, "The Fabric behind the Doll," 31; Rooks, *Hair Raising*, 77.

29. Sabrina Lynette Thomas, "Black Dolls as Racial Uplift," 56.

30. Sabrina Lynette Thomas, "Sara Lee," 43.

31. Sabrina Lynette Thomas, "Sara Lee," 40–42, 45.

32. Bernstein, *Racial Innocence*, 204–5.

33. Haidarali, *Brown Beauty*, 68–69; Michele Mitchell, *Righteous Propagation*, 189–90, explains the early twentieth-century Garveyite discourse that argued having white dolls taught Black girls to desire white babies and white husbands.

34. duCille, *Technicolored*, 29.

35. Chapman, *Prove It on Me*, 6.

36. Wolcott, "Bible, Bath, and Broom"; Chapman, *Prove It on Me*, 10.

37. duCille, *Technicolored*, 62.

38. Parker, *Department Stores and the Black Freedom Movement*, 3.

39. Walker, *Style and Status*; Baldwin, *Chicago's New Negroes*.

40. Chapman, *Prove It on Me*, 17.

Chapter 1. Theorizing Black Women's Cultural Influence through Consumption

1. Althusser, "Ideology," 53–54.

2. Sturken and Cartwright, *Practices of Looking*, 52.

3. Steinhorn and Diggs-Brown, *By the Color of Our Skin*, 56; Shipler, "Integration," 30.

4. Muñoz, *Disidentifications*, 12.

5. Sender, *Business, Not Politics*, 7.

6. Banet-Weiser, *Authentic TM*, 23 (emphasis in original).

7. Althusser, "Ideology"; Hall, "What Is This 'Black' in Black Popular Culture?"; McCracken, "Culture and Consumption"; Sheth, Newman, and Gross, "Why We Buy What We Buy."

8. Steinhorn and Diggs-Brown, *By the Color of Our Skin*, 53.

9. McCracken, "Culture and Consumption," 76.

10. Banet-Weiser, *Authentic TM*, 58; Greer, *Represented*.

11. Banks, *Hair Matters*; Byrd and Tharps, *Hair Story*; Leeds Craig, *Ain't I a Beauty Queen?*; Rooks, *Hair Raising*; Ford, *Liberated Threads*.

12. Ford, *Liberated Threads*, 7.

13. Filling, "Transforming Beauty"; Tate, *Black Beauty*, 13; Thompson, "Black Women, Beauty, and Hair as a Matter of *Being*," 835.

14. Leeds Craig, *Ain't I a Beauty Queen?*, 123.

15. Walker, *Style and Status*, 199.

16. Lindsey, "'One Time for My Girls,'" 30; Walker, *Style and Status*, 207.

17. duCille, *Skin Trade*, 51; Chin, *Purchasing Power*, 25.

18. Sims, Pirtle, and Johnson-Arnold, "Doing Hair, Doing Race"; Lemi and Brown, "Melanin and Curls."

19. Peiss, *Hope in a Jar*. See also Davarian Baldwin's *Chicago's New Negros* for more on Walker and Turnbo Malone.

20. "About Us—Founder Lisa Price."

21. Grigsby Bates, "A Black Cosmetic Company Sells, or Sells Out?"

22. More research on the relationship between shifting notions of professionalism for Black women and the rise of mass-marketed hair products for Black women, and created by Black women, is needed. This history directly corresponds with legislation like the CROWN Act, a law introduced into California's legislature in January 2019 to address discrimination Black women and girls face in workplaces and schools based on their hair. The CROWN Act has become law in thirteen states as of July 2021. See Lemi and Brown, "Melanin and Curls," for how hair impacts Black women's professional perceptions.

23. Gill, "#TeamNatural," 71–72. See also Noliwe Rooks's "Black Women's Status Update" for more on Black women's social media use.

24. Max, "The Oprah Effect."

25. Kwateng-Clark, "Carol's Daughter Founder."

26. Jerkins, "The Whitewashing of Natural Hair Care Lines"; Afrobella, "Know Your Ingredients."

27. Grigsby Bates, "A Black Cosmetic Company Sells, or Sells Out?"

28. Further research should be dedicated to understanding the history of white-owned personal care companies such as L'Oréal that routinely purchase ethnic hair care companies to create a public face of inclusion and catering to communities of color. See Grigsby Bates, "A Black Cosmetic Company Sells, or Sells Out?" for more details about L'Oréal's previous acquisitions.

29. Berg, "These Mother-and-Son Entrepreneurs."

30. "CurlBoxTV, Behind SheaMoisture."

31. Payne and Duster, "Shea Moisture Ad Falls Flat."

32. Jerkins, "The Whitewashing of Natural Hair Care Lines."

33. "Sundial Brands."

34. Hall, Evans, and Nixon, *Representation*; Patierno and Talreja, *Stuart Hall: Representation and the Media*.

35. Shaw, *Gaming at the Edge*.

36. McCracken, "Culture and Consumption," 74.

37. McCracken, "Culture and Consumption," 78.

38. Higginbotham, "African-American Women's History and the Metalanguage of Race," 255.

39. Higginbotham, "'The Metalanguage of Race,' Then and Now," 639.

40. Mirzoeff, *The Right to Look*, 1–3.

41. hooks, *Black Looks*, 7.

42. Byrd and Tharps, *Hair Story*, 227.

43. Carla L. Peterson, Foreword to *Recovering the Black Female Body*, ed. Bennett and Dickerson, x–xi.

44. Peterson, Foreword, xiii.

45. Hall, "What Is This 'Black' in Black Popular Culture?" 30.

46. Halliday, "Centering Black Women in the Black Chicago Renaissance."

47. Greer, *Represented*.

48. Greer, *Represented*, 150.

49. Fleetwood, *Troubling Vision*, 110–11.

50. Hobson, *Venus in the Dark*, 2.

51. McMillan, *Embodied Avatars*, 9.

52. McMillan, *Embodied Avatars*, 11.

53. Bradley, "Contextualizing Hip Hop Sonic Cool Pose," 56.

54. McMillan, *Embodied Avatars*, 11.

55. hooks, *Black Looks*, 25–26.

56. Patricia Hill Collins, *Black Feminist Thought*.

57. Cooper, *Beyond Respectability*, 80.

58. Harris-Perry, *Sister Citizen*, 29.

59. Cooper, *Beyond Respectability*, 81.

60. Gottdiener, *New Forms of Consumption*, 3–4.

61. Lezama, "Status, Votive Luxury, and Labour," 5. Lezama argues for a differing relationship to capitalism for Black women, especially Black women rappers who shift the meaning of luxury goods by reinvesting in themselves.

62. McMillan Cottom, *Thick*, 65.

63. Nash, *Black Body in Ecstasy*; Miller-Young, *A Taste for Brown Sugar*.

64. Nash, *Black Body in Ecstasy*, 3.

65. Miller-Young, *A Taste for Brown Sugar*, 63.

66. Durham, *Home with Hip Hop Feminism*, 88.

67. Halliday, "Envisioning Black Girl Futures," 67.

68. Gaunt, *Games Black Girls Play*, 121.

69. Ruth Nicole Brown, *Black Girlhood Celebration*, 1.

70. Morrison is quoted as saying, "If there's a book you want to read, but it hasn't been written yet, then you must write it." In Hult, *Handy English Grammar Answer Book*, 327.

71. Driscoll, *Girls*, 269.

72. Chin, *Purchasing Power*, 30.

73. Hall quoted in hooks, *Reel to Real*, 274.

74. hooks, *Reel to Real*, 271.

75. James C. Scott, *Domination and the Arts of Resistance*, 19–20.

76. Pew Research Center, "Social Networking Fact Sheet."

Chapter 2. From Riots to Style

1. Rosner, *Playing with History*, 25.

2. Eason, Interview.

3. Richard Henry Boyd, "Negroes Want Negro Dolls," frontpage; Sabrina Lynette Thomas, "Sara Lee," 40.

4. Forman-Brunell, "Barbie in 'Life'"; Gerber, *Barbie and Ruth*; Handler and Shannon, *Dream Doll*; Stern, *Barbie Nation*.

5. Gottschall et al., "The Cyndi Lauper Affect," 33.

6. Cheng, "Does Barbie Have a Future?"; Louise Collins, "Fashion Dolls and Feminism"; Cunningham, "Barbie Doll Culture and the American Waistland"; Dockterman, "A Barbie for Every Body"; Driscoll, "Girl-Doll"; Forman-Brunell, "Barbie in 'Life'"; Golgowski, "Bones So Frail"; Grewal, *Transnational America*; Lord, *Forever Barbie*; MacDougall, "Transnational Commodities as Local Cultural Icons"; Norton et al., "Ken and Barbie at Life Size"; Pearson and Mullins, "Domesticating Barbie"; Rand, *Barbie's Queer Accessories*; Schwarz, "Native American Barbie"; Urla and Swedlund, "The Anthropometry of Barbie"; Wanless, "Barbie's Body Images."

7. "1959 First EVER Barbie Commercial."

8. Ebony Elizabeth Thomas, *The Dark Fantastic*, 5.

9. An advertisement ran in the United States shortly before the Francie dolls were released to the US market in winter 1968. The description of "Colored Francie" simply

states that she is a "beautiful fashion doll," without the colorful detailed wording for how to play with her like that which accompanied the original Francie doll. It's important to note that despite the cultural difference, these dolls are marketed on a dark pink background, establishing their connection to the original 1959 Barbie. Mattel re-created their popular "Twist and Turn" Barbie design with the Francie brand, including the bendable legs and hand-sewn eyelashes that marked the dolls of this period. Colored Francie's box and design was light blue and green, which became important complementary colors in Mattel's marketing schema.

10. Throughout my research, I contacted Mattel marketing representatives several times to locate data and research on doll sales, marketing decisions, and distribution of dolls over time. However, Mattel representatives did not disclose or explain how to find these data points. I believe that this carefully crafted image of Mattel, possible with active surveillance of their data and information accessible to the public or researchers, maintains the fantasy that Barbie is indeed the most sellable doll ever; see Hart, "Introducing the New, Realistic Barbie."

11. "'JULIA' Television Network Introduces First Black Family Series"; George, "Was the 1968 TV Show 'Julia' a Milestone?".

12. George, "Was the 1968 TV Show 'Julia' a Milestone?"

13. Greer, *Represented*.

14. For various reflections on Watts, see Joiner, "Looking Back"; Theoharis, "Echoes of Watts"; Colker and Lacy, "From Watts Riots Ashes."

15. Lord, *Forever Barbie*, 167.

16. "With Our Help These Dolls."

17. It is important to note the centrality of the Kiswahili language in the United States due to the rise of Afrocentric cultural aesthetics in the 1960s. In particular, Maulana Karenga promoted the study and use of the East African language with the harvest festival holiday, Kwanzaa, and his organization, US. Karenga, like Lou Smith, was in Los Angeles during the Watts Riots and saw a need for Black cultural affirmation. Karenga turned to the study of Africa and Black nationalist ideologies to "reconnect" Black Americans to ways of knowing and cultural traditions in Africa. Pleck, "Kwanzaa," 6–7.

18. The cultural impact of Shindana's toys can sparsely be gleaned from ten *Ebony* and two *Jet* magazine issues between 1969 and 1977. These stories, used to market the dolls to readers during the holiday season, communicate some insight into the popularity and growth of Shindana's toys as well as the story behind the creation of the dolls. The Strong National Museum of Play (Rochester, NY) archived four examples of Shindana's marketing material, including wholesale order sheets sent to large retailers like Sears Roebuck.

19. Greaves, *Black Journal* 1969 Part 2.

20. Stride, "Maker of Black Dolls."

21. Gerber, *Barbie and Ruth*. It is unclear how or why Mattel decided to provide financial backing to Shindana because records from Mattel are closed and Shindana's records do not include this information. There seems to be some discrepancy in the amount of the gift as well; some interviews say $150,000 while one says $200,000.

22. Spencer, email to the author.

23. Black Doll Enthusiast (Debbie Garrett), "Moments in Black Doll History—Garvey's UNIA Doll Factory."

24. Tuesday Conner, email to the author, June 17, 2019.

25. Conner, Interview.

26. Greaves, *Black Journal 1969 Part 2* interview with Herman Thompson; "Shindana Toy Company."

27. Chin, *Purchasing Power*, 25.

28. Again, the issue of public records for Shindana and Mattel limits the ability to fully ascertain causes for the downfall of Shindana. Doll collector and author Debbie Garrett (Black Doll Enthusiast) reports Shindana's downfall came in 1983, rather than 1978; however, I found her internet source, a document created by Russ Ellis, to be unreliable. The document has no identifying information or date other than Ellis's name.

29. duCille, "Dyes and Dolls"; "Kitty Black-Perkins."

30. Goldman, "La Princesa Plástica," 267.

31. Ford, *Liberated Threads*, 6.

32. duCille, "Toy Theory," 264.

33. duCille, "Dyes and Dolls," 55–56. Another noted Black designer (the first Black male designer of Barbie clothes) who worked at Mattel in the 1990s was Byron Lars. Lars developed his own dolls and doll fashions that were sold exclusively as collectors' items rather than mass-produced commodities. More research should be done on Lars and the collector culture of Black dolls.

34. O'Connell and Russo, *Women in Psychology*; Powell-Hopson and Hopson, "Implications of Doll Color Preferences," 58; Hraba and Grant, "Black Is Beautiful," 398.

35. Powell Garlington, Interview.

36. Powell-Hopson and Hopson, "Implications of Doll Color Preferences."

37. Bernstein, *Racial Innocence*; Seow, "Black Girls and Dolls." Researcher Janet Seow contemporarily re-creates this argument with Afro-Caribbean girls in Toronto.

38. Powell Garlington, Interview.

39. Powell Garlington, Interview.

40. duCille, "Dyes and Dolls," 56.

41. duCille, "Dyes and Dolls," 55.

42. Perry, *May We Forever Stand*, 37–38.

43. Formerly Negro History Week and established by Carter G. Woodson in 1926, Black History Month became federally recognized by President Gerald Ford in 1976.

44. Eidsheim, "Marian Anderson," 663–65. Nina Sun Eidsheim theorizes sonic blackness as "a combination of interchangeable self-producing modes: a perceptual phantom projected by the listener; a vocal timbre that happens to match current expectations about blackness; or the shaping of vocal timbre to match current ideas about the sound of blackness." She contends that ideas about what blackness sounds like are based in racialized perceptions of value built into our society from enslavement.

45. "Mattel Shani 30 Sec 6:14:91."

46. Powell Garlington, Interview.

47. Powell Garlington, Interview. Jack and Jill is an invitation-only organization founded in 1938 for "African American mothers" to "provide social, cultural, and educational opportunities for youth between the ages of 2 and 19." Jack and Jill of America, Inc.

48. Gilroy, "Sounds Authentic," 131.

49. "Mattel's Latest African-American Doll Sparks Debate."

50. duCille, *Skin Trade*, 27, 38. In many ways, I believe that the quick fix of multiculturalism has propelled the recent discourse of postracialism as an erasure of diverse people.

51. "Mattel's Latest African-American Doll Sparks Debate."

52. Johnson, "'Blackness' and Authenticity," 2–4.

53. McBride-Irby, Interview.

54. McBride-Irby, Interview.

55. McBride-Irby, Interview.

56. Five of the nine historically Black fraternities and sororities within the National Pan-Hellenic Council (NPHC) were formed in the early twentieth century at Howard University, a private federally funded university in Washington, DC, dedicated to the education and success of Black people. The NPHC organizations are Alpha Phi Alpha Fraternity, Inc., Alpha Kappa Alpha Sorority, Inc., Kappa Alpha Psi Fraternity, Inc., Omega Psi Phi Fraternity, Inc., Delta Sigma Theta Sorority, Inc., Phi Beta Sigma Fraternity, Inc., Zeta Phi Beta Sorority, Inc., Sigma Gamma Rho Sorority, Inc., and Iota Phi Theta Fraternity, Inc.

57. Whaley, *Disciplining Women*.

58. Peterson, "New Black Barbies."

59. Gray, "AKAs Induct Michelle Obama."

60. Engelhart, "There's a New Black Barbie in Town."

61. Lovejoy, "So In Style Barbies a Huge Hit for Mattel"; Martin, "Diversity in the Toy Aisle."

62. Urquhart, "Baby Got Phat!"; Higgins, "5 Things We Hope the Baby Phat Relaunch Gets Right"; Annika Harris, "Remembering the Fabulosity That Was Kimora Lee's Baby Phat."

63. See figure 2.6b.

64. McBride-Irby, Interview.

65. Sumner, Interview.

66. hooks, *Black Looks*, 26.

Chapter 3. From Bootstraps to Glass Slippers

1. Strings, *Fearing the Black Body*, 52, 86.

2. Bercovitch, *American Jeremiad*, 84.

3. Weber, *The Protestant Ethic*; Hochschild, *Facing Up*.

4. Bowler, *Blessed*.

5. Petry, *The Street*, 43.

6. Anna Beatrice Scott, "Superpower vs. Supernatural," 296–300.

7. Koritha Mitchell, *From Slave Cabins to the White House*, 3.

8. Arnesen, "The Stuff of History Will Be Your Guide."

9. Burroughs and Hunter, *Twelve Things*.

10. Gaines, *Uplifting the Race*.

11. Baldwin, *Chicago's New Negroes*, 7.

12. Cobb, *Picture Freedom*, 2–3.

13. Glymph, *Out of the House of Bondage*, 207–10.

14. Halliday, "Centering Black Women."

15. Gara, "Disney's 1995 Deal."

16. Storey, *Cultural Theory and Popular Culture*, 11.

17. Madison, "Pretty Woman," 234.

18. Rand, *Barbie's Queer Accessories*.

19. Orenstein, *Cinderella Ate My Daughter*; Wohlwend, "Damsels in Discourse."

20. Wohlwend, "Damsels in Discourse," 58.

21. Orenstein, *Cinderella Ate My Daughter*, 12–16.

22. Tamara Winfrey Harris, *The Sisters Are Alright*, 44–47.

23. James, "It's Possible: An Oral History."

24. Balasubramanyam, "The Rhetoric of Multiculturalism."

25. James, "It's Possible: An Oral History."

26. Producers Guild of America, *Portraits of Diversity*.

27. "Whitney Houston and Brandy Star."

28. Derek Gregory, Ron Johnston, Geraldine Pratt, Michael J. Watts, and Sarah What-more, eds., *The Dictionary of Human Geography*, 5th ed. (Malden, MA: Wiley-Blackwell, 2009), 168. While Disneyfication was coined to articulate the commodification of place, I use it here to represent the commodification of blackness as it is reified in discourses of multiculturalism.

29. James, "It's Possible: An Oral History."

30. Hobson, *Body as Evidence*, 9.

31. Gomer, *White Balance*, 12; Joseph, *Postracial Resistance*; Bonilla-Silva, *Racism without Racists*.

32. James, "It's Possible: An Oral History."

33. Wanzo, "Black Love Is Not a Fairytale," 4.

34. James, "It's Possible: An Oral History."

35. Warner, *Cultural Politics of Colorblind TV Casting*, 13.

36. Kennedy, "Keke Palmer."

37. Kennedy, "Keke Palmer."

38. Bobo, *Black Women as Cultural Readers*, 36–37.

39. "Whitney Houston and Brandy Star."

40. Gehlawat, "Strange Case"; Gregory, "Disney's Second Line"; Parasecoli, "A Taste of Louisiana." These scholars explain much more about the racial implications for the film's racially ambiguous and amphibian-centered narrative.

41. McKittrick, *Demonic Grounds*; Summers, *Black in Place*.

42. Although, later, Tiana's princess status is contingent upon a kiss between Charlotte, a princess of Mardi Gras, and Naveen to undo the Shadowman's curse; there are no other Disney princesses whose husband-to-be is even remotely romantically involved with another woman.

43. Moffitt, "Scripting the Way," 473.

44. Sharp, "Race and Gender."

45. Watts, "Princess Tiana."

46. Moffitt and Harris, "Of Negation," 70–71.

47. Brooks, Martin, and Simmons, "Conjure Feminism."

48. Many scholars have discussed the stereotype of the "strong Black woman" and the debilitating effects of the pervasive ideology. See Beauboeuf-Lafontant, *Behind the Mask*, and Harris-Perry, *Sister Citizen*, for discussions about the psychological, social, and political ways that the stereotype harms Black women.

49. Watts, "Princess Tiana"; Robertson, "Disney's Royal Highness."

50. Hurley, "Seeing White."

Chapter 4. A Black Barbie's Moment

1. Cosimini, "I'm a Motherfuckin' Monster"; Hunter and Cuenca, "Nicki Minaj and the Changing Politics of Hip-Hop"; Kyrölä, "Music Videos as Black Feminist Thought"; McMillan, "Nicki-Aesthetics"; Shange, "A King Named Nicki"; Smith, "'Or a Real, Real Bad Lesbian'"; Theresa Renee White, "Missy 'Misdemeanor' Elliott and Nicki Minaj"; Whitney, "Some Assembly Required."

2. Whitney, "Some Assembly Required," 156.

3. David, "Afrofuturism and Post-Soul Possibility."

4. Larocca, "Cyndi, Barbie, Nicki"; Wallace-Wells, "Shape-Shiftress."

5. Cosimini, "I'm a Motherfuckin' Monster," 48–49.

6. McMillan, "Nicki-Aesthetics," 82.

7. Roach, "Black Respectable Currency," 17; Shange, "A King Named Nicki," 34; Smith, "'Or a Real, Real Bad Lesbian,'" 367–68.

8. Whitney, "Some Assembly Required," 149.

9. Morgan, *Laughing to Keep from Dying*, 2.

10. Kilbane, "Barbie's 60th Birthday Wish."

11. Strings, *Fearing the Black Body*, 6–10.

12. "Nicki Minaj Launches."

13. Raynor, "My First Black Barbie," 180.

14. Hernandez, *Aesthetics of Excess*, 11.

15. hooks, *Black Looks*, 26.

16. Jeffries, *Thug Life*, 118–19; Speers, *Keepin' It Real*.

17. Jeffries, *Thug Life*; Allers and Marrs, "The New Hustle"; Speers, *Keepin' It Real*.

18. Minaj, "Moment 4 Life" music video.

19. Halliday and Brown, "The Power of Black Girl Magic Anthems."

20. A lyric video is a music video that artistically renders the lyrics of the song, using images that represent the artist with the lyrics overlaid.

21. Snorton, "On the Question," 297.

22. Halliday, "Miley, What's Good?"; Neal, *Looking for Leroy*, 3–4.

23. Nakamura, "I WILL DO EVERYthing," 260.

24. Nakamura, "I WILL DO EVERYthing," 261.

25. Milner, "FCJ-156 Hacking the Social," 66–67.

26. Ellis, "Nicki Minaj Points Out Racial Biases with Booty Pics, Chrissy Teigen Responds."

27. Joseph, *Postracial Resistance*, 3.

28. McMillan, "Nicki-Aesthetics"; Jayna Brown, *Babylon Girls*; Hobson, *Venus in the Dark*.

29. Fleetwood, *Troubling Vision*, 112.

30. Fleetwood, *Troubling Vision*, 112.

31. adrienne maree brown, *Pleasure Activism*, 10.

32. Balaji, "Vixen Resistin'," 9.

33. Nash, *The Black Body in Ecstasy*, 2.

34. Nash, *The Black Body in Ecstasy*, 3.

35. Here, my use of "Hottentot Venus" speaks to the iconography of that image and the Western representation (and persecution) of the "Hottentot" that is problematic, rather than the personhood of Saartje Baartman (or Sarah Baartman) and performers like her. For more on the differences between persona and iconography of Sarah Baartman, see Fleetwood, *Troubling Vision*; Hobson, *Venus in the Dark*; Strings, *Fearing the Black Body*.

36. Pough, *Check It*, 77–80.

37. Weheliye, *Habeus Viscus*, 91.

38. Sharpe, *Monstrous Intimacies*, 3.

39. Hunter and Cuenca, "Nicki Minaj," 34–35.

40. Muhammad, "Nicki Minaj Reacts."

41. hooks, *Black Looks*, 21. In her words, "the commodification of Otherness has been so successful because it is offered as a new delight, more intense, more satisfying than normal ways of doing and feeling."

42. Boffone, *Renegades*, 31.

43. Pew Research Center, "Social Networking Fact Sheet"; Murray, "Notes to Self"; Florini, "Tweets, Tweeps"; Florini, *Beyond Hashtags*; Brock, *Distributed Blackness*.

44. Halliday and Brown, "The Power of Black Girl Magic Anthems."

45. Ramirez, "Nicki Minaj's 'Only.'"

46. Hobson, *Venus in the Dark*, 2.

47. Berlatsky, "Why Nicki Minaj."

48. Minaj's hip-hop genre–specific bravado, however, allows her to fire off an assault rifle at men who stare and are unable to provide in the "Looking Ass" music video, released in February 2014.

49. Ramirez, "Nicki Minaj's 'Only.'"

Coda

1. Patel, "Brands Follow Antiracist Statements with Donations"; Eligon and Burch, "Questions of Bias"; Wiggins-Chavis, "We Also Face a Pandemic of Racism"; St. Félix, "The Embarrassment of Democrats Wearing Kente-Cloth Stoles"; "A Restaurant Owner, a Football Star"; Wise, "Protesters Topple Statue of Confederate Leader Jefferson Davis in Richmond"; Siddique and Skopeliti, "BLM Protesters Topple Statue of Bristol Slave Trader Edward Colston."

2. Yep, "Disney Releases Video in Support of Black Lives Matter"; Jenkins, "Disney Makes $5 Million Pledge to Social Justice Organizations"; Mattel, "Barbie Statement."

3. Peralta and Horsley, "Treasury Decides to Put Harriet Tubman on $20 Bill"; Naylor, "Harriet Tubman on the $20 Bill?"; Pruitt, "Should Harriet Tubman Replace Jackson on the $20 Bill?"

4. Ades Stone, "Campaign & Results."

5. Swanson and Ohlheiser, "Tubman Is New Face of $20 Bill."

6. "Harriet Tubman and the Twenty Dollar Bill."

7. Sydney Scott, "Issa Rae Reveals"; Schildhause, "Lena Waithe's Chicago Is 'Really Black, Really Human, and as Authentic as Possible'"; D'Addario, "Why Kasi Lemmons Decided to Direct."

8. Howard, "'Harriet' Producer Debra Martin Chase."

9. Stacia L. Brown, "Seven Stages"; Abdul-Jabbar, "Are 'Harriet' and Slavery Films Good for African Americans?"; Kara Brown, "I'm So Damn Tired"; Hartman, "Twelve Years a Slave."

10. Sims, "Why 'Harriet' Is Really a 'Freedom Movie.'"

11. Desta, "Cynthia Erivo on Bringing Harriet Tubman to the Screen."

12. Branigin, "Cynthia Erivo Responds to Backlash."

13. Branigin, "Cynthia Erivo Responds to Backlash"; Erbland, "Cynthia Erivo Responds to Harriet Tubman Casting Backlash."

14. Toldson, "OpEd: Do These 'I Am Not My Grandparents' Shirts Dishonor Our Forefathers?"; Owens, "Saying 'I Am Not My Ancestors' Blatantly Disrespects How They Lived and Died for Us."

Bibliography

Abdul-Jabbar, Kareem. "Kareem Abdul-Jabbar: Are 'Harriet' and Slavery Films Good for African Americans?" *Hollywood Reporter*, November 18, 2019.

"About Us—Founder Lisa Price." *Carol's Daughter*. Accessed December 2, 2019. https://www.carolsdaughter.com/about-us.html.

Ades Stone, Susan. "Campaign & Results." *Women on 20s*. Accessed November 2, 2020. https://www.womenon20s.org/campaign.

Afrobella. "Know Your Ingredients: The Truth about Glycerin on Natural Hair." *Essence*, October 8, 2014.

Allers, Kimberly L., and Tim Marrs. "The New Hustle." *Essence*, August 1, 2005.

Althusser, Louis. "Louis Althusser, from 'Ideology and Ideological State Apparatuses'" In *A Critical and Cultural Theory Reader*, 2nd ed., edited by Antony Easthope and Kate McGowan, 50–58. Toronto: University of Toronto Press, 2004.

Arnesen, Eric. "The Stuff of History Will Be Your Guide: On the New National Museum of African American History and Culture." *Journal of American Ethnic History* 37, no. 2 (2018): 71–81. https://doi.org/10.5406/jamerethnhist.37.2.0071.

Balaji, Murali. "Vixen Resistin': Redefining Black Womanhood in Hip-Hop Music Videos." *Journal of Black Studies* 41, no. 1 (2010): 5–20.

Balasubramanyam, Rajeev. "The Rhetoric of Multiculturalism." In *Multi-Ethnic Britain 2000+*, edited by Lars Eckstein, Barbara Korte, Eva Ulrike Pirker, and Christoph Reinfandt, 33–42. Leiden, the Netherlands: Brill | Rodopi, 2008.

Baldwin, Davarian. *Chicago's New Negroes: Modernity, the Great Migration, and Black Urban Life*. Chapel Hill: University of North Carolina Press, 2007.

Banet-Weiser, Sarah. *Authentic TM: Politics and Ambivalence in a Brand Culture*. New York: New York University Press, 2012.

Banks, Ingrid. *Hair Matters: Beauty, Power, and Black Women's Consciousness*. New York: New York University Press, 2000.

Beauboeuf-Lafontant, Tamara. *Behind the Mask of the Strong Black Woman: Voice and the Embodiment of a Costly Performance*. Philadelphia: Temple University Press, 2009.

Bennett, Michael, and Vanessa D. Dickerson, eds. *Recovering the Black Female Body: Self-Representations by African American Women*. New Brunswick, NJ: Rutgers University Press, 2001.

Bercovitch, Sacvan. *The American Jeremiad*. Madison: University of Wisconsin Press, 1978.

Berg, Madeline. "These Mother-and-Son Entrepreneurs Went from Selling Soap on Harlem Streets to an $850 Million Fortune." *Forbes*, September 21, 2018.

Berlatsky, Noah. "Why Nicki Minaj Made Herself into a Nazi Superhero." *The Atlantic*, November 11, 2014.

Bernstein, Robin. *Racial Innocence: Performing American Childhood from Slavery to Civil Rights*. New York: New York University Press, 2011.

Black Doll Enthusiast (Debbie Garrett). "Moments in Black Doll History—Garvey's UNIA Doll Factory." *Black Doll Collecting* (blog), February 22, 2010. https:// blackdollcollecting.blogspot.com/2010/02/moments-in-black-doll-history-garveys .html.

Bobo, Jacqueline. *Black Women as Cultural Readers*. New York: Columbia University Press, 1995.

Boffone, Trevor. *Renegades: Digital Dance Cultures from Dubsmash to TikTok*. New York: Oxford University Press, 2021.

Bogle, Donald. *Toms, Coons, Mulattoes, Mammies, and Bucks: An Interpretive History of Blacks in American Films*. 4th ed. New York: Bloomsbury Academic, 2001.

Bonilla-Silva, Eduardo. *Racism without Racists: Color-Blind Racism and the Persistence of Racial Inequality in America*. New York: Rowman & Littlefield, 2013.

Bowler, Kate. *Blessed: A History of the American Prosperity Gospel*. Oxford: Oxford University Press, 2018.

Boyd, Henry Allen. "When You See a Negro Doll," *Nashville Globe*, November 1, 1912.

Boyd, Richard Henry. "Negroes Want Negro Dolls," *Nashville Globe*, December 18, 1908.

Bradley, Regina. "Contextualizing Hip Hop Sonic Cool Pose in Late Twentieth- and Twenty-First-Century Rap Music." *Current Musicology* 93 (2012): 55–71.

Branigin, Anne. "Cynthia Erivo Responds to Backlash over Harriet Tubman Biopic Casting." *The Grapevine*, September 17, 2018.

Brock, André L. *Distributed Blackness: African American Cybercultures*. New York: New York University Press, 2019.

Brooks, Kinitra, Kameelah Martin, and LaKisha Simmons. "Special Issue: Conjure Feminism: Tracing the Genealogy of a Black Women's Intellectual Tradition." *Hypatia* 34, no. 1 (2019): 170–71.

brown, adrienne maree. *Pleasure Activism: The Politics of Feeling Good*. Chico, CA: AK Press, 2019.

Brown, Jayna. *Babylon Girls: Black Women Performers and the Shaping of the Modern.* Durham, NC: Duke University Press, 2008.

Brown, Kara. "I'm So Damn Tired of Slave Movies." *Jezebel,* January 27, 2016.

Brown, Ruth Nicole. *Black Girlhood Celebration: Toward a Hip-Hop Feminist Pedagogy.* New York: Peter Lang, 2008.

Brown, Stacia L. "The Seven Stages of Important Black Film Fatigue." *American Prospect,* October 21, 2013.

Burroughs, Nannie Helen, and Karen Hunter. *Twelve Things the Negro Must Do: With Special Commentary by Karen Hunter.* Jacksonville, FL: Book Bloc Publishing, 2015.

Byrd, Ayana D., and Lori L. Tharps. *Hair Story: Untangling the Roots of Black Hair in America.* New York: St. Martin's Griffin, 2014.

Chapman, Erin D. *Prove It on Me: New Negroes, Sex, and Popular Culture in the 1920s.* New York: Oxford University Press, 2012.

Cheng, Andria. "Does Barbie Have a Future?" *MarketWatch,* July 17, 2014.

Chin, Elizabeth. *Purchasing Power: Black Kids and American Consumer Culture.* Minneapolis: University of Minnesota Press, 2001.

Cobb, Jasmine Nichole. *Picture Freedom: Remaking Black Visuality in the Early Nineteenth Century.* New York: New York University Press, 2015.

Colker, David, and Marc Lacey. "From Watts Riot Ashes: Bright Hopes, Heartaches." *Los Angeles Times,* May 10, 1992.

Collins, Louise. "Fashion Dolls and Feminism." *In Fashion—Philosophy for Everyone,* edited by Jessica Wolfendale and Jeanette Kennett, 151–65. New York: Wiley-Blackwell, 2011.

Collins, Patricia Hill. *Black Feminist Thought: Knowledge, Consciousness, and the Politics of Empowerment.* New York: Routledge. 1990.

Collins, Patricia Hill. "New Commodities, New Consumers: Selling Blackness in a Global Marketplace." *Ethnicities* 6, no. 3 (2006): 297–317. https://doi.org/10.1177/1468796806068322.

Conner, Tuesday. Interview with the author, June 17, 2019.

Cooper, Brittney C. *Beyond Respectability: The Intellectual Thought of Race Women.* Urbana: University of Illinois Press, 2017.

Cosimini, Seth. "'I'm a Motherfuckin' Monster!': Play, Perversity, and Performance of Nicki Minaj." *Feminist Formations* 29, no. 2 (2017): 47–68. https://doi.org/10.1353/ff.2017.0016.

Crenshaw, Kimberlé Williams. "Race, Reform, and Retrenchment: Transformation and Legitimation in Antidiscrimination Law." *Harvard Law Review* 101, no. 7 (1988): 1331–87. https://doi.org/10.2307/1341398.

Cunningham, Kamy. 1993. "Barbie Doll Culture and the American Waistland." *Symbolic Interaction* 16, no. 1 (1993): 79–83. https://doi.org/10.1525/si.1993.16.1.79.

"CurlBOX TV: Behind SheaMoisture." *YouTube.* Accessed December 2, 2019. https://www.youtube.com/watch?v=YPEY8Z6tO6k.

D'Addario, Daniel. "Why Kasi Lemmons Decided to Direct the First Biopic about Harriet Tubman." *Variety,* October 2, 2019.

David, Marlo. "Afrofuturism and Post-Soul Possibility in Black Popular Music." *African American Review* 41, no. 4 (2007): 695–707. https://doi.org/10.2307/25426985.

Desta, Yohana. "Cynthia Erivo on Bringing Harriet Tubman to the Screen in the Trump Era, the Casting Controversy, and More." *Vanity Fair*, October 15, 2019.

Dockterman, Eliana. "A Barbie for Every Body." *Time*, February 8, 2016.

Do Rozario, Rebecca-Anne C. 2004. "The Princess and the Magic Kingdom: Beyond Nostalgia, the Function of the Disney Princess." *Women's Studies in Communication* 27, no. 1 (2004): 34–59. https://doi.org/10.1080/07491409.2004.10162465.

Douglas, Susan J. *Enlightened Sexism: The Seductive Message That Feminism's Work Is Done.* New York: Times Books, 2010.

Driscoll, Catherine. *Girls.* New York: Columbia University Press, 2002.

Driscoll, Catherine. "Girl-Doll: Barbie as Puberty Manual." *Counterpoints* 245 (2005): 224–41.

duCille, Ann. 1994. "Dyes and Dolls: Multicultural Barbie and the Merchandising of Difference." *Differences: A Journal of Feminist Cultural Studies* 6, no. 1 (1994): 47–68.

duCille, Ann. *Skin Trade.* Cambridge, MA: Harvard University Press, 1996.

duCille, Ann. *Techicolored: Reflections on Race in the Time of TV.* Durham, NC: Duke University Press, 2018.

duCille, Ann. "Toy Theory: Black Barbie and the Deep Play of Difference." In *The Consumer Society Reader,* edited by Juliet Schor and Douglas B. Holt, 259–78. New York: The New Press, 2000.

Durham, Aisha. 2014. *Home with Hip Hop Feminism: Performances in Communication and Culture.* New York: Peter Lang, 2014.

Eason, Yla. Interview with the author, June 24, 2019.

Eidsheim, Nina Sun. "Marian Anderson and 'Sonic Blackness' in American Opera." *American Quarterly* 63, no. 3 (2011): 641–71. https://doi.org/10.1353/aq.2011.0045.

Eligon, John, and Audra D. S. Burch. "Questions of Bias in Covid-19 Treatment Add to the Mourning for Black Families." *New York Times*, May 10, 2020, sec. U.S.

Ellis, Stacy-Ann. "Nicky Minaj Points Out Racial Biases with Booty Pics, Chrissy Teigen Responds." *Vibe*, July 26, 2014.

Engelhart, Katie. "There's a New Black Barbie in Town." *Maclean's* 122, no. 31 (2009): 53.

Erbland, Kate. "Cynthia Erivo Responds to Harriet Tubman Casting Backlash: 'I Cannot Tell How Protective I Am of This Woman.'" *IndieWire*, September 18, 2018.

Evans-Winters, Venus E. *Teaching Black Girls: Resiliency in Urban Classrooms.* New York: Peter Lang, 2011.

Filling, Michelle. "Transforming Beauty: Discourses of Race, Icons, and Beauty Culture, 1965–1975." PhD diss., University of Delaware, 2008.

Fleetwood, Nicole R. *Troubling Vision: Performance, Visuality, and Blackness.* Chicago: University of Chicago Press, 2011.

Florini, Sarah. *Beyond Hashtags: Racial Politics and Black Digital Networks.* New York: New York University Press, 2019.

Florini, Sarah. "Tweets, Tweeps, and Signifyin' Communication and Cultural Performance on 'Black Twitter.'" *Television & New Media* 15, no. 3 (2014): 223–37. https://doi.org/10.1177/1527476413480247.

Ford, Tanisha. *Liberated Threads: Black Women, Style, and the Global Politics of Soul.* Chapel Hill: University of North Carolina Press, 2015.

Forman-Brunell, Miriam. "Barbie in 'Life': The Life of Barbie." *Journal of the History of Childhood and Youth* 2, no. 3 (2009): 303–11.

Fry, Richard, Ruth Igielnik, and Eileen Patten. "How Millennials Today Compare with Their Grandparents 50 Years Ago." *Pew Research Center*, March 16, 2018.

Gaines, Kevin. *Uplifting the Race: Black Leadership, Politics, and Culture in the Twentieth Century.* Chapel Hill: University of North Carolina Press, 1996.

Gara, Antoine. "Disney's 1995 Deal for ABC Made Buffett Billions by Marrying Mickey Mouse with SportsCenter." *Forbes*, May 23, 2017.

Gaunt, Kyra D. *The Games Black Girls Play: Learning the Ropes from Double-Dutch to Hip-Hop.* New York: New York University Press, 2006.

Gehlawat, Ajay. "The Strange Case of 'The Princess and the Frog': Passing and the Elision of Race." *Journal of African American Studies* 14, no. 4 (2010): 417–31.

George, Alice. "Was the 1968 TV Show 'Julia' a Milestone or a Millstone for Diversity?" *Smithsonian.com*, September 6, 2018.

Gerber, Robin. *Barbie and Ruth: The Story of the World's Most Famous Doll and the Woman Who Created Her.* New York: HarperCollins, 2009.

Gill, Tiffany M. "#TeamNatural: Black Hair and the Politics of Community in Digital Media." *Nka Journal of Contemporary African Art* 37 (2015): 70–79. https://doi.org/10.1215/10757163-3339739.

Gilroy, Paul. "Sounds Authentic: Black Music, Ethnicity, and the Challenge of a 'Changing' Same." *Black Music Research Journal* 11, no. 2 (1991): 111–36.

Glymph, Thavolia. *Out of the House of Bondage: The Transformation of the Plantation Household.* Cambridge: Cambridge University Press, 2008.

Goldman, Karen. "La Princesa Plástica: Hegemonic and Oppositional Representations of Latinidad in Hispanic Barbie." In *From Bananas to Buttocks: The Latina Body in Popular Film and Culture*, edited by Myra Mendible, 263–78. Austin: University of Texas Press, 2007.

Golgowski, Nina. "Bones So Frail It Would Be Impossible to Walk and Room for Only Half a Liver: Shocking Research Reveals What Life Would Be Like If a REAL Woman Had Barbie's Body." *Daily Mail*, April 13, 2013.

Gomer, Justin. *White Balance: How Hollywood Shaped Colorblind Ideology and Undermined Civil Rights.* Chapel Hill: University of North Carolina Press, 2020.

Gottdiener, Mark, ed. *New Forms of Consumption: Consumers, Culture, and Commodification.* Lanham, MD: Rowman & Littlefield, 2020.

Gottschall, Kristina, Susanne Gannon, Jo Lampert, and Kelli McGraw. "The Cyndi Lauper Affect: Bodies, Girlhood, and Popular Culture." *Girlhood Studies* 6, no. 1 (2013): 30–45.

Gray, Kristin. "AKAs Induct Michelle Obama at International Centennial Celebration." *St. Louis American*, July 19, 2008.

Greaves, William W., prod. "*Black Journal 1969 Part 2*." [New York]: William Greaves Productions, 1969. Accessed December 23, 2019. https://video-alexanderstreet-com. unh.idm.oclc.org/watch/black-journal-1969-part-2.

Greer, Brenna Wynn. *Represented: The Black Imagemakers Who Reimagined African American Citizenship*. Philadelphia: University of Pennsylvania Press, 2019.

Gregory, Sarita McCoy. "Disney's Second Line: New Orleans, Racial Masquerade, and the Reproduction of Whiteness in 'The Princess and the Frog.'" *Journal of African American Studies* 14, no. 4 (2010): 432–49.

Grewal, Inderpal. *Transnational America: Feminisms, Diasporas, Neoliberalisms*. Durham, NC: Duke University Press Books, 2005.

Grigsby Bates, Karen. "A Black Cosmetic Company Sells, or Sells Out?" *NPR*, October 24, 2014.

Haidarali, Laila. *Brown Beauty: Color, Sex, and Race from the Harlem Renaissance to World War II*. New York: New York University Press, 2018.

Hall, Stuart. "What Is This 'Black' in Black Popular Culture?" In *Black Popular Culture*, 1st ed., edited by Gina Dent, 21–33. Seattle: Bay Press, 1992.

Hall, Stuart, Jessica Evans, and Sean Nixon, eds. *Representation: Cultural Representations and Signifying Practices*. Los Angeles: SAGE Publications, 1997.

Halliday, Aria S. "Centering Black Women in the Black Chicago Renaissance: Katherine Williams-Irvin, Olive Diggs, and 'New Negro Womanhood.'" In *Against a Sharp White Background: Infrastructures of African American Print*, edited by Brigitte Fielder and Jonathan Senchyne, 240–58. Madison: University of Wisconsin Press, 2019.

Halliday, Aria S. "Envisioning Black Girl Futures: Nicki Minaj's Anaconda Feminism and New Understandings of Black Girl Sexuality in Popular Culture." *Departures in Critical Qualitative Research* 6, no. 3 (2017): 65–77. https://doi.org/10.1525/dcqr.2017.6.3.65.

Halliday, Aria S. 2018. "Miley, What's Good?" *Girlhood Studies* 11, no. 3 (2018): 67–83. https://doi.org/10.3167/ghs.2018.110307.

Halliday, Aria S., and Nadia E. Brown. 2018. "The Power of Black Girl Magic Anthems: Nicki Minaj, Beyoncé, and 'Feeling Myself' as Political Empowerment." *Souls* 20, no. 2 (2018): 222–38. https://doi.org/10.1080/10999949.2018.1520067.

Handler, Ruth, and Jacqueline Shannon. *Dream Doll: The Ruth Handler Story*. Stamford, CT: Longmeadow Press, 1994.

"Harriet Tubman and the Twenty Dollar Bill." *C-SPAN.org.*, October 7, 2016. Accessed January 25, 2021. https://www.c-span.org/video/?416578-1/harriet-tubman-twenty -dollar-bill.

Harris, Alexis. "Black Millennial Women as Digital Entrepreneurs." In *Black Women and Popular Culture: The Conversation Continues*, edited by Adria Goldman, VaNatta Ford, Alexis Harris, and Natasha Howard, 247–71. Lanham, MD: Lexington Books, 2014.

Harris, Annika. "Remembering the Fabulosity That Was Kimora Lee's Baby Phat." *Uptown Magazine*, March 11, 2019.

Harris, Tamara Winfrey. *The Sisters Are Alright: Changing the Broken Narrative of Black Women in America.* Oakland, CA: Berrett-Koehler Publishers, 2015.

Harris-Perry, Melissa V. *Sister Citizen: Shame, Stereotypes, and Black Women in America.* New Haven: Yale University Press, 2013.

Hart, Anna. "Introducing the New, Realistic Barbie: 'The Thigh Gap Has Officially Gone.'" *The Telegraph*, January 28, 2016, sec. News.

Hartman, Hermene. "Twelve Years a Slave: I Am Sick of the Slave Movies." *HuffPost*, October 28, 2013.

Hartman, Saidiya. *Wayward Lives, Beautiful Experiments: Intimate Histories of Social Upheaval.* New York: W. W. Norton, 2019.

Hernandez, Jillian. *Aesthetics of Excess: The Art and Politics of Black and Latina Embodiment.* Durham, NC: Duke University Press, 2020.

Higginbotham, Evelyn Brooks. "African-American Women's History and the Metalanguage of Race." *Signs: Journal of Women in Culture and Society* 17, no. 2 (1992): 251–74. https://doi.org/10.1086/494730.

Higginbotham, Evelyn Brooks. "'The Metalanguage of Race,' Then and Now." *Signs: Journal of Women in Culture and Society* 42, no. 3 (2017): 628–42. https://doi.org/10.1086/689893.

Higginbotham, Evelyn Brooks. *Righteous Discontent: The Women's Movement in the Black Baptist Church, 1880–1920.* Cambridge, MA: Harvard University Press, 1994.

Higgins, Keenan. "5 Things We Hope the Baby Phat Relaunch Gets Right." *The Source*, March 17, 2019.

Hobson, Janell. *Body as Evidence: Mediating Race, Globalizing Gender.* Albany: SUNY Press, 2012.

Hobson, Janell. *Venus in the Dark: Blackness and Beauty in Popular Culture.* New York: Routledge, 2005.

Hochschild, Jennifer L. *Facing Up to the American Dream: Race, Class, and the Soul of the Nation.* Princeton, NJ: Princeton University Press, 1995.

Hoffower, Hillary. "15 Ways Millennials Changed the World in the 2010s." *Business Insider*, December 30, 2019.

Hoffower, Hillary. "5 Things Millennials Are Paying for That Their Parents Never Would Have Dreamed of Spending Money On." *Business Insider*, January 27, 2020.

hooks, bell. *Black Looks.* Boston: South End Press, 1992.

hooks, bell. *Reel to Real: Race, Sex, and Class at the Movies.* New York: Routledge, 1996.

Howard, Annie. "'Harriet' Producer Debra Martin Chase on Her 7-Year Fight to Get the Film Made: 'As Hollywood Changes, the World Changed.'" *Hollywood Reporter*, November 23, 2019.

Hraba, Joseph, and Geoffrey Grant. "Black Is Beautiful: A Reexamination of Racial Preference and Identification." *Journal of Personality and Social Psychology* 16, no. 3 (1970): 398–402. https://doi.org/10.1037/h0030043.

Hult, Christine A. *The Handy English Grammar Answer Book.* Canton, MI: Visible Ink Press, 2015.

Hunter, Margaret, and Alhelí Cuenca. "Nicki Minaj and the Changing Politics of Hip-Hop: Real Blackness, Real Bodies, Real Feminism?" *Feminist Formations* 29, no. 2 (2017): 26–46. https://doi.org/10.1353/ff.2017.0015.

Hurley, Dorothy L. "Seeing White: Children of Color and the Disney Fairy Tale Princess." *Journal of Negro Education* 74, no. 3 (2005): 221–32.

Jack and Jill of America, Inc. "About Us." 2019. https://jackandjillinc.org/about-us/.

James, Kendra. "It's Possible: An Oral History of 1997's 'Cinderella.'" *Shondaland*, November 2, 2017.

Jeffries, Michael P. *Thug Life: Race, Gender, and the Meaning of Hip-Hop.* Chicago: University of Chicago Press, 2011.

Jenkins, Aric. "Disney Makes $5 Million Pledge to Social Justice Organizations." *Fortune*, June 4, 2020.

Jerkins, Morgan. "The Whitewashing of Natural Hair Care Lines." *Racked*, April 5, 2017.

Johnson, E. Patrick. "'Blackness' and Authenticity: What's Performance Got to Do with It?" In *Appropriating Blackness: Performance and the Politics of Authenticity*, edited by E. Patrick Johnson, 1–16. Durham, NC: Duke University Press, 2003.

Joiner, Lottie. "Looking Back: 40 Years after the 1965 Watts Riots." *The Crisis*, August 2005.

Jones, Nikki. *Between Good and Ghetto: African American Girls and Inner-City Violence.* New Brunswick, NJ: Rutgers University Press, 2009.

Joseph, Ralina L. *Postracial Resistance: Black Women, Media, and the Uses of Strategic Ambiguity.* New York: New York University Press, 2018.

"'JULIA' Television Network Introduces First Black Family Series." *Ebony*, November 1968.

Kennedy, Mark. "Keke Palmer to Be Broadway's 1st Black Cinderella." *AP News*, August 4, 2014.

Kilbane, Brennan. "Barbie's 60th Birthday Wish Was to Be More Inclusive. Now What?" *Allure*, May 2, 2019.

"Kitty Black-Perkins." *South Carolina African American History Calendar*. January 2002. Accessed August 14, 2019. http://scafricanamerican.com/honorees/kitty-black-perkins/.

Kwateng-Clark, Danielle. "Carol's Daughter Founder, Lisa Price, Sets the Record Straight on Being Called a 'Sell Out.'" *Essence*, July 1, 2017.

Kyrölä, Katariina. "Music Videos as Black Feminist Thought—From Nicki Minaj's Anaconda to Beyoncé's Formation." *Feminist Encounters: A Journal of Critical Studies in Culture and Politics* 1, no. 1 (2017): 1–13. https://doi.org/10.20897/femenc.201708.

Ladson-Billings, Gloria. "Landing on the Wrong Note: The Price We Paid for *Brown.*" *Educational Researcher* 33, no. 7 (2004): 3–13. https://doi.org/10.3102/0013189X033007003.

Larocca, Amy. "Cyndi, Barbie, Nicki." *NYMag*, February 12, 2012. Accessed September 3, 2018. http://nymag.com/fashion/12/spring/nicki-minaj-interview-2012-2/.

Leeds Craig, Maxine. *Ain't I a Beauty Queen?: Black Women, Beauty, and the Politics of Race.* Oxford: Oxford University Press, 2002.

Lemi, Danielle Casarez, and Nadia E. Brown. "Melanin and Curls: Evaluation of Black Women Candidates." *Journal of Race, Ethnicity and Politics* 4, no. 2 (2019): 259–96. https://doi.org/10.1017/rep.2019.18.

Lezama, Nigel. "Status, Votive Luxury, and Labour: The Female Rapper's Delight." *Fashion Studies* 1, no. 2 (2019): 1–23. https://doi.org/10.38055/FS010202.

Lindsey, Treva B. "'One Time for My Girls': African-American Girlhood, Empowerment, and Popular Visual Culture." *Journal of African American Studies* 17 (2013): 22–34. https://doi.org/10.1007/s12111-012-9217-2.

Lord, M. G. *Forever Barbie: The Unauthorized Biography of a Real Doll*. Somerville, MA: Walker Books, 2009.

Love, Bettina L. *Hip Hop's Li'l Sistas Speak: Negotiating Hip Hop Identities and Politics in the New South*. New York: Peter Lang, 2012.

Lovejoy, Christy. "So In Style Barbies a Huge Hit for Mattel." *Daily Word Buzz*, July 14, 2015.

MacDougall, J. Paige. "Transnational Commodities as Local Cultural Icons: Barbie Dolls in Mexico." *Journal of Popular Culture* 37, no. 2 (2003): 257–75. https://doi.org/10.1111/1540-5931.00067.

Madison, D. Soyini. "Pretty Woman through the Triple Lens of Black Feminist Spectatorship." In *From Mouse to Mermaid: The Politics of Film, Gender, and Culture*, edited by Elizabeth Bell, Lynda Haas, and Laura Sells, 224–35. Bloomington: Indiana University Press, 1995.

Martin, Michel. "Diversity in the Toy Aisle." *NPR*, December 1, 2009.

Mattel. "Barbie Statement." *Barbie.Mattel.com*, June 12, 2020.

"Mattel Shani 30 Sec 6:14:91." *Red Car Channel, YouTube*. Accessed November 23, 2019. https://www.youtube.com/watch?time_continue=14&v=7J70YnDHkuU&feature=emb_logo.

"Mattel's Latest African-American Doll Sparks Debate." *Orlando Sentinel*, November 21, 1991.

Max, D. T. "The Oprah Effect." *New York Times*, December 26, 1999, sec. Magazine.

McBride-Irby, Stacey. Interview with the author, June 10, 2019.

McCracken, Grant. "Culture and Consumption: A Theoretical Account of the Structure and Movement of the Cultural Meaning of Consumer Goods." *Journal of Consumer Research* 13 (June 1986): 71–84.

McKittrick, Katherine. *Demonic Grounds: Black Women and the Cartographies of Struggle*. Minneapolis: University of Minnesota Press, 2006.

McMillan, Uri. "Nicki-Aesthetics: The Camp Performance of Nicki Minaj." *Women & Performance* 24, no. 1 (2014): 79–87. https://doi.org/10.1080/0740770X.2014.901600.

McMillan, Uri. *Embodied Avatars: Genealogies of Black Feminist Art and Performance*. New York: New York University Press, 2015.

McMillan Cottom, Tressie. *Thick: And Other Essays*. New York: New Press, 2019.

Miller-Young, Mireille. *A Taste for Brown Sugar: Black Women in Pornography*. Durham, NC: Duke University Press, 2014.

Milner, Ryan M. "FCJ-156 Hacking the Social: Internet Memes, Identity Antagonism, and the Logic of Lulz." *Fibreculture Journal* 22 (2013): 62–92.

Mirzoeff, Nicholas. *The Right to Look: A Counterhistory of Visuality*. Durham, NC: Duke University Press, 2011.

Mitchell, Koritha. *From Slave Cabins to the White House: Homemade Citizenship in African American Culture.* Urbana: University of Illinois Press, 2020.

Mitchell, Michele. *Righteous Propagation: African Americans and the Politics of Racial Destiny after Reconstruction.* Chapel Hill: University of North Carolina Press, 2004.

Moffitt, Kimberly R. "Scripting the Way for the 21st-Century Disney Princess in *The Princess and the Frog.*" *Women's Studies in Communication* 42, no. 4 (2019): 471–89. https://doi.org/10.1080/07491409.2019.1669757.

Moffitt, Kimberly R., and Heather E. Harris. "Of Negation, Princesses, Beauty, and Work: Black Mothers Reflect on Disney's *The Princess and the Frog.*" *Howard Journal of Communications* 25, no. 1 (2014): 56–76. https://doi.org/10.1080/10646175.2014.865354.

Morgan, Danielle Fuentes. *Laughing to Keep from Dying: African American Satire in the Twenty-First Century.* Urbana: University of Illinois Press, 2020.

Muhammad, Latifah. "Nicki Minaj Reacts to Miley Cyrus 'Anaconda' Pic." *BET*, August 11, 2014.

Muñoz, José Esteban. *Disidentifications: Queers of Color and the Performance of Politics.* Minneapolis: University of Minnesota Press, 1999.

Murray, Derek Conrad. "Notes to Self: The Visual Culture of Selfies in the Age of Social Media." *Consumption Markets & Culture* 18, no. 6 (2015): 1–27. https://doi.org/10.1080/10253866.2015.1052967.

Nakamura, Lisa. "'I WILL DO EVERYthing That Am Asked': Scambaiting, Digital Show-Space, and the Racial Violence of Social Media." *Journal of Visual Culture* 13, no. 3 (2014): 257–74. https://doi.org/10.1177/1470412914546845.

Nash, Jennifer Christine. *The Black Body in Ecstasy: Reading Race, Reading Pornography.* Durham, NC: Duke University Press, 2014 .

Naylor, Brian. "Harriet Tubman on the $20 Bill? Not during the Trump Administration." *NPR*, May 22, 2019.

Neal, Mark Anthony. *Looking for Leroy: Illegible Black Masculinities.* New York: New York University Press, 2013.

"Nicki Minaj Launches 'Pink Friday' Perfume in NYC." *Vibe*, September 25, 2012. http://www.vibe.com/2012/09/nicki-minaj-launches-pink-friday-perfume-in-nyc/.

"1959 First EVER Barbie Commercial." *YouTube.* Accessed October 28, 2019. https://www.youtube.com/watch?v=h8-avPUxyno.

Norton, Kevin I., Timothy S. Olds, Scott Olive, and Stephen Dank. 1996. "Ken and Barbie at Life Size." *Sex Roles* 34, no. 3–4 (1996): 287–94. https://doi.org/10.1007/BF01544300.

O'Connell, Agnes N., and Nancy Felipe Russo. *Women in Psychology: A Bio-Bibliographic Sourcebook.* Greenwood Publishing Group, 1990.

Orenstein, Peggy. *Cinderella Ate My Daughter: Dispatches from the Front Lines of the New Girlie-Girl Culture.* New York: Harper Paperbacks, 2012.

Orenstein, Peggy. *Schoolgirls: Young Women, Self Esteem, and the Confidence Gap.* New York: Doubleday Anchor, 1995.

Orr, Lisa. "'Difference That Is Actually Sameness Mass-Reproduced': Barbie Joins the Princess Convergence." *Jeunesse: Young People, Texts, Cultures* 1, no. 1 (2009): 9–30. https://doi.org/10.1353/jeu.2010.0026.

Owens, Ja'Loni. "Saying 'I Am Not My Ancestors' Blatantly Disrespects How They Lived and Died for Us." *Black Youth Project*, July 31, 2018.

Parasecoli, Fabio. "A Taste of Louisiana: Mainstreaming Blackness Through Food in *The Princess and the Frog.*" *Journal of African American Studies* 14, no. 4 (2010): 450–68.

Parker, Traci. *Department Stores and the Black Freedom Movement: Workers, Consumers, and Civil Rights from the 1930s to the 1980s.* Chapel Hill: University of North Carolina Press, 2019.

Patel, Sahil. "Brands Follow Antiracist Statements with Donations. What's Next?" *Wall Street Journal*, June 6, 2020, sec. C Suite.

Patierno, Mary, and Sanjay Talreja. *Stuart Hall: Representation and the Media.* Video file. Media Education Foundation, 1997.

Payne, Amber, and Chandelis R. Duster. "Shea Moisture Ad Falls Flat under Backlash." *NBC News*, April 25, 2017.

Pearson, Marlys, and Paul R. Mullins. "Domesticating Barbie: An Archaeology of Barbie Material Culture and Domestic Ideology." *International Journal of Historical Archaeology* 3, no. 4 (1999): 225–59.

Peiss, Kathy. *Hope in a Jar: The Making of America's Beauty Culture.* Philadelphia: University of Pennsylvania Press, 2011.

Peralta, Eyder, and Scott Horsley. "Treasury Decides to Put Harriet Tubman on $20 Bill." *NPR*, April 20, 2016.

Perry, Imani. *May We Forever Stand: A History of the Black National Anthem.* Chapel Hill: University of North Carolina Press, 2018.

Peterson, Latoya. "New Black Barbies, Same Old Controversy." *Jezebel*, October 20, 2009.

Petri, Alexandra. "Barbie Is Past Saving." *Washington Post*, January 30, 2016.

Petry, Ann. *The Street.* Boston: Beacon Press, 1985.

Pew Research Center. "How Millennials Approach Family Life." *Pew Research Center*, May 27, 2020.

Pew Research Center. "Millennials Don't Switch Jobs Any More Than Gen Xers Did." *Pew Research Center*, April 19, 2017.

Pew Research Center. "Social Networking Fact Sheet." *Pew Research Center*, December 27, 2013.

Pew Research Center. "Views on Race in America 2019." *Pew Research Center*, April 9, 2019.

Pleck, Elizabeth. "Kwanzaa: The Making of a Black Nationalist Tradition, 1966–1990." *Journal of American Ethnic History* 20, no. 4 (2001): 3–28.

Pough, Gwendolyn D. *Check It While I Wreck It: Black Womanhood, Hip-Hop Culture, and the Public Sphere.* Boston: Northeastern University Press, 2015.

Powell Garlington, Darlene. Interview with author, December 13, 2019.

Powell-Hopson, Darlene, and Derek S. Hopson. "Implications of Doll Color Preferences among Black Preschool Children and White Preschool Children." *Journal of Black Psychology* 14, no. 2 (1988): 57–63.

Producers Guild of America. *Portraits of Diversity—Debra Martin Chase.* YouTube. Accessed February 27, 2016. https://www.youtube.com/watch?v=4nDOoDI3eHA.

Pruitt, Sarah. "Should Harriet Tubman Replace Jackson on the $20 Bill?" *History*, May 12, 2015. https://www.history.com/news/should-harriet-tubman-replace -jackson-on-the-20-bill.

Ramirez, Erika. "Nicki Minaj's 'Only' Video Director: 'Sorry I'm Not Sorry.'" *Billboard*, November 11, 2014.

Rand, Erica. *Barbie's Queer Accessories*. Durham, NC: Duke University Press, 1995.

Raynor, Sharon. "My First Black Barbie: Transforming the Image." *Cultural Studies– Critical Methodologies* 9 (March 2009): 179–85.

"A Restaurant Owner, a Football Star: The People Killed as Protests Spread." *The Guardian*, June 3, 2020.

Richardson, Elaine. "Developing Critical Hip Hop Feminist Literacies: Centrality and Subversion of Sexuality in the Lives of Black Girls." *Equity & Excellence in Education* 46, no. 3 (2013): 327–41. https://doi.org/10.1080/10665684.2013.808095.

Roach, Shoniqua. "Black Respectable Currency: Reading Black Feminism and Sexuality in Contemporary Performance." *Journal of American Culture* 42, no. 1 (2019): 10–20. https://doi.org/10.1111/jacc.12970.

Robertson, Regina R. "Disney's Royal Highness: Anika Noni Rose." *Essence*, November 25, 2009.

Rooks, Noliwe M. *Hair Raising: Beauty, Culture, and African American Women*. New Brunswick, NJ: Rutgers University Press, 1996.

Rooks, Noliwe. "Black Women's Status Update." *Chronicle of Higher Education*. June 26, 2014.

Rose, Tricia. *Black Noise: Rap Music and Black Culture in Contemporary America*. Hanover, NH: Wesleyan University Press, 1994.

Rosner, Molly. *Playing with History: American Identities and Children's Consumer Culture*. New Brunswick, NJ: Rutgers University Press, 2021.

Rottenberg, Catherine. "The Rise of Neoliberal Feminism." *Cultural Studies* 28, no. 3 (2014): 418–37. https://doi.org/10.1080/09502386.2013.857361.

Schildhause, Chloe. "Lena Waithe's Chicago Is 'Really Black, Really Human, and as Authentic as Possible.'" *Vanity Fair*, January 4, 2018.

Schwarz, Maureen Trudelle. "Native American Barbie: The Marketing of Euro-American Desires." *American Studies* 46, no. 3–4 (2005): 295–326.

Scott, Anna Beatrice. 2006. "Superpower vs. Supernatural: Black Superheroes and the Quest for a Mutant Reality." *Journal of Visual Culture* 5, no. 3 (2006): 295–314. https://doi.org/10.1177/1470412906071364.

Scott, James C. *Domination and the Arts of Resistance: Hidden Transcripts*. New Haven: Yale University Press, 1990.

Scott, Sydney. "Issa Rae Reveals How HBO Supports 'Insecure' to Make It Really Authentic." *Essence*, January 31, 2020.

Sender, Katherine. *Business, Not Politics: The Making of the Gay Market*. New York: Columbia University Press, 2004.

Seow, Janet. "Black Girls and Dolls Navigating Race, Class, and Gender in Toronto." *Girlhood Studies* 12, no. 2 (2019): 48–64. https://doi.org/10.3167/ghs.2019.120205.

Shange, Savannah. "A King Named Nicki: Strategic Queerness and the Black Femmecee." *Women & Performance* 24, no.1 (2014): 29–45. https://doi.org/10.1080/0740770X.2014 .901602.

Sharp, Gwen. "Race and Gender in 'The Princess and the Frog.'" *Sociological Images* (blog), August 27, 2009. https://thesocietypages.org/socimages/2009/08/27/race -and-gender-in-the-princess-and-the-frog/.

Sharpe, Christina. *Monstrous Intimacies: Making Post-Slavery Subjects*. Durham, NC: Duke University Press, 2009.

Shaw, Adrienne. *Gaming at the Edge: Sexuality and Gender at the Margins of Gamer Culture*. Minneapolis: University of Minnesota Press, 2015.

Sheth, Jagdish N., Bruce I. Newman, and Barbara L. Gross. "Why We Buy What We Buy: A Theory of Consumption Values." *Journal of Business Research* 22, no. 2 (1991): 159–70. https://doi.org/10.1016/0148-2963(91)90050-8.

"Shindana Toy Company—Changing the American Doll Industry." *Lost L.A.*, KCET, Los Angeles, 2019. https://www.kcet.org/shows/lost-la/episodes/shindana-toy -company-changing-the-american-doll-industry.

Shipler, David K. "Integration: Together and Separate." In *A Country of Strangers: Blacks and Whites in America*, 23–53. New York: Vintage Books, 1997.

Siddique, Haroon, and Clea Skopeliti. "BLM Protesters Topple Statue of Bristol Slave Trader Edward Colston." *The Guardian*, June 7, 2020, sec. UK news.

Sims, David. "Why 'Harriet' Is Really a 'Freedom Movie.'" *The Atlantic*, October 30, 2019.

Sims, Jennifer Patrice, Whitney Laster Pirtle, and Iris Johnson-Arnold. "Doing Hair, Doing Race: The Influence of Hairstyle on Racial Perception across the US." *Ethnic and Racial Studies* (2019): 1–21. https://doi.org/10.1080/01419870.2019.1700296.

Smith, Marquita R. "'Or a Real, Real Bad Lesbian': Nicki Minaj and the Acknowledgement of Queer Desire in Hip-Hop Culture." *Popular Music and Society* 37, no. 3 (2014): 360–70. https://doi.org/10.1080/03007766.2013.800680.

Snorton, C. Riley. "On the Question of 'Who's Out in Hip Hop.'" *Souls* 16, no. 3–4 (2014): 283–302. https://doi.org/10.1080/10999949.2014.968974.

Speers, Laura. *Keepin' It Real: Authenticity Debates and Global Hip Hop*. New York: Routledge, 2017.

Spencer, Carol. Email to the author, February 15, 2015.

Starr, Madison Peterson. "The Fabric behind the Doll—The Performance of the Black Doll in Early 20th-Century America." Thesis, Trinity College, 2016.

Steinhorn, Leonard, and Barbara Diggs-Brown. *By the Color of Our Skin: The Illusion of Integration and the Reality of Race*. New York: Dutton, 1999.

Stern, Susan, dir. *Barbie Nation: An Unauthorized Tour*. San Francisco: El Rio Productions; New York: New Day Films, 2007.

St. Félix, Doreen. "The Embarrassment of Democrats Wearing Kente-Cloth Stoles." *New Yorker*, June 9, 2020.

Storey, John. *An Introductory Guide to Cultural Theory and Popular Culture*. Athens: University of Georgia Press, 1993.

Stride, David. "Maker of Black Dolls Finding Profits in Attitude Changes." *New York Times*, December 24, 1976.

Strings, Sabrina. *Fearing the Black Body: The Racial Origins of Fat Phobia*. New York: New York University Press, 2019.

Sturken, Marita, and Lisa Cartwright. *Practices of Looking: An Introduction to Visual Culture*. New York: Oxford University Press, 2001.

Summers, Brandi Thompson. *Black in Place: The Spatial Aesthetics of Race in a Post-Chocolate City*. Chapel Hill: University of North Carolina Press, 2019.

Sumner, Stephen. Interview with the author, June 10, 2019.

"Sundial Brands Announces Game Changing Partnership with Unilever—The Next Chapter." SheaMoisture, *YouTube*, November 27, 2017. https://www.youtube.com/watch?v=eojn7zhOR4Q.

Swanson, Ana, and Abby Ohlheiser. "Tubman Is New Face of $20 Bill." *Washington Post*, April 21, 2016, sec. A.1.

Tate, Shirley Anne. *Black Beauty: Aesthetics, Stylization, Politics*. London: Routledge, 2009.

Theoharis, Jeanne. "Echoes of Watts, 50 Years Later." *New York Times*, August 11, 2015, Opposing Viewpoints in Context edition, sec. A23.

Thomas, Ebony Elizabeth. *The Dark Fantastic: Race and the Imagination from Harry Potter to the Hunger Games*. New York: New York University Press, 2019.

Thomas, Sabrina Lynette. "Black Dolls as Racial Uplift: A Preliminary Report." *Transforming Anthropology* 13, no. 1 (2005): 55–56. https://doi.org/10.1525/tran.2005.13.1.55.

Thomas, Sabrina Lynette. "Sara Lee: The Rise and Fall of the Ultimate Negro Doll." *Transforming Anthropology* 15, no. 1 (2007): 38–49. https://doi.org/10.1525/tran.2007.15.1.38.

Thompson, Cheryl. "Black Women, Beauty, and Hair as a Matter of *Being*." *Women's Studies* 38, no. 8 (2009): 831–56. https://doi.org/10.1080/00497870903238463.

Toldson, Ivory. "OpEd: Do These 'I Am Not My Grandparents' Shirts Dishonor Our Forefathers?" *NBC News*, November 21, 2016.

Urla, Jacqueline, and Alan C. Swedlund. "The Anthropometry of Barbie: Unsettling Ideals of the Feminine Body in Popular Culture." In *Deviant Bodies: Critical Perspectives on Difference in Science and Popular Culture*, edited by Jennifer Terry and Jacqueline Urla, 240–87. Bloomington: Indiana University Press, 1998.

Urquhart, Tira. "Baby Got Phat! Kimora Lee Simmons Buys Back and Relaunches Her Iconic Label, Baby Phat." *BET*, March 11, 2019.

Wade, Ashleigh Greene. "Indigo Child Runnin' Wild: Willow Smith's Archive of Black Girl Magic." *National Political Science Review* 19, no. 2 (2018): 21–33.

Wallace-Wells, David. "Shape-Shiftress." *NYMag*, February 12, 2012. Accessed October 18, 2015. http://nymag.com/fashion/12/spring/nicki-minaj-2012-2/.

Walker, Susannah. *Style and Status: Selling Beauty to African American Women, 1920–1975*. Lexington: University Press of Kentucky, 2007.

Wanless, Mary Dorsey. "Barbie's Body Images." *Feminist Media Studies* 1, no. 1 (2001): 125–27. https://doi.org/10.1080/14680770120042909.

Wanzo, Rebecca. "Black Love Is Not a Fairytale." *Poroi* 7, no. 2 (2011): article 5. https://doi.org/10.13008/2151-2957.1096.

Warner, Kristen J. *The Cultural Politics of Colorblind TV Casting.* New York: Routledge, 2015.

Watts, Jenisha. "Princess Tiana Continues Her Reign on DVD." *Essence,* March 14, 2010.

Weber, Max. *The Protestant Ethic and the Spirit of Capitalism.* Routledge Classics. London: Routledge, 2001.

Weheliye, Alexander G. *Habeas Viscus: Racializing Assemblages, Biopolitics, and Black Feminist Theories of the Human.* Durham, NC: Duke University Press, 2014.

Whaley, Deborah Elizabeth. *Disciplining Women: Alpha Kappa Alpha, Black Counterpublics, and the Cultural Politics of Black Sororities.* Albany: SUNY Press, 2010.

White, E. Frances. *Dark Continent of Our Bodies: Black Feminism and the Politics of Respectability.* Philadelphia: Temple University Press, 2001.

White, Shane, and Graham White. *Stylin': African American Expressive Culture, from Its Beginnings to the Zoot Suit.* Ithaca, NY: Cornell University Press, 1999.

White, Theresa Renee. "Missy 'Misdemeanor' Elliott and Nicki Minaj Fashionistin' Black Female Sexuality in Hip-Hop Culture—Girl Power or Overpowered?" *Journal of Black Studies* 44, no. 6 (2013): 607–26. https://doi.org/10.1177/0021934713497365.

Whitney, Jennifer Dawn. "Some Assembly Required: Black Barbie and the Fabrication of Nicki Minaj." *Girlhood Studies* 5, no. 1 (2012): 141–59.

"Whitney Houston and Brandy Star in TV Movie 'Cinderella.'" *Jet,* November 3, 1997.

Wiggins-Chavis, Linda. "We Also Face a Pandemic of Racism." *Progressive.org,* May 11, 2020.

Willis, Deborah, Ellyn Toscano, and Kalia Brooks Nelson. *Women and Migration: Responses in Art and History.* Cambridge: Open Book Publishers, 2019.

Wise, Justin. "Protesters Topple Statue of Confederate Leader Jefferson Davis in Richmond." *TheHill,* June 11, 2020.

"With Our Help These Dolls Are Making a Profit for These Guys in Watts." *Ebony,* September 1971.

Wohlwend, Karen E. "Damsels in Discourse: Girls Consuming and Producing Identity Texts through Disney Princess Play." *Reading Research Quarterly* 44, no. 1 (2009): 57–83.

Wolcott, Victoria W. "'Bible, Bath, and Broom': Nannie Helen Burrough's National Training School and African-American Racial Uplift." *Journal of Women's History* 9, no. 1 (1997): 88–110.

Wolcott, Victoria W. *Remaking Respectability: African American Women in Interwar Detroit.* Chapel Hill: University of North Carolina Press, 2001.

Yep, Kristin. "Disney Releases Video in Support of Black Lives Matter." *Inside the Magic,* June 13, 2020.

Index

ARIA S. HALLIDAY is an assistant professor in the Department of Gender and Women's Studies and Program in African American and Africana Studies at the University of Kentucky.

FEMINIST MEDIA STUDIES

Queer Migration Politics: Activist Rhetoric and Coalitional Possibilities   Karma R. Chávez
Sexting Panic: Rethinking Criminalization, Privacy, and Consent   Amy Adele Hasinoff
Cupcakes, Pinterest, and Ladyporn: Feminized Popular Culture
    in the Early Twenty-First Century   Edited by Elana Levine
Gendered Asylum: Race and Violence in US Law and Politics   Sara L. McKinnon
Football and Manliness: An Unauthorized Feminist Account of the NFL   Thomas P. Oates
Alice in Pornoland: Hardcore Encounters with the Victorian Gothic   Laura Helen Marks
Homeland Maternity: US Security Culture and the New Reproductive Regime
    Natalie Fixmer-Oraiz
Buy Black: How Black Women Transformed US Pop Culture   Aria S. Halliday

The University of Illinois Press
is a founding member of the
Association of University Presses.

———————————————

Composed in 10.75/13 Arno Pro
with Adrianna Extended display
by Kirsten Dennison
at the University of Illinois Press
Manufactured by Versa Press

University of Illinois Press
1325 South Oak Street
Champaign, IL 61820-6903
www.press.uillinois.edu